Can Japan Compete?

Also by Michael E. Porter:

On Competition (1998). Boston: Harvard Business School Press

The Competitive Advantage of Nations (1990). New York: The Free Press. Republished with a new introduction, 1998

Competition in Global Industries (ed.) (1986). Boston: Harvard Business School Press

Competitive Advantage: Creating and Sustaining Superior Performance (1985). New York: The Free Press. Republished with a new introduction, 1998

Competitive Strategy: Techniques for Analyzing Industries and Competitors (1980). New York: The Free Press. Republished with a new introduction, 1998

Also by Hirotaka Takeuchi (with Ikujiro Nonaka):

The Knowledge-Creating Company: How Japanese Companies Create the Dynamics of Innovation (1995). New York: Oxford University Press

Can Japan Compete?

Michael E. Porter

Hirotaka Takeuchi

Mariko Sakakibara

palgrave

First published 2000 by
PALGRAVE
Houndmills, Basingstoke, Hampshire RG21 6XS and
175 Fifth Avenue, New York, N. Y. 10010
Companies and representatives throughout the world

PALGRAVE is the new global academic imprint of
St. Martin's Press LLC Scholarly and Reference Division and
Palgrave Publishers Ltd (formerly Macmillan Press Ltd).

ISBN 0–333–78658–0 hardback

This book is printed on paper suitable for recycling and
made from fully managed and sustained forest sources.

A catalogue record for this book is available
from the British Library.

10   9   8   7   6   5   4   3
09 08 07 06 05 04 03 02 01

Editing and origination by
Aardvark Editorial, Mendham, Suffolk

Printed and bound in Great Britain by
Creative Print & Design (Wales) Ebbw Vale

CONTENTS

LIST OF FIGURES

List of Tables

PREFACE

This book, which has been a long time in the making, grew out of a puzzle. It dates back to the late 1980s, when we were conducting research on Japan as part of a larger study, which was published as *The Competitive Advantage of Nations* (1990). Japan was then seen as the world's preeminent economic power. In fact, a series of widely read books credited Japan with creating a new and superior form of capitalism that would supplant the West.[1]

While studying some of Japan's most formidable industries, however, we discovered a Japan that no one was talking about. Alongside the highly competitive industries were other industries that were highly uncompetitive. It was as if there were two Japans. As time passed, the uncompetitive Japan remained obscure and often hidden, and it never showed signs of improvement.

This, then, was the puzzle: if Japanese government policies and practices in fact accounted for the nation's extraordinary competitiveness – as so many people believed, why wasn't Japan competitive in large, important industries where those policies and practices had been explicitly and prominently implemented?

In the face of the overwhelming acceptance of the government-led explanation for Japan's success, we knew that any challenge to the conventional wisdom would require an extraordinary body of evidence. So we embarked on a process of detailed case study and empirical research that spanned almost eight years and involved a large team of graduate students and others. We conducted in-depth examinations of twenty competitive Japanese industries as well as less detailed studies of many more. More important, we also studied Japan's failures, a topic that other investigators had overlooked. We examined a large cross-section of Japan's uncompetitive sectors and industries.

To complement the case study evidence, we also developed original statistical evidence covering the entire economy on areas such as government-sponsored cooperative research and legalized cartels, which figured prominently in the accepted model of Japan's success.

As our work progressed, we began to see other dimensions to the puzzle. Even 'successful' companies and industries showed signs that Japan's competitive performance was not as it should be, and that performance was slipping. In addition, it was surprising that in a nation so admired for its strengths as an exporter, virtually no new export industries were developing. All this was reflected in a persistent productivity gap between Japan and other advanced nations, together with high domestic costs that dragged down the Japanese standard of living.

Careful study of Japan's successes and failures has helped us unscramble the puzzle. The emerging picture challenges the conventional wisdom on the drivers of national competitiveness in Japan, or in any nation that follows a similar path. We will demonstrate in the pages that follow that Japan is not a special case after all. Its industries succeed not when the government manages competition but when it allows competition to flourish. And Japanese companies succeed when they follow the accepted principles of strategy.

This book aims first and foremost to offer a theory that can explain and interpret Japan's postwar economic trajectory. Because of the influence of Japan's success on economic thinking and practice worldwide, it is vital to set the record straight on exactly what did and did not happen in Japan. Our theoretical framework can also be applied elsewhere, and it will be especially useful for countries that have tried to emulate the 'Japanese miracle'.

Our second goal is to offer an outline of what steps will be necessary to restore Japan's economic vitality, at a time when a new direction for the nation is far from clear. Current policy prescriptions are incomplete, to say the least. The enormous public cost of bailouts and macroeconomic stimulation is putting the nation's macroeconomic stability at risk. And the current foot dragging on reforms, such as in financial reporting and deposit insurance limits, is only heightening the ultimate cost.

We began this research at the peak of the Japanese boom and completed it during the seemingly never-ending economic recession. We believe our message is equally viable for both periods. Finishing this book has required us to chase a rapidly moving target, especially when we charted a course for Japan's future. As the nation's economic difficulties have become increasingly clear, a steady stream of books, articles, government reports, corporate restructurings, and policy announcements have followed. We have outlined the elements of a new direction for companies and for government without attempting to summarize all the recent developments.

Two of us are Japanese citizens, and all of us care deeply about the future of this important nation. We recognize that Japan's situation will continue to evolve and policy changes will continue to occur, for better or for worse. Our hope is that this book will provide a compelling framework in which to understand and evaluate those changes.

This research would not have been possible without a large team of collaborators. We owe special thanks to Yoshinori Fujikawa, Satoshi Akutsu, Tomohiro Doai, Lucia Marshall, Kyoko Suetsugu, Reiko Kinoshita, Michael Stephenson and Ken Serwin for their leadership in the research process. We are grateful to Dawn Sylvester, Daniel Vasquez, and Elizabeth King for their research assistance. We are also appreciative of Ryozo Hayashi, Chihiro Watanabe, Kazuhiro Fuchi, Takahiro Fujimoto, and Kinji Gonda for assisting us collect data and conduct interviews.

This research is partly funded by the Division of Research of the Harvard Business School, the School of Commerce at Hitotsubashi University, the Center of International Business Education and Research at the UCLA Anderson Graduate School of Management, the Academic Senate of the University of California, and the Alfred P. Sloan Foundation.

We are very grateful to Shinji Fukukawa, Yoko Ishikura, Yoshihiko Miyauchi, Iwao Nakatani, Ikujiro Nonaka, and Hugh Patrick for helpful comments. Joan Magretta and Nan Stone acted as consulting editors and added immeasurably to the book. Thanks are due to Eileen Roche for her skillful editing. Lyn Pohl not only assembled the manuscript but also served as an outstanding project manager throughout this arduous effort.

MICHAEL E. PORTER
Boston
HIROTAKA TAKEUCHI
Tokyo
MARIKO SAKAKIBARA
Los Angeles

Notes

1. Examples included *Containing Japan* (Fallows, 1989), *Trading Places* (Prestowitz, 1988), and *The Enigma of Japanese Power* (Van Wolferen, 1989).

CHAPTER 1

The Japanese Model of Competitiveness

Not so long ago, the entire world stood in awe of Japan's postwar economic miracle. Japan was heralded as a country that could do no wrong. Some Japanese policy makers boasted of inventing a superior form of capitalism. Japanese companies were admired for practicing a better approach to management, one that has been widely emulated. Just ten years ago, it would have been unthinkable to write a book with the title, *Can Japan Compete?*

Today it is a question worth posing. Japan is mired in a seemingly endless slump. In 1998, economic growth turned negative for an unprecedented second consecutive year, and 1999 growth was anemic at best. The banking industry is showing few signs of recovering from its bad loans. Real estate prices, after skyrocketing during the late 1980s, have plummeted by as much as 78%. The Nikkei stock price index, which peaked at ¥38,915 in December 1989, fell below ¥13,000 in October 1998 and had only recovered to the 20,000 range by early 2000. Unemployment hit a record high in 1999, topping the US jobless rate for the first time.

In Japanese policy circles, there is some talk of a defeat by Anglo-Saxon capitalism. Considering the depth and the persistence of Japan's slide, however, there is remarkably little questioning of the country's underlying economic model. Yes, everyone agrees, some reforms are needed. But most believe the economic engine is basically sound, if only the government would jump-start it with a massive dose of credit and demand stimulation.[1] Only recently, after being confronted with company failures and huge losses, have many Japanese begun to realize that a structural problem exists. And even now, there is a persistent tendency for premature optimism at any sign of restructuring.

The emerging consensus attributes Japan's economic problems to three causes. The first is the collapse of the so-called bubble economy of overvalued equities and real estate. Imploding asset prices sent shock waves through the banking system and the rest of the economy, making credit scarce. As the value of collateral plummeted, banks, corporations, and even households found themselves heavily in debt, which suppressed consumption and investment.

The second explanation is over-regulation and overprotection by meddlesome government ministries. Government intervention distorts companies' behavior, drives up their costs, and reduces their flexibility, thus undermining their competitiveness.

The third explanation also faults government. By raising taxes, failing to stimulate domestic demand, and clinging to their policy of export-led growth for too long, Japanese bureaucrats mismanaged macroeconomic policy. As Japanese companies encountered limits on exports and expanded their foreign investment, slow domestic investment and sluggish domestic demand have undermined economic growth.

We agree that stimulating the economy and restoring the flow of capital would be beneficial. But quick fixes and macroeconomic adjustments alone will not restore economic vitality. Japan has tried these tactics and failed. The Bank of Japan slashed its short-term discount rate to zero. Nearly $1.5 trillion worth of public-works spending, tax cuts, bank bailouts, government loans for cash-strapped companies, and even shopping vouchers have had little effect. Nothing seems to work.

That is because what ails Japan goes beyond macroeconomics. Japan's problem is rooted in *microeconomics*, in how the nation competes industry by industry. If Japanese policy makers and business leaders hope to restore the nation's long-term economic health, they must address the underlying causes of its decline. That means beginning with an accurate reading of what drove Japan's success in the first place.

Arriving at this is easier said than done. Since the 1980s, a continuous stream of articles and books has created what is, by now, a widely accepted view of Japan's unparalleled rise in competitiveness. It consists of two related explanations. One has to do with a specific set of government policies, the other, with a set of management practices common to Japanese corporations. Both have been repeated so often that they are deeply ingrained in the minds of the public.

This prevailing view has had a profound impact, not only within Japan but also on the rest of the world. Policy makers and business leaders in other countries have tried to emulate the Japanese model or borrow parts of it. For various political and cultural reasons, it has been appealing to believe that Japan had invented a new and intrinsically superior form of capitalism, one more controlled and egalitarian than the Western version.

What we have found is that almost none of the conventional wisdom is true. Japan's much-celebrated bureaucratic capitalism is *not* the cause of Japan's success; in fact, it is most closely associated with the nation's failures. As we will demonstrate, the core of the problem is that the government mistrusts competition and therefore is prone to intervene in the economy in ways that harm the nation's productivity and prosperity. The received wisdom about Japan's past corporate success has more merit, but it is dangerously incomplete. What was once a viable approach to competition no longer works in today's global marketplace. Hampered by the wrong approach to competing, Japanese companies undermine their own profitability.

Early Warning Signs

In retrospect, it is possible to identify a number of inconsistencies that should have raised fundamental questions about Japan's competitive success – and about its sustainability. Ultimately, a nation's competitiveness depends on its productivity, or the value of the goods and services produced per unit of labor or invested capital. Well before the bubble burst, there were clear signs that Japanese productivity was not what it should be, and that the process of upgrading and productivity growth was faltering.[2]

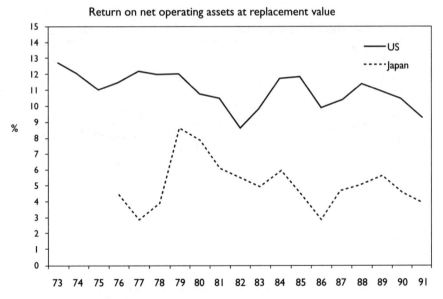

Figure 1-1   Return on assets for Japanese
manufacturing companies relative to US companies

Source: G.N. Hatsopoulos and J.M. Poterba, 'America's Investment Shortfall: Probable Causes and Possible Fixes,' draft manuscript January 1993

The first sign that all was not what it was believed to be is the relatively small number of industries in which Japan is competitive in world markets. For such a large economy, modern Japan is a player in a surprisingly narrow array of significant export industries. In fact, its export concentration more closely resembles that of smaller economies such as Canada and Korea than peers like Germany and the United States. Something has long been holding back competitiveness and productivity in many parts of the Japanese economy.

Second, Japanese corporate profit rates have long been chronically low by international standards, even in competitive industries and even after controlling for accounting differences. As Figure 1-1 shows, Japan's return on assets for all manufacturing companies was roughly half that of the United States. Another telling indicator is that the profitability of US subsidiaries in Japan has been higher than that of Japanese-owned companies. Measured by the use of capital, then, Japanese companies were much less competitive than many Western companies.

Data on overall capital productivity lead to the same conclusion. While labor productivity in Japan grew rapidly in the 1960s through the 1980s, capital productivity was far less attractive. Japanese capital productivity,

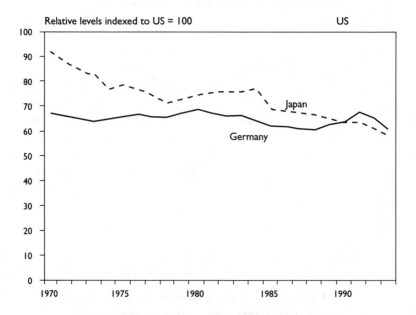

Figure 1-2   Market sector physical capital productivity, 1970–93

Source: Capital Productivity, Washington, DC: McKinsey Global Institute (June 1996)

which was close to that of the United States in the early 1970s, declined sharply through the 1970s, 80s, and 90s (see Figure 1-2). Poor capital productivity has offset advances in Japanese labor productivity, so that total factor productivity relative to the United States has changed little since the early 1970s.

The low returns to capital persisted because Japan operated largely outside the international capital markets. For years, foreign investors were held at bay. The Japanese government discouraged foreign companies from taking stakes in Japanese companies, establishing Japanese facilities of their own, or buying Japanese stocks on the open market. The dominant owners of Japanese companies have been Japanese banks, insurance companies, and other domestic companies that sought stable business relationships through cross-shareholdings held in perpetuity. Banks and insurance companies, in turn, were insulated from pressures to earn attractive returns on their capital by regulation and by market protection orchestrated by the Ministry of Finance. Foreign financial services firms were not allowed to compete effectively with Japanese banks and other institutions for funds, and Japanese investors were limited in where they could invest. Even though Japanese citizens saved heavily, the system caused the rates of return they earned on these savings to be extremely low.

The investment incomes of Japanese citizens were thus held down in favor of making cheap capital abundantly available. Beginning in the second half of the 1970s, regulation brought interest rates in Japan well below those in the United States, and the Bank of Japan provided capital to commercial banks at subsidized rates.[3]

A third, and in many cases the most telling, sign that Japanese competitive performance was not what it was believed to be was the pattern of industry performance *within* the economy. Looking at the performance of Japanese industries over the past three decades, it is no exaggeration to say that there have been two Japans. The Japan familiar to Westerners – the unstoppable Japan – was highly competitive. Industries such as consumer electronics and cars carried the entire economy, driving growth in both exports and productivity. But such industries were relatively few in number, and they existed alongside a very different, inefficient Japan.

The uncompetitive Japan consists of the large number of industries that have been a chronic drag on overall productivity. This Japan has two segments. One is the group of internationally traded industries in which Japan has never achieved a significant world export position. Included under this heading are huge sectors such as agriculture, chemicals, consumer-packaged goods, medical products, software, and virtually all services. Japanese firms in these industries have often been protected by

Table 1-1   Comparative dollar price levels of selected
services and goods, 1993 (OECD average = 100)

	Japan	US	UK
Food	205	78	74
Restaurants, cafés and hotels	178	68	121
Household equipment and operation	171	81	101
Clothing and footwear	165	77	73
Rent, fuel and power	156	91	78
Construction	155	84	74
Transport and communication	141	81	110
Medical and health care	87	136	70

Source: OECD (1995)

trade barriers and other restraints to competition, under the theory that they needed to be nurtured until they were strong enough to export. In reality, these industries remained perpetually uncompetitive, and many are still protected.

The other segment of the uncompetitive Japan consists of 'domestic' industries such as retailing, wholesaling, transportation and logistics, construction, energy, health care services, and food preparation. These industries, virtually all highly inefficient, have generated large numbers of jobs and acted as a sort of social welfare system. Consolidation and restructuring in these industries have been blocked by a wide array of government policies and forms of intervention.

One consequence of the two Japans has been an extraordinarily high cost of living. Japanese workers' high wages are offset by the high cost of necessities, including food, housing, gasoline, apparel, consumer-packaged goods, and services in general. Table 1-1 compares the prices of selected goods and services in Japan, the United Kingdom, and the United States in 1993, expressed as an index relative to the OECD average. Japanese prices are staggeringly inflated in every area but health care, where government price caps hold costs down but work against quality, innovation in treatment, and new drug development.

The Japanese pay too much for almost everything. They allocate 20% of household spending to food, compared with 12% in the United States. Buying a home is a once-in-a-lifetime event for most Japanese – the bulk of home purchases are made upon retirement.

As a result, the Japanese standard of living has been and is far lower than the nation's *per capita* income would suggest. Table 1-2 presents data on

Table 1-2   GNP *per capita* 1998, unadjusted and adjusted
for purchasing power parity, selected countries

Ranking	Economy	Unadjusted (US dollars)	Ranking	Economy	Purchasing power parity adjusted (US dollars)
1	Switzerland	40,080	1	United States	29,340
2	Norway	34,330	2	Singapore	28,620
3	Denmark	33,260	3	Switzerland	26,620
4	Japan	32,380	4	Norway	24,290
5	Singapore	30,060	5	Canada	24,050
6	United States	29,340	6	Denmark	23,830
7	Austria	26,850	7	Belgium	23,480
8	Germany	25,850	8	Japan	23,180
9	Sweden	25,620	9	Austria	22,740
10	Belgium	25,380	10	France	22,320
11	France	24,940	11	Hong Kong, China /b	22,000
12	Netherlands	24,760	12	Netherlands	21,620
13	Finland	24,110	13	Germany	20,810
14	Hong Kong, China /b	23,670	14	United Kingdom	20,640
15	United Kingdom	21,400	15	Finland	20,270
16	Australia	20,300	16	Italy	20,200
17	Italy	20,250	17	Australia	20,130 c
18	Canada	20,020	18	Sweden	19,480
19	Ireland	18,340	19	Ireland	18,340
20	Israel	15,940	20	Israel	17,310
21	New Zealand	14,700	21	Spain	16,060
22	Spain	14,080	22	New Zealand	15,840

Source: World Development Indicators database, World Bank, 7/1/99

reported GNP *per capita* (expressed in dollar terms) compared with GNP per capita *adjusted for purchasing power parity.* Purchasing power parity involves careful estimates of differences in the cost of living as well as local business costs. Adjusted for effective income *per capita*, the United States jumps to the top of the income ladder while Japan drops substantially.

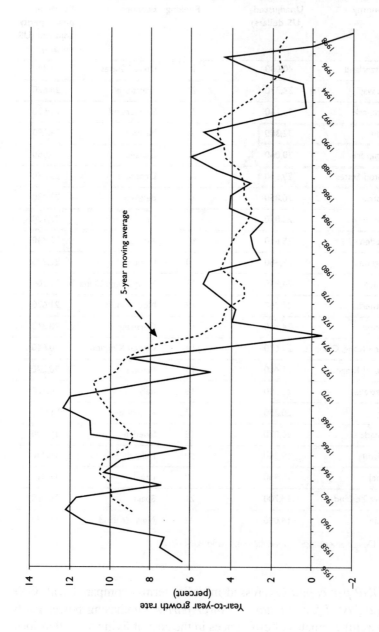

Figure 1-3   Real Japanese GDP growth rate, 1956–98

Note: Real GDP is 1990 prices. 1996 figures are estimates.

Source: *Economic Statistics Annual*, 1995, Research and Statistics Department, Bank of Japan

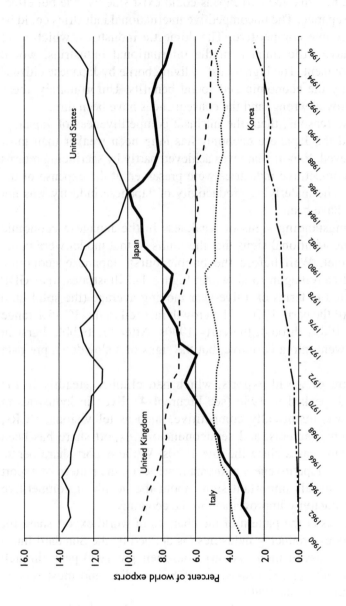

Figure 1-4 Japanese share of world exports, 1960–97

Note: World export share figures are derived from constant 1995 US$ for all countries in all reported years.

Source: World Bank National Accounts, authors' calculations

Does it matter that Japan's consumers carry such a heavy burden? Does it affect the nation's productivity and competitiveness? The policy makers assumed it did not, that the two Japans could exist side by side but effectively remain separate. The uncompetitive international industries could be nurtured to become competitive. The domestic industries, which were assumed to have little impact on the international industries, would generate employment. The higher cost of living borne by Japanese citizens was justified by the economic and social benefits. Unfortunately, these assumptions proved wrong, and the consequences have been dire.

For all these reasons, then, the intrinsic competitiveness of Japanese companies and the Japanese economy has long been weaker than most observers believed. Export share was achieved partly by sacrificing returns to capital. Uncompetitive industries were preserved at the expense of the cost of living. The underlying productivity of Japanese industry was not what it should have been.

To these longstanding signs of weakness in the Japanese economic model are some additional signs that the limits of that model were being increasingly met. Well before the bubble burst, Japanese economic growth had already begun to slow. As Figure 1-3 illustrates, real GDP growth measured in terms of a five-year moving average (the solid line) was robust until the early 1970s. The growth rate fell to the 3%–5% range from the mid-1980s through the early 1990s. After the bubble burst in 1991, growth went into a nosedive; but the signs of a slowdown pre-date the bubble.

Japan's share of world exports, which had climbed steadily in the postwar period, peaked in 1986 (see Figure 1-4). Even in industries in which Japan was historically competitive, such as televisions, VCRs, audio equipment, cameras, and semiconductors, export share has been declining in some cases since the late 1970s. While export share per se does not define competitiveness at the national level, the pattern of export share changes reveals important signs about the health of competitive vitality and productivity improvement in the economy.

Table 1-3 looks at the pattern of the changes in world export share for all Japanese goods-producing industries (as defined by the Standard International Trade Classification system) from their pre-1990 peak through 1996. Textiles and apparel peaked in 1978 or earlier, and most sectors peaked in the mid- to late 1980s.

The pattern is striking: of the 1,618 internationally traded industries in which Japan participates, its world export share has declined in 1,250 industries and risen in only 166. Industries with declining share include former juggernauts like copiers (down from 70.6% to 40.7%), still

Table 1-3   Change in world export share since the
pre-1990 peak (number of SITC industries)

Broad sector	Industries gaining share (>.1 points)	Industries losing share (<-.1 points)	No change (<.1 points to >-.1 points)	Japan does not participate	Total
Office	4	33	1	1	39
Semiconductors/computers	0	12	0	0	12
Entertainment/leisure	5	59	3	0	67
Transportation	9	88	2	2	101
Power	2	37	0	0	39
Telecommunications	0	6	0	0	6
Multiple business	10	130	1	0	141
Materials/metals	40	149	27	10	226
Health care	4	24	2	0	30
Petroleum/chemicals	40	134	5	8	187
Textiles/apparel	26	200	17	3	246
Personal	2	55	9	0	66
Defense	2	5	4	0	11
Housing/household	4	126	6	0	136
Forest products	4	55	11	0	70
Food/beverages	14	137	114	21	286
Total	166	1250	202	45	1663

Source: UN trade statistics, authors' analysis

cameras (72.2% to 34.8%), videotape recorders (89.5% to 25.8%), and line telephone equipment (52.6% to 11.2%).

In part, those fall-offs are explained by the fact that Japanese companies have established factories abroad, increasing their outward foreign direct investment. Part of this trend was driven by benign factors such as trade friction and commercial concerns (for example, the desire to be closer to customers). However, the sheer imbalance reveals deep underlying barriers to productivity and competitiveness of operating in Japan. Many companies, for example, moved activities out of Japan because inefficiencies there were simply too high.

Industry by industry, Japan's competitive advantages have eroded. In televisions, VCRs, and audio equipment, for example, Japanese companies built their dominance on analog technologies. They were masters at producing stand-alone, home-entertainment products that converted analog waves into sounds and images. US companies pioneered digital technology, in which audio and video signals are translated into the zero-one language of computers. Because Japanese companies are still playing catch-up in digital technology, US firms have made inroads not only into consumer electronics but also into other industries such as cameras.

Finally, Japan's economy stopped renewing itself in the form of new, globally competitive export industries. Throughout the 1950s, 60s, 70s, and into the early 1980s, Japanese companies entered a succession of higher value, more technologically sophisticated industries, moving from textiles to steel, automobiles, and semiconductors. This is one of the fundamental mechanisms by which productivity in an economy increases and the standard of living rises, and a major driving force behind the Japanese economy. In the late 1980s and throughout the 1990s, however, the pace of industry rejuvenation in Japan stalled, a striking indication that something was fundamentally amiss.

Of the 166 Japanese industries that have increased their world export share since the pre-1990 peak, most fall into one of two categories: industries with export positions that were well established by the 1980s, so their growth since then has been moderate; or industries accounting for such low levels of exports that the rise in export share is insignificant. We identified just 47 *emerging* export industries, defined as those where Japan had little or no exports in the late 1970s and 80s but grew exports significantly in the late 1980s and 90s – as shown in Table 1-4.

Consider the industries on this list. Twelve involve scrap or recycled materials, hardly an encouraging sign of competitive vitality. Two produce spare parts for other industries. The remaining industries are diverse but show little evidence of being major new export engines. Printing equipment and printing ink represent the only cases in which Japanese firms have recently gained an important share of a significant industry. The other industries are either small or, if they are large, industries in which Japan has only a tiny share and the growth may well be a statistical anomaly.

With few new growth industries, Japan has fallen behind the United States in fields such as wireless communications, multimedia, software, microprocessors, and networking, which are spawning grounds for new companies and new export opportunities. Japan also shows no signs of breakthrough advances in biotechnology, environmental technologies, or the entire broad and growing sector of services. Something has been increasingly holding back innovation and renewal in Japan.

Japan's actual competitive performance, then, has been mixed for decades. Even in successful industries, market share gains may have resulted more from low returns to capital than from true competitive advantages. A broad array of inefficient, uncompetitive industries and the

Table 1-4   Emerging Japanese export industries in the 1990s

Broad sector Japan	Industry	1996 export value ($000s)	1996 share of total world export
Office	Printing machinery not elsewhere specified	323,556	20.96
	Printing inks	310,136	13.99
	Bookbinding machinery	124,495	13.86
Transportation	Parts not elsewhere specified of reaction engines, turbo-propellers	388,114	3.74
Multiple business	Parts not elsewhere specified of machine tools for working stone, ceramics, concrete, asbestos, etc.	61,089	5.99
Materials/metals	Rolled silver	14,899	32.59
	Unwrought tantalum waste	41,191	20.1
	Unwrought tungsten waste	7,526	9.88
	Nickel matte, sinters, etc.	34,399	8.27
	Mica and mica waste	3,928	8.24
	Nickel waste and scrap	10,283	5.5
	Other unwrought platinum metal	24,700	5.17
	Natural quartz and quartzite	4,097	3.94
	Waste and scrap of pig or cast iron	7,959	3.17
	Tin waste and scrap	733	2.63
	Unwrought molybdenum waste	1,233	2.35
	Gold sweepings, waste, etc.	22,697	2.19
	Precious metal scrap and waste	13,568	1.78
	Industrial diamonds	1,691	1.03
	Unwrought beryllium waste	12	0.94
	Aluminum waste and scrap	9,337	0.44
	Medicaments containing hormones	224,666	3.72
Petroleum/chemicals	Vinyl chloride	144,781	20.22
	Compounds of other nitrogen compounds not elsewhere specified	384,799	17.25
	Halogen compounds, nonmetal	26,808	15.93
	Styrene	411,850	14.3
	Salts of inorganic acids not elsewhere specified	16,771	11.22
	Waste and scrap	7,317	10.03
	Tetrachloroethylene	4,535	7.63
	Petroleum bitumen, etc.	25,289	3.03
	Gas oils	425,830	2.46
	Fuel oils not elsewhere specified	497,668	2.34
	Chlorine	2,276	1.68
	Motor aviation spirit	196,867	1.65

Table 1-4 (cont'd)

Broad sector Japan	Industry	1996 export value ($000s)	1996 share of total world export
Textiles/apparel	Regenerated fiber monofilament, etc.	3,424	26.21
	Woven card wool, fine hair	63,826	7.29
	Yarn of discontinuous synthetic fibers	2,260	7.1
	Pile, etc. wool fabrics	1,901	2.43
	Other vegetable texturized fiber and waste	111	0.72
	Raw bovine, equine hides	11,835	0.36
Defense	Propellant powders	883	0.95
Housing/household	Other glass articles not elsewhere specified	148,551	21.29
Food/beverages	Yeasts and baking powders	9,784	2.18
	Fish fillets, fresh, chilled	8,724	0.93
	Animal, vegetable fertilizer, crude	1,077	0.89
	Cereal flaked, rolled, etc.	2,956	0.59

Note: Emerging industries are those whose world export share has risen since the pre-1990 peak and in which Japan did not have significant exports before the mid-1980s.
Source: UN trade statistics (Rev 2), authors' analysis

lack of new industries reveals deep-seated challenges. The bubble certainly has had a major negative impact on the economy, but its prominence has obscured other, deeper problems. Something more fundamental is wrong with the Japanese model of competitiveness, both as an explanation for past success and as a prescription for the future.

Challenging the Conventional Wisdom

Where did the conventional wisdom about Japan come from? And on what grounds do we challenge it?

The prevailing view of Japan's success has come overwhelmingly from studies of a relatively small number of industries. Observers who looked only at success stories made the intellectual leap that what happened in those cases must be the reason for the nation's success. The same industries – including semiconductors, machine tools, and steel – were examined over and over again. In most cases, the competitive gains occurred more than a decade ago. And it is notable that many of the success stories look far less robust today. Japan is no longer the leader in semiconductors, for example, the United States has supplanted it.

To complicate matters, much of the previous research focused, understandably, on identifying those aspects of firm and industry competition that were *different* in Japan rather than searching for similar underlying principles. Some of the most influential accounts were written by Western political scientists and political economists, who were primarily interested in the role of government. It was therefore natural for them to note different or unusual Japanese government practices and then conclude that those practices explained business success. Students of competition and management also gravitated to practices that were unique to Japan, such as *kanban* and total quality management, and ascribed heavy weight to them in explaining the nation's success.

Finally, there is the question of historical context. Many of Japan's government practices were instituted in the early postwar period, when the nation was devastated. Extreme measures were needed to rebuild the nation quickly. As Japan became more advanced, many of these practices remained the guiding model, but they actually hindered further development. But because research focused on only a few success cases, these problems were largely overlooked.

Much research on Japan likewise fails to account for changes in the global economy and Japan's position within it. Japan's rise to prominence began during the buoyant 1960s and early 70s, when Western companies were prospering. Few of them took the threat of competition from Japan seriously. Western companies shared their knowledge freely and readily entered into partnerships that gave Japanese firms access to markets and technologies. Back then, Japan was the only Asian participant in global markets, and its management practices were largely unheard of in the West.

By the 1980s, however, the picture was very different. Japanese companies were considered formidable rivals. By the 1990s, Western companies had emulated the best of Japan's management practices and even surpassed them in important respects. At the same time, other Asian and non-Asian nations with lower wages had copied Japan and were competing in a similar fashion in the same industries. Approaches that may have worked in the earlier context were no longer sufficient to maintain competitive success and keep productivity in the nation rising.

The Structure of this Study

We approached the question of the sources of Japan's competitive rise in a different way. First, we studied its failures as well as successes. Japan has always had many uncompetitive industries with virtually no share of international markets, which have received little attention. However, only by examining the uncompetitive Japan could we discriminate among explanations for competitive success. Prescriptions to fix Japan must be based on a clear understanding not only of what is working but also of what is not working.

Second, we revisited a broader array of Japanese success cases. Even in the midst of today's recession, a number of industries in Japan remain globally competitive. To understand why, we examined twenty industries, representing all the important parts of the Japanese economy. To ensure that our findings are representative, we included competitive industries that developed in different decades, from the 1940s to the 1990s.

Third, for central elements of Japanese policy, we supplemented case studies with statistical analyses covering the entire economy. We sought to verify the link between legal cartels, government-sponsored cooperative R&D, intensity of local rivalry, and other variables with international success. Our findings contradict the conventional wisdom in each case.

The rest of the book is organized as follows: Chapter 2 outlines the Japanese government model and its rationale. We then explore the role the government model has actually played in both competitive and uncompetitive industries. The true test of the model is whether its application discriminates between those industries that were productive and prosperous and those that were competitive failures. We also examine two widely discussed policies – legal cartels and government-sponsored cooperative R&D – in more detail. We present data on all the legal cartels and cooperative R&D projects in the post-World War II period to the mid-1990s and discuss their surprising relationship to Japan's competitiveness.

Chapter 3 turns to the Japanese corporate model. We describe the elements of the Japanese approach to competition and management, explain how they fit together, and then evaluate them in light of new learning about the sources of competitive advantage. Although the Japanese corporate model is correct as far as it goes, Japanese companies lack strategies that set them apart from rivals. As Western companies have emulated Japanese management practices, Japan's strategic weaknesses have become painfully evident.

If the Japanese model does not account for the nation's competitive successes and failures, what does? In Chapter 4, we outline a theory of competitiveness drawn from the study of many nations, which explains both success and failure among our case studies. Japan does not operate by different rules; it is governed by the same rules that determine competitive success elsewhere. In addition to our case studies, we present statistical evidence to support the framework in a wide cross-section of Japanese industries.

Drawing on the previous chapters, Chapter 5 examines the implications of our research for the Japanese government. While some aspects of government policy should continue, a major reorientation of economic policy is required. We outline some of the most important changes that will be needed along with the supporting policy priorities.

Chapter 6 turns to the implications for Japanese companies. We outline the elements of a new approach to competition and management. We also illustrate how this approach is being embraced by several highly competitive, emerging Japanese companies.

Finally, Chapter 7 confronts the questions of Japan's ability to change. Can Japan compete? We think it can. There is much that works in Japan, and many companies and industries remain competitive. Moreover, the nation has already demonstrated its capacity to respond to challenges. To renew and broaden its competitiveness and restore its economic vitality, however, Japan must come to terms with the real roots of its past success and the changing character of international competition. Recent macroeconomic solutions are easy cures that may provide temporary relief. Fixing what really ails Japan, however, will require fundamental changes in how Japan competes. For Japan to prosper again, many elements of government and corporate practice must be overhauled.

Notes

1. To be fair, there have been some calls for 'restructuring', especially in the financial sector, but no consensus on what the restructuring should look like.
2. For a discussion of the causes of national prosperity, and a discussion of the differences between the competitiveness of a nation and the competitiveness of a firm, see Porter (1990), Chapter 1.
3. Ito (1992).

CHAPTER 2

Challenging the Japanese Government Model

Conventional wisdom attributes the lion's share of Japan's postwar competitive success to the actions of its government: to the set of economic policies so prominently associated with Japan that they are universally known as the Japanese government model. But conventional wisdom is wrong.

At the core of the Japanese government model is a particular conception of the process of economic development and the bases of competitiveness. It embodies an implicit aversion to certain forms of competition and an effort to channel competition in various ways.

The underlying rationale for the Japanese government's active role in the economy is that it enjoys an overarching perspective no firm possibly could. The government model is premised on the beliefs that exports drive economic growth; that certain industries should be targeted and supported because they offer better prospects for growth, exports, and a rising standard of living; that Japan should conserve resources and avoid the wasteful and destructive aspects of competition; and that industries need to be sheltered to allow them to gain the scale needed to compete internationally. Japan's rapid economic growth and competitiveness are widely credited to a set of policy initiatives that have grown out of this general framework.

The Japanese government model was articulated from actual practices documented in a number of successful industries, which were studied again and again: coal in the 1950s, steel and shipbuilding in the 1960s, semiconductors in the 1970s, and computers in the 1980s. That approach was flawed, however, because these cases are not representative of the economy overall. Our much wider study found that each decade also gave rise to internationally competitive industries in which virtually none of the practices of the government model was employed. Consider, for example, motorcycles in the 1960s, audio equipment in the 1970s, automobiles in the 1980s, and game software in the 1990s. We found, indeed, that the core practices of the government model were almost nonexistent in the majority of Japan's competitive industries. Conversely, the model was pervasive in industries that have been competitive failures. It also led to a huge and unproductive domestic sector that has grown to be a profound drag on the economy overall. Our case study evidence is reinforced by economywide evidence on the impact of two core practices of the government model – legalized cartels and cooperative research. Again, the accepted interpretation proves to be wrong.

The Roots of the Japanese Government Model

The recent history of Japanese government intervention in industrial development begins in the early post-World War II period, when the nation was in shambles and the government sought to rebuild the economy and restore its balance of payments. As time passed, proponents of the government model justified continuing intervention by arguing that late developer countries, such as Japan, needed government participation in industry to catch up to their more developed rivals.

Initially, the government focused on basic sectors – steel, electric power, chemicals, and coal. In the chemical sector, for example, the government prioritized the allocation of foreign exchange for nylon and vinyl production through the Plan for the Rapid Establishment of the Synthetic Fiber Industry in 1949, and set forth plans to foster scale-up of synthetic fiber production through the Synthetic Fiber Industry Promotion Plan in 1953. In 1955, the government set out to reduce synthetic fiber raw material prices through the Countermeasures to Develop the Petrochemical Industry, which provided incentives and loans to establish petrochemical production in Japan.

Extensive government guidance and approval mechanisms became institutionalized during this period. For example, the government set price ceilings for chemicals through the Temporary Law to Stabilize Fertilizer Demand and Supply in 1954 and encouraged cooperation among producers to set selling prices to farmers through a similar law in 1964. The government also allowed designated companies to form cartels to scrap excess capacity through the Law on Temporary Measures for Stabilizing Specified Depressed Industries in 1978 and the Structural Improvement Law in 1983. These laws covered many basic industries.

Government was not involved in every industry. Instead, it singled out certain industries for 'targeting', including frequently studied industries such as coal, steel, shipbuilding, semiconductors, and computers. In an effort to achieve faster economic growth, the government targeted industries with high income elasticity of demand, such as machinery, elec-

tronics, and automobiles, rather than industries such as textiles in which
Japan had a comparative advantage.[1] In the 1970s, the government began
targeting high-technology industries to ensure that Japan would be at the
forefront of technological development, where financial rewards were
believed to be the highest.

The person who first codified the Japanese government model was
Chalmers Johnson. Johnson, who is sometimes called the father of the
Japanese development state concept, argued that in Japan, the government
actually nurtured industrial development whereas in Western economies,
the government simply set the rules of play. Johnson credited this developmental orientation with the massive shifts that occurred in Japan's industrial structure. Between the first half of the 1950s and the first half of the
1960s, fibers and textiles declined from 30% of exports to 8%, while
machinery increased from 14% of exports to 39%. Johnson claimed that
the rapid growth in output and labor productivity that occurred during the
1960s and the early 1970s could not be explained by economic, institutional, or cultural explanations alone, asserting that 'the government's
industrial policy made the difference in the rate of investment in certain
economically strategic industries'.[2]

Responsibility for guiding economic growth lay with the central ministry
bureaucrats who created and implemented industrial policies. As the chief
formulator of industrial policies, the Ministry of International Trade and
Industry (MITI) was identified as the catalyst for the Japanese 'miracle'.
MITI's success, Johnson concluded, could be attributed to its formulation
of practical, market-conforming industrial policies that stimulated investment and rapid growth. This view became widely accepted. Among the
industries frequently cited as the beneficiaries of Japan's unique industrial
policies were steel, large ships, automobiles, and computers.

Johnson emphasized MITI to the point of minimizing the role of other
actors in the Japanese economy. Subsequent work has stressed the importance of the complex web of networks through which Japanese institutions
simultaneously competed and cooperated. These institutions included the
Ministry of Finance (MOF), the Ministry of Posts and Telecommunications, the Bank of Japan, the Economic Planning Agency, the Liberal
Democratic Party, industry associations, the keiretsu (business groups), the
Keidanren and other economic federations, large corporations, multilay-
ered distribution channels, national labor unions, and enterprise labor
unions. These networks offered MITI the crucial mechanisms through
which it affected industrial policies and coordinated policy initiatives.[3]
They also provided a highly developed and institutionalized system of
conflict resolution, where disputes between Japanese domestic interest

groups were settled by having the winning side compensate the losing side in some way.[4]

At the same time, these networks made it difficult for foreigners to enter Japan. In particular, networks involving suppliers, wholesalers, and retailers kept foreign firms from competing on an equal footing with Japanese counterparts. As we will see, however, some of these same networks became the Achilles' heel for industries such as consumer-packaged goods, prepared foods, and apparel in the long run, virtually precluding them from becoming competitive in international markets.

Not all economists, it should be noted, ascribed the same importance to the Japanese government in the nation's postwar development. Hugh Patrick and Henry Rosovsky argued, for example, that while the government provided a favorable environment, the main impetus to growth was private. Government intervention often accelerated trends already put in motion by private market forces. Patrick and Rosovsky identified the well-educated labor force, an ample supply of managerial and technical skills, high rates of investment, and rapid technological improvement as the causes of rapid growth.[5] Our own work also suggested an alternative model, but such points of view represented a tiny minority.[6] Especially in the West, the Japanese industrial policy approach was seen as a grave threat to established orthodoxy.

Elements of the Government Model

The building blocks of the Japanese government model are listed in Figure 2-1. When scholars and others talk about the model, these are the developmental policies they most often cite.

- *Activist, central government with a stable bureaucracy*

The belief that government should actively guide the economy is the cornerstone of the Japanese government model. The principal agents for playing this role were powerful ministries, notably MITI and MOF. Staffed by elite, career bureaucrats, these ministries ensured the continuity of policy well beyond the terms of elected officials. Indeed, politicians did not even have to answer questions in the Japanese Diet, which were handled by the bureaucrats. Retiring at a relatively young age, bureaucrats then took key posts in other public institutions or the private sector.

- Activist, central government with a stable bureaucracy (most of all MITI)
- Targeting of priority industries to enhance economic growth
- Aggressive promotion of exports
- Extensive 'guidance', approval requirements, and regulations
- Selective protection of the home market
- Restrictions on foreign direct investment
- Lax antitrust enforcement
- Government-led industry restructuring
- Official sanctioning of cartels
- Highly regulated financial markets and limited corporate governance
- Government-sponsored cooperative R&D projects
- Sound macroeconomic policies

Figure 2-1   The Japanese government model

- *Targeting of priority industries to enhance economic growth*

Government targeted desirable industries for support. Targeting was manifested in laws, policy guidance provided to companies, and in the official 'visions' for the economy prepared by MITI (and to a lesser extent other agencies) that were disseminated widely. In the 1950s and 60s, targeting was accompanied by financial measures to promote the affected industries. After the 1970s, targeting sometimes involved more of a signaling role, highlighting the importance of an industry (and influencing private investment) without explicitly offering subsidies or tax incentives. Government intervention in particular industries has continued, however, often in the name of goals such as promoting information technologies or conserving energy.

- *Aggressive promotion of exports*

Japan grew its economy with a single-minded emphasis on growing exports in the targeted industries. Government was obsessed with the concept that Japan, as a small country with no natural resources, could survive only by producing exportable goods. Targeted industries were favored in numerous export promotional measures, including special tax incentives such as accelerated depreciation in proportion to export increases, below market-rate financing, and low-interest loans to establish parts and raw material production.

The sewing machine industry, for example, was promoted as an export industry immediately following World War II. Because the US Occupation Command did not allow Japanese civilians to deal directly with foreign customers at the time, the government even acted as a trading company for Japanese manufacturers. In addition, the government temporarily set the exchange rate at 415 yen to the dollar in 1948 (versus 170 yen to the dollar previously) to bolster exports and offered additional incentives for sewing machine manufacturers to allocate production for export, even though the domestic market was growing rapidly due to pent-up demand and the necessity of home sewing.

● *Extensive 'guidance', approval requirements, and regulations*
Extensive government regulations ranged from official approval requirements to so-called 'administrative guidance' to 'voluntary' rules set in consultation with industry associations. In the securities industry, for example, firms not only needed a license to operate but also MOF approval for decisions such as setting up new branches, pursuing mergers, and entering businesses outside of traditional securities services. In addition to the formal laws and rules, MOF officials promulgated numerous guidelines, many given verbally. Indeed, industry observers commented that 'MOF regulates even how to use chopsticks in this industry.' The Japan Securities Dealers Association, a voluntary regulatory body, also set scores of rules.

● *Selective protection of the home market*
To protect domestic companies from competitive imports, foreign firms were often excluded from the Japanese market. Trade and foreign exchange controls were designed to allow domestic firms to 'catch up' to their international competitors in selective growth industries. The vast majority of industries, from raw materials to final goods, were subject to protection. For example, Singer, the largest sewing machine manufacturer in the world at the time, was temporarily excluded from participating in the booming Japanese sewing machine market in the early postwar period.

These restrictions have been eased only grudgingly and incompletely, as pressure from other countries and international organizations has mounted. Japan began to liberalize imports in 1964 in order to gain the status of an Article Eight member of the International Monetary Fund (IMF). Industries where protection was considered necessary were liberalized most slowly. Import quotas, the most draconian form of protection, were abolished in color TV in 1964, passenger automobiles in 1965, color photo film in 1971, electronic calculators and cash registers in 1973, integrated circuits in 1974, and computers in 1975. However, the Japanese market remains far from open.[7]

● **Restrictions on foreign direct investment**

Strict restrictions on foreign direct investment and arduous rules governing local ownership also deterred foreign companies from entering the Japanese market. Government reasoned that infant industries and industries with high spillover effects to other industries need protection.[8] In the detergent industry, for example, the Japanese government prohibited foreign ownership of Japanese corporations throughout the 1950s and 60s. It was not until 1970 that the government allowed 50–50 joint ventures. In the securities industry, foreign direct investment was not liberalized until 1967, and membership in the Tokyo Stock Exchange was extended to only six foreign firms in 1986.

The gradual liberalization of overall formal restrictions to inward foreign direct investment began in 1956 and was largely completed in 1973. Other industries with prolonged protection included automobiles (1971); integrated circuits (1974); pharmaceuticals and computers (1975); and information processing and photo film (1976).

● **Lax antitrust enforcement**

In Japan's targeted growth industries, the goal was to establish a few players big enough to compete effectively in the world market. A notable example is Nippon Steel, formed in 1970 by the merger between Fuji Steel and Yahata Steel. Originally one company, Fuji and Yahata Steel had been broken up by the Allied Occupation Command deconcentrating Japanese business after World War II. MITI welcomed the merger, which would produce a company that controlled more than 30% of the market for major steel products. Although the Fair Trade Commission (FTC) initially opposed the merger, it was eventually approved with only a few conditions. Observers commented that if the FTC could approve this merger, it would approve any kind of merger.

In addition to allowing large mergers that concentrated major industries, government also coordinated the allocation of new plant investment. This occurred in petrochemicals, synthetic fibers, and pulp and paper, among other industries.[9] The aim was to minimize overcapacity and 'excessive' competition.

Several attempts to tighten antitrust enforcement in the 1970s and 80s failed due to political opposition. An illustrative example is the bid-rigging cases on public construction projects brought in 1981. While the FTC investigated, the construction industry persuaded the ruling Liberal Democratic Party to officially express the opinion that the FTC should relax antitrust enforcement in construction. The FTC was forced to cease proceedings.[10]

The FTC has had a limited budget and limited human resources to pursue antitrust cases. In the 1970s and 80s, it published guidelines that defined illegal acts, but compliance by industry was essentially voluntary. The guidelines were not accompanied by sanctions or punishment. Up until 1977, for example, even if the FTC found a cartel illegal, it imposed no fine. Only in the 1990s did the FTC become more active, under pressure from the United States for stronger antitrust enforcement during the Structural Impediment Initiative talks in 1989.[11]

• Government-led industry restructuring

Government planners believed that regulating capacity and preventing excessive competition were necessary for long-term industry success. Bureaucrats were also concerned that Japanese companies were too small to take advantage of the economies of scale necessary for international competitiveness. To achieve these economies, companies were strongly encouraged to cooperate through dividing up product lines in order to increase the scale of their production. Mergers were especially encouraged, because they were the most effective means to achieve scale economies quickly.[12] These ideas were first advanced by MITI in 1963, but they remained firmly in the government mind-set well into the 1990s, despite the fact that Japanese companies had become large, significant global players.

To increase scale and limit excessive competition, government sometimes actively facilitated mergers. In the marine shipping industry, for example, government forgave the interest on Japan Development Bank loans in the mid-1960s and led a process through which the fragmented industry was consolidated into six groups. In the banking industry, MOF facilitated mergers and allowed the merged banks to rearrange branches, resulting in the creation of the Daiichi Kangyo Bank and the Taiyo Kobe Bank.

• Official sanctioning of cartels

Government also sought to address business cycles, enhance scale through the vehicle of legal cartels, and aid troubled industries. These regulated how reductions in production volume and capacity would be allocated across competitors in economic downturns. One type of cartel, the *recession cartel*, was designed to keep industries alive and aid companies in weathering hard times. The rationale was to avoid the unemployment (at both manufacturers and their suppliers) that would accompany bankruptcy, a high priority given the immobility of labor in Japan. Protecting employment was seen by the government as socially less costly than forming cartels.

During the 1965 recession, for example, many industries were allowed to form cartels, including automobile tires, cameras, chemicals, paper, steel, sugar, and yarn. The 1981 recession led to the formation of cartels in asbestos slate, cement, ethylene, glass fiber products, paper, polyethylene, polyvinyl chloride, and yarn. During the 1987 recession, cartels were approved in ships and diesel engines. In all, the Japanese government approved 81 recession cartels between 1953 and 1989, when the last such cartel was approved. A number of other types of cartels were also legalized in Japan, including rationalization cartels and export–import cartels. We will explore these more fully below.

● *Highly regulated financial markets and limited corporate governance*
During the immediate postwar period, a series of laws were introduced to regulate the financial markets, including the separation of banks and securities firms and the establishment of specialized financial institutions (such as banks for long-term loans and banks concentrating on loans to small- and medium-sized companies). The regulations were intended to allocate scarce financial resources to necessary sectors while the capital market was still undeveloped and bank loans represented the dominant form of corporate financing. Although efforts toward deregulation continued, this basic framework was still intact in the 1990s, even though Japanese firms had free access to overseas capital markets.

Japanese capital market regulation was designed to 'protect shareholders' by ensuring that securities firms stayed in business. The approach has been referred to as the 'convoy system', in which all ships are slowed down so the slow ships (the weakest financial institutions) can maintain the pace. This was accomplished by guaranteeing profitability to the securities firms through fixed commissions. The costs, of course, were borne by buyers and sellers of shares in the capital markets. The Ministry of Finance closely supervised the operation of securities firms, issuing guidance. Senior executives from financial institutions would visit the MOF desk once or twice a day, and lobby MOF bureaucrats at expensive restaurants. MOF maintained tight control over information. Shareholder returns, market efficiency, and transparency were not top priorities.

Government policy also conferred little power on shareholders, whose goals were seen as different from those of firms and the economy as a whole. For example, disclosure rules were lax, so companies had wide latitude in reporting. Rules made takeover bids far more difficult than in countries like the United States. The practice of cross-shareholding also shielded companies from the pressure of the capital markets. Corporate boards had very limited monitoring power, since the rules permitted all board members

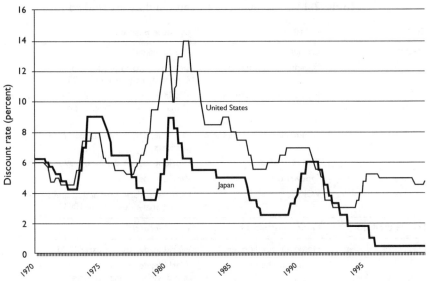

Figure 2-2   Official discount rate, Japan and the United States (1970–99)

to be insiders. Almost all the companies had their shareholders' meetings on the same day, so that shareholder activists (some of whom were opportunists seeking compensation) could not concentrate on a single company.

● *Government-sponsored cooperative R&D projects*
The Japanese government has played a heavy role in organizing and financing cooperative R&D projects. The rationale was to spread the fixed costs of R&D among many participants and to avoid wasteful duplication of effort by allocating research tasks among the participants. A celebrated example of government-sponsored cooperative R&D was the VLSI (Very Large-Scale Integrated circuit) project, designed to help Japan catch up in semiconductor technology. The project, conducted between 1975 and 1985, involved all the major Japanese semiconductor manufacturers, and the government shouldered 22% of the cost. It is widely believed that this project helped Japanese semiconductor companies gain world leadership in the industry. As we will see, however, the experience of the VLSI project was not typical, and Japanese leadership in semiconductors was lost.

● *Sound macroeconomic policies*
In parallel to the other policies, the Japanese government maintained a set of generally sound macroeconomic policies. Aided by low defense

Table 2-1   Competitive Japanese industries studied

Sector	Industry	Japanese position
Electronics	Car audio	World leader
	Facsimile machines	Dominate world production and world export share (just under 100%)
	Home audio equipment	World leader in the production and export of many home electronics products
	Microwave and satellite communications equipment	World leader in satellite communications products
	Semiconductors	World leader in the early 1990s
	Typewriters	World leader
	VCRs	Dominate world production and world export share (just under 100%)
Leisure products	Musical instruments	World leader
Machinery	Home air conditioners	World leader by the early 1980s
	Sewing machines	World leader in the production and export of industrial sewing machines
	Robotics	World leader
Materials	Carbon fiber	Share the leading position with the United States
	Continuous synthetic weaves	World leader
Optical and precision instruments	Cameras	Dominate world production and world export share (just under 80%)
Prepared foods	Soy sauce	World leader
Software	Video games	World leader
Transportation	Automobiles	World leader
	Forklift trucks	World leader
	Tires for trucks and buses	Share the leading position with the United States
	Trucks	World leader

spending, the government sustained a budget surplus for many years. Individual savings rates were high, partly because of government policy and partly because citizens needed to save heavily to buy a home and to provide for their retirement. The net result was an ample supply of low-cost capital that the corporate sector could invest in growth.[13] Figure 2-2 compares the official discount rates in Japan and the United States from 1970 to 1999. By 1987, capital in Japan was virtually free, even before adjustment for inflation.

Other government policies – political stability, a bureaucracy that brought about long-term policy consistency, and high standards for primary education – were also believed to contribute to Japan's success.

The Role of Government in Japan's Competitive Successes

Does the Japanese government model explain the nation's success? To answer this question, we sought to understand whether the application of the model and some of its key practices actually discriminated between Japan's competitively successful and unsuccessful industries. To explore the role of the government model in successful industries, we examined the twenty competitive Japanese industries shown in Table 2-1. These industries were drawn from all the sectors of the economy in which Japan has been especially competitive: machinery (robotics, home air conditioners, and sewing machines); electronics (semiconductors, VCRs, facsimile machines, home audio, car audio, typewriters, and microwave and satellite communications equipment); instruments (cameras); materials (carbon fiber and continuous synthetic weaves); transportation equipment (automobiles, trucks, truck and bus tires, and forklift trucks); and leisure products (musical instruments). In addition, we examined the two most notable and successful exceptions in two sectors where Japan is generally weak: software (video games) and prepared foods (soy sauce). The sources used in the case research are summarized in Appendix A.

In this broad sample of competitive industries, we found that the government model was almost entirely absent. Table 2-2 (at the end of the chapter) details the salient government policies industry by industry. There were no major subsidies and little or no intervention in competition. We found one partial exception, sewing machines, an older industry that was targeted in the early years after World War II to meet domestic demand for clothing and provide employment. Yet even here, Japan today is competitive not in household but in industrial sewing machines, where targeting and the other practices were largely absent. The Japanese government model, then, does not explain Japan's competitive success.

Looking deeper at the internationally competitive industries, we found that the government was indeed involved, but in various unexpected roles. Through a slew of initiatives, government *stimulated early demand* for new products, helping to foster the competitiveness of some industries. In fax machines, for example, NTT, then the Japanese government telephone company, heavily promoted the use of fax technology for the office. In the early 1970s, Japan was one of the first countries to allow facsimile transmission over general phone lines. In 1976, NTT began giving 'type approvals' (blanket approvals for facsimile machine models that met NTT standards) for individual models. Previously, approvals had been required for each individual facsimile installation, and many countries banned facsimile hookups altogether. NTT also invested heavily in marketing facsimile machines and dedicated facsimile lines. Government agencies such as the Self Defense Force, the police, the Japanese National Railroad, and the Weather Service were early adopters. The government and the private sector quickly agreed to global G3 fax standards to ensure that all fax machines could communicate with one another.

In 1977, MITI reduced the depreciable life for fax machines from ten years to five years, thereby encouraging users to buy more expensive, higher value-added models. The Japanese government also encouraged facsimile use by accepting documents sent by facsimile. In 1985, for example, the Patent Office approved faxed applications as legal documents. In contrast, the US Patent and Trademark Office treated facsimiles as documents that lacked a signature and did not file them. Although the Japanese government did not give legal standing to every document sent by facsimile, its policies lent credibility to the emerging communications medium. Cumulatively, these practices helped to create an early market for facsimile; this, in turn, sparked demand for more sophisticated versions, which spurred Japanese companies to invest in the industry and to improve their products.

A similar story can be told in robotics. The Japan Robot Leasing Company was established to encourage robot use among small- and medium-sized companies. Special financing was also made available by the Small Business Finance Corporation and the People's Finance Corporation to help small- and medium-sized firms introduce robots that enhanced worker safety. In addition, depreciation rates on high-performance robots involving computers were cut. The special depreciation allowance reached a peak in 1978–79 when buyers could write off 25% of the value of high-performance robots in the first year. In 1982–83, the special allowance fell to 10%, and it was later phased out as the penetration of robotics was well established. As with facsimile machines, Japanese government policy encouraged not only early demand but also demand for more sophisticated varieties of products, which spurred manufacturers to innovate and upgrade. In Japan and elsewhere, stimulating demand has proved far more successful than subsidizing supply.

In other cases, government regulation triggered innovation through setting *stringent standards*. In home air conditioners, for example, the 1979 Japanese Energy Conservation Law aimed to reduce energy consumption by an average of 17% by 1983 through the use of strict energy targets. This law led to a flurry of efforts to reduce energy usage and, among other things, to the invention of the rotary compressor, a technological breakthrough that reduced power consumption. In addition to achieving world leadership in compressor technology, Japan also became competitive in other refrigeration technologies, including freezing, air equalizing, and condensing.

To these government policies that encouraged competitive success, three other cross-cutting Japanese government practices can be added: *policies to encourage patient capital, a universal and rigorous basic educational system, and a supply of engineering graduates from universities.* Although not figuring prominently in the traditional model, these practices are important in the success cases.

Overall, then, as Table 2-2 illustrates, government did play a variety of roles in the successful Japanese industries. However, these roles were very different from what is most closely associated with Japan, and they were not the Japanese policies that have been the most widely emulated. Not only was there little of the intervention in competition associated with the received government model; in some successful industries, such as automobiles, the industry actually spurned government's efforts to suppress competition. In the early 1960s, for example, MITI tried to reduce the number of automobile competitors by forming three groups, consisting of two to three firms each, that would each specialize in different product categories. The companies were not interested, and the attempt failed.[14]

Table 2-3   Japanese failure cases

Sector	Industry	Japanese position in 1998
Advanced manufacturing	Civil aircraft	Less than 1% of world export share. Huge trade deficit in civil aircraft
	Chemicals	6% of world export share. Accounts for 14% of total world production but most is for the protected home market
Services	Securities	Lagged behind the United States and Europe in areas such as financial advisory services, derivatives, and venture capital. International involvement is overwhelmingly based on the low interest rates and serving the offshore needs of Japanese companies. Marred by fraud and bankruptcies
	Software	Not a single Japanese firm is included in global top 20 software vendors list*
Consumer goods	Detergents	Kao and Lion hold 70% of the Japanese market but have virtually no international presence
	Apparel	Less than 1% of world export share. Huge trade deficit in apparel
Prepared foods	Chocolate	Less than 0.1% share of world exports

*Source: Economist, May 25, 1996

MITI also tried to discourage Honda from entering the industry, as we will discuss in Chapter 3. Fortunately, Honda did not listen, and it has become one of Japan's most successful companies.

The Role of Government in Japan's Failures

Ironically, it is the failure cases that argue most strongly against the received government model. Our sample of uncompetitive Japanese sectors and industries (see Table 2-3) covers a wide swath of large, important sectors of the economy, ranging from consumer goods (apparel and detergents) to advanced manufacturing (civil aircraft and chemicals) to services (securities and software) to prepared foods (chocolate). Chemicals, software, apparel, and financial services comprise a huge portion of the economy. Aircraft is a large manufacturing industry involving the complex coordination usually seen as a Japanese strength, and Japan was a leader in aircraft technology during World War II. Chocolate is typical of the uncompetitive prepared food sector, where Japan is internationally successful in just one product, soy sauce, and somewhat successful in one other (instant noodles). Similarly, the detergents industry reveals a set of issues common to consumer-packaged goods, where Japan has enjoyed virtually no international success, with the partial exception of Shiseido in skin care.

What did we learn from these unsuccessful industries? Table 2-4 (at the end of the chapter) details the role of government in Japan's uncompetitive industries, and the contrast with the competitive industries is striking. The policies at the core of the government model figured prominently in the competitive failures. In civil aircraft, for example, the industry was essentially a single consortium. All the major development projects – for example, the YS-11 mid-size transport turboprop aircraft and the YX project (Boeing 767) – were cooperative ventures among all the Japanese competitors. The government, not competitive forces, determined which company worked on what. There was virtually no competition among the companies on any dimension.

In chemicals, an MITI-targeted sector, price controls were common. Prices were controlled for chemical fertilizers from 1946 to 1989. Favorable tax incentives and government loans were provided to chemical fertilizer, synthetic resin, synthetic fiber, and petrochemical products. MITI approvals were required to enter the sector. Capacity expansion was coordinated, and companies took turns adding plants. Joint investment in facilities was encouraged. Whenever the chemical sector hit a serious downturn in the market, recession cartels were approved (for example, in petrochemicals, synthetic resins, and synthetic fibers). In the late 1970s and 1980s, the reduction of excess capacity in petrochemicals, synthetic fibers, and chemical fertilizers was coordinated via cartels. Other kinds of targeting assistance since the 1980s included the formation of joint sales companies for polyvinyl chloride and polyolefins, which resulted in a monopoly.

In securities, a stringent licensing system by line of business blunted competition after 1965. Commissions for brokerage and underwriting were fixed, and corporate and government bond-underwriting market shares were allocated. Foreign firms were not granted branch-office licenses until 1971, neither were they granted membership in the Tokyo Stock Exchange until 1986. Emergency loans were provided to the industry during the 1964 securities panic and again during the market downturn in the 1990s.

In software, there were extensive subsidies and tax incentives for sales, product development, and systems integration. The Information-Technology Promotion Agency provided loan guarantees to computer service companies.

The chocolate industry had import quotas until 1974. These were replaced by high tariffs, which were gradually reduced from 35% to 10% by 1988. The import quotas imposed on ingredients (sugar and milk) beginning in 1961 later became 35% tariffs. Domestic ingredient producers were subsidized but remained highly uncompetitive.

We found a similar array of policies in the other failure industries. In fact, the policies widely believed to explain Japan's success were far more prevalent in the nation's failures than in its successes. Instead of encouraging productivity, exports, and national prosperity, they worked against them.

Looking deeper into the unsuccessful industries, we found some characteristic, and unexpected, problems. The first was a *shortage of trained talent*. Japan is often praised, and rightly so, for its strong basic education system and its large pool of well-trained engineers. But although Japanese universities produce many graduates in fields such as electrical and production engineering, they are surprisingly weak in fields that are important to the poorly performing industries we studied: chemistry and chemical engineering, finance, software engineering, and aeronautical engineering. More broadly, the Japanese employment system – with its flexible job descriptions, on-the-job training, and rotation of workers within the firm – excels at developing multiskilled workers, but it is much less effective at developing specialists. This proved to be particularly problematic in industries such as securities and software, which require highly specialized workers – and the ranks of such industries seem to be rising in an increasingly knowledge-intensive economy.

A second unexpected commonality was that *local industries exerted a profound drag* on the competitiveness of the traded industries. Time and again, we saw that inefficiencies in domestic sectors such as retailing, wholesaling, agriculture, and logistics exacted a heavy toll. In wholesaling, for example, there were 34 wholesalers per 10,000 people in Japan in the mid-1980s versus 16 in the United States.[15] The high cost and idiosyncratic nature of Japanese wholesaling was a major reason Japanese companies in the chocolate, apparel, and detergents industries were uncompetitive relative to American rivals.

The inefficiencies in local industries were usually due to government regulatory or licensing rules that protected inefficient firms from competition. In trucking, for example, licenses were required to enter the industry, and the Ministry of Transport approved rates long after deregulation had taken place in the United States.

Japanese companies dependent on these sectors faced high costs of doing business. More important, however, was that the structure of these sectors is idiosyncratic to Japan, so Japanese companies were forced to operate in ways that were incompatible with foreign markets. As a result, competitiveness in many export industries was weakened.

Third, many of the failures occurred in sectors or industries in which *basic and applied research and innovation* are important to competition. Despite Japan's high overall rate of R&D spending and its celebrated system of R&D consortia, industries heavily dependent on basic and applied research came up lacking. This was a chronic problem in chemicals, aircraft, software, and securities. Even in industries where formal research was not prominent in competition but innovation in design was essential for success, Japanese firms did poorly. In the Japanese apparel industry, for example, there was a striking lack of original design; the vast majority of designs were licensed from abroad. These weaknesses reflect fundamental problems in Japan's university research system as well as barriers to innovation in Japanese companies and institutions.

Finally, almost all the failures involved *misalignment between Japanese home customer needs and the needs of the global market*. In chemicals, for example, local consumers insisted on custom specifications, leading to unnecessary grades of products and driving up costs. In plastics, for example, there were literally thousands of grades. Japanese consumers are very sensitive to appearance and packaging. For instance, supermarket and other shopping bags had to be made of 'flawless' high-density polyethylene; bags with tiny spots that had no impact on product performance were rejected. Facing high packaging costs and needs for flawless surfaces or enclosures, Japanese products were uncompetitive relative to other Asian (or US) products.

In apparel, Japanese customers were preoccupied with attributes such as appearance of fabric, texture, and stitching and indifferent to qualities such as comfort, ease of care, and color coordination. In software, Japanese customers strongly preferred custom software, which was often bundled with mainframe computers by Japanese computer companies. Because they expected software to come 'free' with the computer, Japanese customers resisted paying for pre-packaged software separately. That inhibited development of the much more cost-effective software solutions that were widely accepted in the United States and elsewhere.

Sometimes limits on local demand or demand misalignment were the result of government intervention. In aircraft, for example, government discouraged air travel to promote ground (especially rail) travel. Government blocked the development of airports in Tokyo, Osaka, and other Japanese cities. Opportunities for the Japanese aircraft industry to serve the potentially huge but largely short-haul local market, whose needs were similar to Europe's and could have led to export opportunities, were all but eliminated. Even where government did not actually worsen home demand conditions, it ignored opportunities to improve them. In chocolate, for example, government set much looser product quality standards for the amount of cocoa and cocoa butter required in chocolate than other leading nations did, reinforcing the tendency of Japanese producers to proliferate low-quality products.

Competition among ministries, and among bureaus within ministries, sometimes discouraged new market needs, inhibited the birth of new industries, or delayed the shift to innovative new products. In the Ministry of Finance, for example, a strong rivalry between the Banking Bureau and the Securities Bureau existed. Because each bureau tried to protect the territory of the firms it traditionally supervised, new products such as floating rate notes and medium-term notes that might blur the demarcation between banks and securities firms were never introduced. As a result, Japan was uncompetitive in financial services, and Japanese companies were hindered in accessing modern financial products.

The information technology (software, computer, semiconductors) and telecommunications services industries were among the casualties of another rivalry – the so-called 'Telecom War' between MITI and the Ministry of Post and Telephone (MPT). MITI did not want MPT to influence the computer industry, while MPT wanted MITI to stay away from the telecommunications industry. This rivalry seriously hindered advancements that involved the combination of information technology and telecommunications.

Testing the Japanese Government Model

To supplement these detailed industry case studies, we examined two core practices of the Japanese government model more deeply and systematically across the entire economy. These are legal cartels and cooperative R&D.

Cartels and Japanese Competitiveness

It is widely believed that Japan's international success is due in part to the government's role in tempering local rivalry through weak antitrust enforcement and legalized cartels. These policies, it is held, avert the 'destructive' competition ascribed particularly to American industries and foster the collective action and cooperative activity that were believed to make Japanese companies more efficient. In some areas, such as cooperative research and joint production, American antitrust laws have been relaxed to emulate Japanese practices. Competition policy in other parts of the world has also been affected.

Antitrust policy in Japan was a US import: the Allied Occupation Command introduced the concept to Japan immediately after World War II. The first Japanese Antitrust Law, as strict as, or stricter than US laws, was enacted in 1947. The goal was to break up the Zaibatsu groups, which were considered obstacles to democratization and competition in postwar Japan. Over time, however, the law was relaxed and enforcement proved to be lax.

Small- and medium-sized company cartels were sanctioned in the original law. They were intended to protect companies from large buyers or sellers by creating collective bargaining power. Protecting small companies in this way was seen as pro-competitive because it limited the power of big business. In this type of cartel, companies are allowed to agree on almost anything, including production volume, price, terms of sale, and capacity expansion. The conditions under which these cartels were allowed were more expansive than those governing other cartels.

In 1953, in response to the recession after the Korean War, so-called *recession cartels* were sanctioned to deal with severe downturns. In recession cartels, which were open both to small and large firms, companies can agree on production levels, prices, and restrictions on capacity expansion. As noted earlier, the goal was to avoid unemployment.

Rationalization cartels, also introduced in 1953, were designed to aid in cost reduction or quality enhancement. In this type of cartel, companies

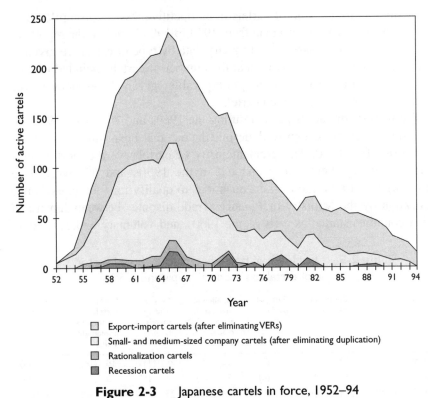

☐ Export-import cartels (after eliminating VERs)
☐ Small- and medium-sized company cartels (after eliminating duplication)
▨ Rationalization cartels
■ Recession cartels

Figure 2-3 Japanese cartels in force, 1952–94

Source: FairTrade Commission Annual Report, various years, authors' analysis

were permitted to agree on standards, allocate models among participants, share storage and transportation facilities, share technology, and collectively dispose of scrap or by-products. Rationalization cartels sought to minimize the overall level of industry investment in a particular technology or manufacturing process. It was thought that this practice was required to allow Japanese industries to catch up with the West.

Finally, *export–import trading cartels*, introduced in 1952, were originally intended to discourage 'dumping' of exports by small companies at low prices. The Japanese government worried that dumping reduced foreign exchange revenue, a critical concern in the early postwar period. Under export–import cartels, companies can agree on the quantity, price, and quality of exported goods.

In addition to the four general categories of cartels, industry-specific cartels were occasionally permitted through special laws such as the Machinery Industry Promotion Temporary Measures Law and the Electronic Industry Promotion Temporary Measures Law.

To investigate the role of cartels in competitiveness, we compiled data on all registered cartels in Japan from 1953 to 1994 based on the reports of the Fair Trade Commission.[16] Summary data by type of cartel are given in Figure 2-3 and Table 2-5. Note that the number of cartels included in each category is not always directly comparable, given differences in the breadth of products of a given cartel.

The number of cartels peaked during the 1960s and 70s. After 1989, no recession cartels were approved, despite the fact that Japan suffered a severe recession after 1990. The great majority of cartels were export–import cartels. Among them, those enacted in the 1950s and 60s were used primarily to set minimum export quantities to qualify for foreign exchange allocation by the Ministry of Finance. Trade disputes between Japan and other countries started as early as the 1960s, and voluntary export restraint

Table 2-5   Incidence of Japanese cartels by broad sector
(number of cartelized products in parentheses)

Cluster name	Recession cartels		Rational-ization cartels		Small- and medium-sized company cartels*		Export trading cartels		Export cartels (formed to implement VERs)		Total	
Materials/metals	17	(13)	2	(2)	12	(8)	29	(21)	18	(14)	60	(44)
Forest products	12	(7)	0	(0)	22	(7)	11	(6)	0	(0)	45	(20)
Petroleum/chemicals	14	(8)	0	(0)	4	(3)	25	(20)	0	(0)	43	(31)
Semiconductors/computers	0	(0)	0	(0)	0	(0)	0	(0)	0	(0)	0	(0)
Multiple business	5	(3)	1	(1)	7	(6)	17	(10)	3	(2)	30	(20)
Transportation	4	(3)	1	(1)	6	(6)	18	(6)	2	(1)	29	(16)
Power gen. and dist.	3	(1)	0	(0)	0	(0)	2	(2)	0	(0)	5	(3)
Office	0	(0)	0	(0)	0	(0)	2	(1)	0	(0)	2	(1)
Telecommunications	0	(0)	0	(0)	0	(0)	1	(1)	1	(1)	1	(1)
Defense	0	(0)	0	(0)	0	(0)	0	(0)	0	(0)	0	(0)
Food/beverages	4	(4)	2	(2)	86	(14)	27	(22)	0	(0)	119	(42)
Housing/household	16	(6)	7	(7)	569	(37)	183	(54)	39	(18)	775	(104)
Textiles/apparel	5	(2)	0	(0)	68	(29)	43	(15)	0	(0)	116	(46)
Health care	0	(0)	0	(0)	1	(1)	2	(2)	0	(0)	3	(3)
Personal	0	(0)	0	(0)	16	(11)	8	(4)	0	(0)	24	(15)
Entertainment/leisure	1	(1)	13	(13)	8	(8)	40	(9)	4	(2)	62	(31)
Not elsewhere classified			70	(17)	8	(8)	78	(25)				
TOTAL	81	(48)	13	(13)	869	(147)	416	(181)	67	(38)	1379	(389)

* After eliminating duplication in regions and purposes.
Source: Calculated from the Fair Trade Commission Annual Report, various years. The number of approval by FTC by products. When a cartel is approved for more than two product categories, it is counted for each included product category

agreements (VERs) with the United States began in 1969. Of the export cartels formed after 1962, 67 were created to implement VERs.

Cartels have tended to occur in a limited number of industries, where they have been formed repeatedly (see Table 2-5). The sectors in which cartels have appeared most frequently are textiles/apparel, food/beverages, materials/metals (especially steel), and petroleum/chemicals. Of all cartels, 64% (including 46% of products that have at some time experienced a cartel) fell into these four sectors. These heavily cartelized sectors are largely uncompetitive. In contrast, there have been no cartels in highly competitive sectors such as semiconductors and computers; just one in telecommunications equipment; and just two in office products. Only a small number of competitive Japanese industries have ever been involved in cartels. The majority were industries where the cartel implemented a VER agreement and was designed to allow the government to control and slow exports.

The competitive industries in which cartels occurred were steel (cartelized 1962–64, 1965–66, 1971–73, 1975–77), automobile tires (1965), shipbuilding (1979–82), cameras (1965–66), and ball bearings (1956–66). However, did these industries become competitive because of cartels or in spite of them? We investigated three representative cases in some detail: steel, automobile tires, and cameras (see Appendix B for summaries). In steel, cartels had neither a material influence on production nor a stabilizing effect on prices. None of the cartels in automobile tires achieved its intended purpose of limiting competition. The majority of cartels in cameras were export–import cartels, whose objective was to discourage the export of cheap, low-end Japanese cameras. None had a significant impact on export prices or volume.

Overall, then, cartels are rarely found in competitive industries. In the relatively few competitive industries in which cartels were formed, they were not strong enough to significantly limit rivalry because of the industry's structure. Conversely, cartels were common in uncompetitive Japanese industries. Legalized cartels, then, were not a source of competitiveness; they actually contributed to uncompetitiveness. This finding is confirmed by the statistical analysis discussed in Chapter 4.

Cooperative R&D and Japanese Competitiveness

Government-sponsored cooperative R&D projects are another widely celebrated and emulated element of the Japanese government model. Many believe that R&D consortia spread the fixed costs of R&D and avoid wasteful duplication of effort by allocating tasks among participants.

The Japanese government organizes the projects, 'encourages' companies to participate, and plays a major role in financing.

Perhaps the most celebrated Japanese cooperative research project is the VLSI (Very Large-Scale Integration) project, which was designed to help Japan catch up in semiconductor technology. The project, conducted from 1975 to 1985 with a budget of ¥130 billion ($591 million at the then-current exchange rate of 220 yen to the dollar), involved all the major Japanese semiconductor manufacturers. The government financed about 22% of the cost. The project developed state-of-the-art semiconductor manufacturing technology, and Japanese semiconductor companies gained world leadership soon after. These events have been seen as cause and effect, and it is widely believed that this success story is just one of many.

Other countries have emulated 'Japanese-style' cooperative research. The National Cooperative Research Act, enacted in the United States in 1984, relaxed antitrust regulations (among other things) to encourage the formation of research joint ventures. Sematech, a consortium of fourteen US semiconductor companies, was established in 1987 to jointly develop semiconductor production technology. As of 1995, the total Sematech budget had reached $1.6 billion, half of which was financed by the US government. The National Cooperative Production Amendments of 1993 encouraged joint ventures in production by further relaxing antitrust laws. Government-supported cooperative efforts were initiated in flat-panel displays, electric vehicles, and computer-integrated manufacturing. The results of these consortia have been decidedly mixed.

In Europe, the drive for collaboration was earlier and greater. Stimulated by the Japanese Fifth Generation Computer Project, the multibillion dollar European Strategic Programme for Research and Development of Information Technology project (ESPRIT) was initiated in 1984 to bolster European competitiveness in computers and information technology. As of 1999, the 26-member European Research Coordination Agency (EURECA) had sponsored 764 completed and 682 ongoing joint R&D programs since 1985 in technologies ranging from semiconductors to mobile phones to biotechnology. The cumulative investment under the EURECA program reached $21.5 billion by 1999, including an eight-year $5 billion Joint European Submicron Silicon (JESSI) semiconductor program. In the United Kingdom, the Alvey project, begun in 1983, sought to develop a fifth-generation computer. The project involved 113 companies, 55 universities and polytechnics, and five national laboratories. The $470 million budget was financed by both government and industry. It is notable that European companies have made little headway in most of these areas.

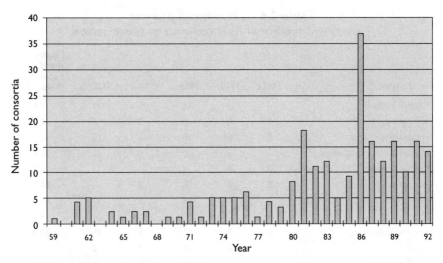

Figure 2-4   Number of R&D consortia started each year, 1959–92

Like many aspects of the Japanese model, arguments about the role of R&D cooperation in Japanese industry competitiveness have been based on anecdotal evidence or on accounts of a few highly publicized projects.[17] To examine the role of cooperative R&D more systematically, we collected data on all 237 government-sponsored R&D consortia in Japan between 1959 and 1992.[18] Most projects were sponsored by MITI, but some were sponsored by the Ministry of Transport, the Ministry of Agriculture, Forestry, and Fisheries, the Ministry of Post and Telecommunications, and the Ministry of Health and Welfare. The total budget for all projects over the 34-year period was ¥2.3 trillion, or $10.5 billion, with an average project size of $45 million. The number of projects begun in each decade increased from eighteen in the 1960s to 143 in the 1980s (see Figure 2-4). On average, 42 projects were active per year during the 1959–92 period.

Projects have taken place in a wide variety of industries. Big-budget projects were concentrated in semiconductors/computers, power generation and distribution, and petroleum/chemicals. The government budget per project is by far the greatest in power generation and distribution, due to several large energy-related undertakings.

Contrary to popular perception, however, overall Japanese government spending to support R&D consortia has been surprisingly moderate. The total government budget was $7.5 billion over 34 years, or $220 million per year and $32 million per project. In contrast, Sematech alone received $800 million from the US government between 1987 and 1995.

Table 2-6   Number of Japanese
government-sponsored R&D consortia by broad sector

Broad sector	~ 1960s	1970s	1980s	1990–92	TOTAL	Japan's world export share, 1992
Materials/metals	4	3	14	0	21	7.8
Forest products	0	0	6	2	8	2.2
Petroleum/chemicals	5	6	18	3	32	4.7
Semiconductors/computers	2	5	20	5	32	22.6
Multiple business	0	6	9	4	19	12.2
Transportation	2	6	8	2	18	18.0
Power generation and distribution	0	6	9	2	17	14.5
Office	0	0	0	0	0	19.0
Telecommunication	0	0	21	5	26	26.3
Defense	0	0	0	0	0	4.2
Food/beverages	1	1	14	12	28	1.3
Housing/household	1	1	5	0	7	4.0
Textiles/apparel	2	0	5	0	7	4.6
Health care	0	2	14	5	21	5.8
Personal	0	0	0	0	0	4.7
Entertainment/leisure	1	0	0	0	1	18.0
TOTAL	18	36	143	40	237	10.4

Note: This table covers government-sponsored R&D consortia in Japan from 1959 to 1992. Projects are assigned to the year they were launched.
Source: Sakakibara (1994)

There is no clear link between cooperative R&D projects and competitiveness. As Table 2-6 shows, there are many projects in uncompetitive sectors such as petroleum/chemicals and food/beverages. Conversely, highly competitive sectors such as entertainment/leisure and office products and services have had few, and in many cases no, R&D consortia.

Detailed data on the contribution of R&D consortia to competitiveness as perceived by Japanese managers support this indeterminate finding. We surveyed high-level corporate R&D managers from 67 companies who had participated in 86 government-sponsored cooperative R&D projects. Based on 398 responses, a typical project was evaluated as a modest success. Japanese managers did *not* perceive R&D consortia to be important to the development of their competitive positions.[19]

Perceptions of the role of cooperative R&D have been heavily influenced by the VLSI project, but this is perhaps the only project that was a consensus success. In contrast, many projects are widely recognized as failures. One – ironically, given its effect on other countries – is the Fifth Generation

Computer project, undertaken between 1982 and 1992 to develop a parallel-processing computer. The total budget was ¥54.15 billion ($361 million), of which 100% was financed by government. Distributed processing emerged during the life of the project, making large computers far less important. The architecture developed by the project was never commercialized.

Another notable example is the HDTV project. NHK spent about $110 million over 30 years to develop core equipment such as transmitters, decoder ICs, and cameras for an HDTV system. Even though the analog specifications for HDTV, which were adopted in 1964, became obsolete, NHK was unable to modify the project goal to incorporate rapidly developing digital technology. US competitors leapfrogged analog technology and developed superior digital systems. These cases reveal common flaws in Japanese-style cooperative R&D: rigidity and the need for consensus, which slow down progress and stymie innovation.

If cooperative R&D is cumbersome and not an important source of Japanese competitiveness, why do companies participate? There are Japan-specific reasons which reveal important weaknesses in Japan's innovation system. One explanation is that entry into new businesses in Japan often takes place through internal diversification by large, established firms.[20] These companies participate in cooperative R&D projects to obtain the new technology they need. Also, cooperative R&D projects are a partial substitute for the labor mobility and high degree of informal inter-firm communications that take place among R&D personnel in the United States. These are limited in Japan by the practice of lifetime employment.[21]

Finally, and most important, the limited research capabilities in Japanese universities and national laboratories, together with the weak linkages among these organizations and Japanese corporations, have made the need for knowledge transfer among firms through cooperative R&D important. In the United States, strong university research and extensive university–firm linkages both create and diffuse technical knowledge rapidly. Cooperative R&D in Japan, then, may well not be the best policy choice but rather a pragmatic alternative.

The motives of Japanese companies for participating in cooperative R&D are also misunderstood. It is commonly believed that cooperative R&D allows firms to share fixed costs and to avoid wasteful R&D duplication. However, our survey found that the primary motive is sharing complementary knowledge, which is especially crucial in system-oriented fields such as industrial robotics. In contrast, spreading the fixed costs of R&D and avoiding duplication were among the least important reasons Japanese managers cited for participating. Indeed, there is evidence that government-sponsored cooperative R&D projects actually stimulate private R&D, especially when participants bring complementary knowledge. A cooperative project legitimizes and brings attention to a technology and puts all companies on notice that others are working on it. Also, it is difficult and time consuming to hire research personnel, and mergers and acquisitions have been rare. Cooperation with other companies thus becomes the most practical way for all companies to obtain technology outside of their areas of particular expertise.

Even in Japan, cooperative R&D is a difficult and costly process. It encounters all the problems associated with the management of cooperative ventures in general, such as communication difficulties, cultural differences among participants, incentive problems, and fear of benefiting rivals. Statistical research reveals that Japanese cooperative R&D projects did not yield productive outcomes when they involved close competitors.[22]

Cooperative R&D also carries grave risks for the competitiveness of individual companies within an industry. If all companies pursue symmetric research paths, their technologies and products are likely to converge. Competition will be blunted and innovation slowed. Hence, the prevalence of cooperative R&D may well be one reason that Japanese companies rarely have distinctive strategies (see Chapter 3).

Summary

The true test of the Japanese government model is whether its application discriminates between competitive and uncompetitive industries. Our evidence suggests overwhelmingly that it does not. In the competitive industries, the government model usually played little, if any, role. There was little intrusion in competition, few cartels, and few cooperative R&D projects. In the uncompetitive industries, the government model was prevalent. There was rampant intervention in competition, numerous cartels, and often widespread cooperation.

Some argue that Japanese government intervention was necessary in certain industries precisely *because* they were failures, and that the failure had prior causes. Although that may be true, the fact remains that the intervention did not work. Therefore, the government model could not have been the driver of Japanese competitiveness. Moreover, the case for the government model was argued in terms of its benefits in enhancing competitiveness. Despite conventional wisdom and the fact that the Japanese government has fought hard to preserve its approach, the great preponderance of evidence points to the Japanese government model as a cause of failure, not the source of the Japanese miracle.

Table 2-2 The role of government in competitive Japanese industries

	Entry	Rivalry	Operating subsidies	Technology	Suppliers	Demand
	Import controls; foreign entry restrictions; entry restrictions	Cartels; price controls; capacity controls	Subsidies; low-interest loans; tax incentives	R&D support; standards setting	Intervention in supplier industries	Government procurement; influence on demand
Automobiles	• GM and Ford were prohibited from car assembly in Japan, and imports were banned in 1936 • Import quotas were abolished in 1963 • Tariffs were set to protect small domestic cars. Tariff rates were gradually reduced and abolished in 1978 • Liberalization of inward FDI began in 1971	• MITI sought to standardize products in 1955 to exploit economies of scale, and in 1961 to reduce the number of competitors (forming three groups of product category, of two to three firms each). This effort failed • Japan Development Bank loans were provided to promote mergers (1966–71). Little consolidation occurred • Voluntary export restraints since 1981	• Japan Development Bank loans for capital equipment (1954–71) • Accelerated depreciation (beginning in 1951) • Tariff exemptions for production equipment	• R&D subsidies to the industry association (1951–59) • R&D consortia beginning in 1971 on various issues (emission control, electric car, automated control system, combustion system) • Subsidies for the electric car were paid back to the government, indicating the success of the project	• Auto suppliers were designated as one of the targeted industries under the Temporary Law for the Machinery Industry (1956–70). About 500 companies received favorable loans of a total of $100 million over 15 years, as well as incentives such as accelerated depreciation • Between 1960 and 1965, firms that received favorable loans achieved 4% higher growth rate than non-receiving firms, but the stronger firms might have been the ones to receive support. (Cole and Yakushiji, 1984, p. 87)	• Commodity tax favored small cars in the 1950s, which was disadvantageous for imported large cars. Tax rates were gradually reduced from 1962 and abolished in 1989

(cont'd)

Table 2-2 The role of government in competitive Japanese industries (cont'd)

	Entry	Rivalry	Operating subsidies	Technology	Suppliers	Demand
Cameras	None	• Recession cartel to limit production volume in 1965 lasted nine months. Firms directed their efforts to exports	None	• R&D consortia on optical technology, members include all the major companies in optical technology including small companies (1962–81). Total budget ¥1.66 billion ($8 million by $1=220 yen)	None	None
Car audio	None	None	None	None	• Support provided to the semiconductor industry	None
Carbon fibers	None	None	None	• Dr. Shindo at the Osaka Industrial Technology Testing Institute discovered the world's first PAN-based carbon fiber in 1961	None	None
Continuous synthetic weaves	None	• Attempt to scrap-and-build capacity in the mid-1980s led to capacity expansion since newer looms generally were of higher capacity than old looms	None	None	• Synthetic fiber (1949) – tax incentive and favorable loan • Attempt to reorganize and reduce capacity in the synthetic textile industry: recession cartels (1975, 1978–79, 1981)	• Government procurement of synthetic fibers (1953) – effect unknown

| **Facsimile machines** | None | None | • Low-interest loan to reduce production costs and to shorten transmission time (existed at least in 1979) | • MPT accelerated the standardization of facsimiles in the early 1970s – ensured that all facsimiles were based on the same technology

• NTT began issuing 'type approvals,' blanket approvals for facsimile machine models that met NTT standards in 1976 – stimulated demand

• NTT lab conducted research on technology that directly transmitted thick documents using a technology called 'Book Facsimile technology' in the early 1980s. NTT also lab developed an ultra-high speed facsimile that transmitted a page in three seconds – assisted existing manufacturers in helping build a stronger technological foundation | • Support to the semiconductor industry | • NTT allowed full facsimile transmission over the public telephone system using dedicated lines in 1973 and over regular phone lines in 1974

• NTT advertised and marketed facsimile machines in the 1970s

• MITI reduced the depreciable life for facsimiles from ten years to five years in 1977. This stimulated the purchases of newer, higher priced, higher value-added machines

• Patent Office approved applications sent by facsimile as legal documents in 1985. This gave credibility to the facsimile's existence as a valid communications method in Japan |

(cont'd)

Table 2-2 The role of government in competitive Japanese industries (cont'd)

	Entry	Rivalry	Operating subsidies	Technology	Suppliers	Demand
Forklift trucks	• Import barriers were completely lifted in 1964–65, spurring improvement by Japanese competitors	None	• Small loans were made to a few manufacturers in 1954 to upgrade quality • Some low-interest loans were made available to smaller lift truck companies in 1964, enabling the company to improve the confidence of its banks, and loans from banks became easier	None	None	None
Home air conditioners	None	None	None	None	None	• The Energy Conservation Law of 1979 led to efforts to reduce energy usage. Led to the invention of the rotary compressor
Home audio equipment	None	None	None	None	• Support to the semiconductor industry	None
Microwave and satellite communications equipment	• No official entry restriction, but 'NTT family' companies (NEC, Mitsubishi, Oki, and Hitachi) received favorable treatment	None	None	• NTT developed microwave systems jointly with NEC, Mitsubishi, Oki, and Hitachi • NTT Telecommunications	None	• Government was a major buyer for microwave equipment: NTT (government owned until 1985) accounted for over 50% of sales. Other major buyers were

government agencies. Though purchases were conducted through international open tender, it became a mere formality since NTT knew the technological capability of each manufacturer
• Government agencies or government-related organizations were major buyers for domestic and regional satellite communication
• Large demand for microwave and satellite communication equipment in Japan because of topography contributed to the development of the industry

Laboratories conducted basic research on microwave and satellite communication technology

None

None

None

None

None

Musical instruments

None | None | None | None | • Government stimulated early demand for instruments through musical education programs in elementary schools

(cont'd)

Table 2-2 The role of government in competitive Japanese industries (cont'd)

	Entry	Rivalry	Operating subsidies	Technology	Suppliers	Demand
Robotics	None	None	• Low-interest loans made available for robot manufacturers in the 1970s. Few companies availed themselves of these loans because the interest rate differential was small and companies had adequate resources	• Government sponsored research – at a level far below that undertaken by the companies themselves • R&D consortia on the development of special-purpose robots for use in space, under water, and in nuclear power plants (1983–1991). Total government contribution of ¥20 billion ($16 million)	None	• Establishment of a leasing system and of Japan Robot Leasing Co. designed to popularize industrial robots among small- and medium-sized enterprises in 1980 • Special finance to small and medium enterprises for introducing industrial robots designed to insure worker safety in 1980 • Establishment of a special depreciation system for high performance industrial robots provided with computers in 1980 • Application of loans and leasing programs to industrial robots by local governments to help minor enterprises in modernizing their equipment in 1980

- Establishment of the FMS leasing system using special interest rates for government finance in 1984

- Establishment of a tax system for promoting investment in advanced equipment provided with electronics for smaller enterprises in 1984

- It was believed that these measures were not very important in the growth of the industry

(cont'd)

Table 2-2 The role of government in competitive Japanese industries (cont'd)

	Entry	Rivalry	Operating subsidies	Technology	Suppliers	Demand
Semiconductors	• Successfully delayed the entry of Texas Instruments into Japan. By agreement reached in 1968, MITI did not allow the establishment of 100% subsidiary (50–50 JV with Sony; later became a 100% subsidiary) • Liberalization of import and foreign investment in December 1974, which was later than other industries	None	• Japan Development Bank provided low-interest loans for capital investment from 1966. Amounted to only ¥6 billion ($14 million) in 10 years • Accelerated depreciation of production equipment from 1960s	• MITI electronic research lab produced the first domestic IC in 1956 • 50% subsidy for LSI development: 1973–74, ¥3.5 billion ($9.7 million) • VLSI project (1976–86) ¥130 billion – 22% that was financed by the government led to advancement in the manufacturing technology • Intellectual property rights for the design of LSI strengthened in 1985 • The number of college graduates with electronics engineering degree was 1.8 times higher than that in the US in the 1970s	• Semiconductor manufacturing equipment suppliers benefited from the VLSI project (though not official members)	• Establishment of the computer leasing company (JECC) in 1961 – Japan Development Bank loan for the purchase of computer – JECC accounted for 30%–70% of the domestic computer demand until 1980s • Series of computer joint development projects since 1962

Sewing machines					
• Little or no allocation of foreign exchange for the import of light machinery in the early postwar period. Sheltered the domestic industry	• Price controls: fixed the manufacturer's selling price and the resale price of the standardized model, HA-1, at the low level from 1946 to 1951. Helped stimulate demand, forced manufacturers to cut costs	• Temporarily set the exchange rate at 415 yen to the dollar in 1948, versus 170 yen to the dollar previously, to provide incentives for manufacturers to allocate production for export. Not specific to sewing machines	• The Sewing Machine Technology Council, under the guidance of MITI, set uniform standards for sewing machines and components and created the first standardized model, the HA-1, with 130 components in 1947. Allowed the entry of numerous small- and medium-sized subcontractors into the industry, reducing costs • Voluntary inspection councils judged products on a number of dimensions in 1947. This stimulated product quality improvement and upgrades	(See Technology)	• Mandatory sewing classes for girls at public elementary and junior high schools, Ministry of Education provided subsidies toward sewing machine purchases – helped stimulate demand • MITI designated four companies to manufacture 800 household sewing machines for export, and MITI served as a trading company in 1947 – stimulated exports and opened the industry to international competition early on • Elimination of cumbersome paperwork and government approval procedures for export in 1948 – drove exports further • Termination of the export quality inspection system in 1960 – government involvement came to an end

(cont'd)

Table 2-2 The role of government in competitive Japanese industries (cont'd)

	Entry	Rivalry	Operating subsidies	Technology	Suppliers	Demand
Soy sauce	None	None	None	None	None	• Establishment of product standards in 1953 to ensure consistency of product quality
Tires for trucks and buses	None	• Recession cartel in 1965. Restriction of production volume/allocation of market share • Government 'guidance' encouraged reduction in the number of tire varieties from 167 to 58. Encouraged revision of the production system in 1965	None	None	None	None

Trucks	None	• Restriction on the number of trucks produced by foreign makers in Japan in 1936 • Tariff increase in 1936 • Required permits for production: only Toyota, Nissan, and Isuzu received permits in 1936. This policy encouraged industry consolidation during the pre-war period • Import prohibition was lifted in 1961. Few imports occurred because of the low domestic price and different local needs (small trucks)	None	• Prioritized allocation of materials, capital and labor; special loans in the immediate postwar years helped the development of the industry • Low-interest loans, a reduction or exemption from taxes, special depreciation rules, reduction or exemption of taxes related to importing of equipment from 1951. Loans only accounted for a small percent of total investment	None	• Low-interest loans to parts manufacturers from 1956 – accounted for 30% of total equipment investment	None
Typewriters	None	None	None	None	None	Support to the semiconductor industry	None

(cont'd)

Table 2-2 The role of government in competitive Japanese industries (cont'd)

	Entry	Rivalry	Operating subsidies	Technology	Suppliers	Demand
VCRs	None	None	None	• MITI provided an R&D subsidy in 1958. Sony and NHK copied Ampex's (US) VCR, learning the technology • Government attempted through guidance to build an industry consensus around the beta standard. The effort failed	• Support to the semiconductor industry	None
Video games	None	None	None	None	• Support to the semiconductor industry	None

Table 2-4 The role of government in uncompetitive Japanese industries

	Entry	Rivalry	Operating subsidies	Technology	Suppliers	Demand
	Import controls; foreign entry restrictions; entry restrictions	Cartels; price controls; capacity controls	Subsidies; low-interest loans; tax incentives	R&D promotion, standards	Intervention to suppliers	Procurement; intervention to buyers; sales promotion
Apparel	None	None	None	• R&D consortia on the automated sewing system (1983–91)	• Support to synthetic fiber industries	• Large-Scale Retail Store Act limited the development of alternative channels, encouraging strong relationship between apparel makers and department stores

(cont'd)

Table 2-4 The role of government in uncompetitive Japanese industries (cont'd)

	Entry	Rivalry	Operating subsidies	Technology	Suppliers	Demand
Chemicals	• Government-owned plants to provide raw material for the chemical fertilizer industry dating back to the 1870s • Petrochemicals: entry approval (1956–72). Though virtually all the applications were ultimately approved, this policy hindered competition. Even though a minimum scale was set for the approval, many plants did not achieve economies of scale	• Chemical fertilizers: price control (1946–89) and supply control (1946–89). Delayed the chemical sector's shift to petrochemicals • Petrochemicals – approval of capacity expansion, promotion of joint investment (1956–87) • Recession cartels for petrochemicals (1972, 1982), synthetic resin (1959, 1966, 1972, 1977, 1982), and fiber (1975, 1978–79, 1981) • Excess capacity scrap by petrochemicals (1978–88), synthetic fiber and chemical fertilizers (1978) through cartel formation, with favorable loans and tax incentives • Promotion of mergers, joint production, and sales	• Prioritized foreign exchange allocation to the chemical fertilizer industry in 1946 • Chemical fertilizers: aid for production facilities, low-interest loans, preferred allocation of raw materials, subsidies and low-interest loans for the introduction of new production facilities since 1954 • These policies delayed the chemical sector's shift to petrochemicals • Synthetic resin and fiber (1949), petrochemicals: tax incentive and favorable loans • Petrochemicals: low-interest loans, accelerated depreciation, approval of the import of technologies,	• Approval to import foreign technology through foreign exchange allocation (1949–72) • Process patents prior to 1975. This discouraged new product development • Cooperative R&D to reduce energy, reduce raw materials costs, and develop new products since 1967 • Favorable loans for new technology commercialization (1951–)	• Support to the Iran–Japan Petrochemical project (1973–mid-1980s) – discontinued after the Iran–Iraq war • Petroleum industry: approvals for entry, production, capacity expansion, allocation of crude oil throughput to each company (1934–92) – petroleum industry remained uncompetitive • Insufficient number of college graduates with chemical degrees • Weak research in chemicals – limited new product development	• Government procurement of synthetic fibers (1953) – effect unknown • Formation of joint sales companies for polyvinyl chloride (four companies from 1982) and polyolefins (four companies from 1983) – MITI's intention was to induce industry consolidation and promote competition between joint sales companies, but in effect the policy worked to establish a joint monopoly

• All these practices nurtured the cartel nature of the industry, let the weakest players survive, removed upgrading pressure, delayed product innovation, and reduced rivalry, resulting in few strategy differences among companies

allocation of foreign exchange, and tariff exemption for the import of equipment were provided for the government-approved investment plans since 1956

(cont'd)

Table 2-4 The role of government in uncompetitive Japanese industries (cont'd)

	Entry	Rivalry	Operating subsidies	Technology	Suppliers	Demand
Civil aircraft	• Licensing requirements for manufacturers and repairers. Though virtually all the companies that had planned to enter did enter, this practice fostered the cartel nature of the industry	• All aircraft and engine development projects since 1953 are collaborative with predetermined work allocation. No rivalry developed	None	• Limited support for basic research facilities and university research	• Small military demand	• Military procurement since 1930, restarted in 1956 – helped the development of the industry, but limited supply of pilots (compared with US and European countries) as a springboard to develop commercial aircraft. Domestic development of the military aircraft largely ceased by 1977 • Prohibition of exports of military aircraft in 1967. Firms could only serve domestic markets • Heavily regulated airline industry and stunted domestic demand because of the policy choice to promote public ground transportation and the limited capacity at major airports and commuter airports – limited demand for commuter airlines

Chocolate						
• Import quota abolished in 1974 • 35% tariff since 1974 – reduced to 20% in 1983 and to 10% in 1988	None	None	• Export promotion: subsidy (1939–40) and tariff relief on primary ingredients in the 1930s. Limited success in promoting exports	None	• Promotion of the establishment of sugar and cacao plantations in Japanese colonies in 1939 • Abolition of import tariffs on cacao beans in 1929. Helped the development of the industry, but did not continue because of WWII • Restriction of imports of cacao beans in 1937; imports prohibited in 1941 • Import quotas on cocoa in the 1950s. Abolished in 1960 • Import quotas and domestic subsidies on sugar and milk since 1961 •35% tariff on sugar and milk since 1974. Made essential chocolate ingredients more expensive, Japanese companies were driven to develop a chocolate substitute	• Lax regulation of the percentage requirements of cocoa and cocoa butter in grades of chocolate. Indirectly sanctioned the domestic production of inferior quality products

(cont'd)

Table 2-4 The role of government in uncompetitive Japanese industries (cont'd)

	Entry	Rivalry	Operating subsidies	Technology	Suppliers	Demand
Detergents	• Restriction of inward FDI until 1970. Delayed foreign entry	• Abolition of the Resale Price Maintenance System in 1973. Invited price reduction, made the industry even less profitable	None	• Process patent (not product patent) on chemicals prior to 1975 discouraged new product development	• Support of the petrochemical industry	None
Securities	• Registration system from 1948 to 1965 • Licensing system by the line of business since 1965 • Branch office licenses were not granted to foreign firms until 1971 • Tokyo Stock Exchange membership was not granted to foreign firms until 1986 • These policies all effectively worked as entry barriers and suppressed competition	• Allocation of corporate bond underwriting shares since 1951 • Allocation of government bond underwriting shares (1965–77) • Approval or guidance for setting up new branches, mergers, entry to new businesses since 1965 • Fixed commission for brokerage and underwriting until the mid-1980s • Fixed pricing scheme for bond issues • Division of work between banks and	• Emergency loans during the 1964 securities panic and the stock market crash in the 1990s – allowed the weakest player to survive, though Yamaichi eventually went bankrupt	None	None	• Securities purchase during the 1964 securities panic – effectively weathered the market downturn • Lenient disclosure requirements and complicated rules for takeover bids – discouraged M&A and related businesses • Restrictions on overseas issuance of debt securities by Japanese firms until 1973 – discouraged overseas business

securities firms since
1948

● All of these policies
allowed the weakest
player to survive, and
discouraged
innovation

● No 'Chinese Walls'
to separate
underwriting from
brokerage until 1988.
Encouraged the
sales-driven nature of
the business and
contributed to stock
price manipulation

(cont'd)

Table 2-4 The role of government in uncompetitive Japanese industries (cont'd)

	Entry	Rivalry	Operating subsidies	Technology	Suppliers	Demand
Software	• MITI represented computer makers in negotiating with IBM for licensing agreements in return for allowing IBM production in Japan in 1960. Government approval requirements delayed IBM's full-fledged entry to the Japanese market	None	• Loan guarantees by IPA to computer service company • Tax incentives for software companies to promote after-sales maintenance, packaged software development (1979), and system integrators. Effects hard to quantify, but apparently did not yield visible results	• R&D subsidy • R&D consortia since 1962 • Formation of three groups to develop new computers in 1971, 50% subsidy provided. Contributed to the establishment of computer businesses and software business to some extent, but market forces (that is, US dominance in software) are far stronger than what Japanese companies can do to obtain *de facto* standards	• Training center for programmers, SEs • Qualification exam for programmers • Lagged in software research and education at the university level. Shortage of programmers and software engineers, low productivity • The Law for Labor-Dispatching Business in 1986 discouraged the practice of dispatching software engineers to client companies for custom software development. This contributed to correct the 'body shop' nature of the industry	• Establishment of a government-sponsored computer leasing company, low-interest loan provided – contributed to increase the installed base of computers • Prohibition of on-line data transmission until 1972, data exchange via computer until 1982 – regulation lasted longer than the US (allowed the connection of computers in 1968, total deregulation of data communication in 1980), discouraged on-line data processing and the development of computer networking • Promotion of general-purpose software development and sales through IPA in

1979 – did not play a major role

• Copyright law to protect software in 1986 – discouraged illegal software copying

• Promotion of computer education at junior and senior high school level in 1993 – came much later than the US

Appendix A: How the Case Studies were Developed

The case studies of the twenty competitive Japanese industries and seven uncompetitive Japanese sectors and industries were prepared by Michael E. Porter, Hirotaka Takeuchi, and Mariko Sakakibara, with assistance from Michael J. Enright (now at the University of Hong Kong), and a large research team including Yoshinori Fujikawa, Satoshi Akutsu, and Tomohiro Doai at Hitotsubashi University. Lucia Menzer Marshall helped develop data on Japan's competitive performance and in rewriting the summary case study documents.

The case research is based on myriad published sources including books, academic and trade journals, newspapers, reports by nonprofit research organizations, MITI, and various trade associations. The authors and the team also conducted numerous interviews with industry participants, industry observers, trade association officials, and government officials.

The sheer quantity of sources is such that detailed citations for all the case studies are not included in this book. Complete references are available from the authors upon request.

Appendix B: Case Studies of the Role of Cartels in Competitive Industries

The Japanese steel industry consists of six integrated steelmakers with blast furnaces and approximately 60 other companies that operate electric furnaces. Rivalry was intense among the top six companies until 1970. Market share fluctuated frequently, with Kawasaki and Sumitomo gaining shares at the expense of the market leader, Yawata. Several attempts by companies and the government to control prices and ensure orderly capacity investments failed. A recession cartel, formed in 1965, was one such attempt. It was intended to limit the production of thick and medium plate. Another cartel was formed in 1971 to limit production of stainless steel, thick and medium plate, thin plate, wires, tubes, and structural alloy steel. Neither cartel had a material influence on production or stabilized prices.

In automobile tires, there were seven Japanese competitors: Bridgestone, Yokohama Rubber, Sumitomo Rubber, Toyo Tire & Rubber, Ohtsu Tire & Rubber, Michelin Okamoto, and Ryoto Tire in 1994. Fierce rivalry characterized the industry, and market shares of competitors changed markedly between 1955 and 1991. Tire companies participated in three cartels in the post-World War II period. A 1963 rationalization cartel was formed to reduce the number of SKUs, but unit prices kept declining. A 1965 recession cartel was intended to restrict output, but production actually increased. A 1967 export–import cartel was formed to increase export price, but the export price did not rise though export volume increased. None of the cartels in automobile tires achieved its intended purpose of limiting competition.

The Japanese camera industry has a highly competitive history, with frequent market share fluctuations. It has had one recession cartel and twelve export–import cartels. A recession cartel was formed in 1965 to cope with sluggish domestic demand. This cartel, which lasted nine months, aimed to limit production volume. Production did decline from the level of the previous year, though demand was also lower. Export–import cartels seem to have been directed at discouraging the sale of cheap, low-end Japanese cameras. Many cartels were terminated by 1972. Voluntary export restraint agreements with foreign governments to restrict camera exports began in February 1973. Nevertheless, the export value and volume of Japanese cameras continued to increase.

Overall, then, cartels are rarely found in the most competitive industries. And in the handful in which they do occur, they were not sufficient to significantly limit rivalry because of the underlying structure of the industry.

Notes

1. Tyson and Zysman (1989).
2. See pages 9 and 31 in Johnson (1982).
3. Okimoto (1989).
4. Calder (1988).
5. Patrick and Rosovsky (1976). See also Eads and Yamamura (1987) for competing views of the role of government in the Japanese development. For an excellent comparison of the business–government relationship between Japan and the United States in historical perspective, see McCraw (1986).
6. See Chapter 8 in Porter (1990).
7. For a discussion of how Japan managed import liberalization, see Yoffie (1986).
8. Ito and Kiyono (1984).
9. Kisugi (1999).
10. Koshiro (1999).
11. Koshiro (1999).
12. MITI (1963).
13. For a discussion of how the Japanese government encouraged saving, see McCraw (1986).
14. Tsuruta (1984).
15. Ad Hoc Administration Reform Promotion Council Coordination Office (1988).

16. Fair Trade Commission Annual Report, (various years). Reiko Kinoshita and Kyoko Ichijo provided assistance in the analysis.
17. Callon (1995), for example, presents a mixed view of Japanese R&D consortia based on case studies.
18. For more detailed discussion of the research summarized in this section, see Sakakibara (1994, 1997a, b, 1999a, b), Branstetter and Sakakibara (1998), and Sakakibara and Branstetter (1999b).
19. See Sakakibara (1997b). Statistical analysis also shows that the participation to R&D consortia had a positive but only moderate effect on the R&D productivity of partici-pating firms (see Branstetter and Sakakibara, 1998).
20. Porter (1992).
21. Saxonhouse (1985).
22. Sakakibara and Branstetter (1999b).

CHAPTER 3

Rethinking Japanese Management

According to conventional wisdom, Japan's unique management model is the other leg of its postwar economic success. We agree – in part. The model stresses attributes such as teamwork, a long time horizon, and dedication to continuous quality improvement, all of which remain important Japanese strengths. But it has also encouraged conformity and a conception of competition that is dangerously incomplete.

The model of Japanese corporate success is built on the notion that a company can achieve both the highest quality and lowest cost simultaneously by employing fundamentally better managerial practices than its rivals do. Companies compete by relentlessly staying at the frontier of best practice through continuous improvement. This model is not an abstract theory; it derives from the extraordinary advances made by Japanese companies through pioneering a host of by now well-known managerial practices, such as total quality management (TQM), lean production, and close supplier relationships. These produced persistent cost and quality advantages over Western companies.

The Japanese Corporate Model

The corporate model consists of a series of production practices, human resource policies, organizational and leadership approaches, and modes of diversification, all guided by a distinctive set of corporate goals. Although various accounts differ in emphasis, most, if not all, name the elements in Figure 3-1. Characteristic product, channel, and other policies grew from this model. The benefits of the Japanese corporate model, identified by both Western and Japanese scholars, include rapidly improving the skills of employees, creating a strong sense of community, building employee loyalty, and encouraging managers to take a long-term view of business decisions.

- High quality and low cost
- Wide array of models and features
- Lean production
- Employees as assets
- Permanent employment
- Leadership by consensus
- Strong intercorporate networks
- Long-term goals
- Internal diversification into high-growth industries
- Close working relationship with government (discussed in Chapter 2)

Figure 3-1   The Japanese corporate model

• *High quality and low cost*
The Japanese corporate model is based on the belief that competitive advantage can be gained by simultaneously offering superior quality and lower cost. At the core of this approach are process improvements that reduce cost but, through reducing defects, rework, the number of parts, or delay, also improve product quality. The insight embraced by Japanese companies was that standardization, mass production, and eliminating unnecessary process steps were not only tools for cost reduction but the best way to achieve very high levels of quality in terms of consistency and timeliness. For example, the use of automated parts-insertion machines to produce electronic products by Japanese companies in the early 1980s resulted in unheard-of low levels of defects.

• *Wide array of models and features*
Japanese companies sought to provide a wide line of models offering multiple features. Typically, a set of standard products was offered with a wide range of options or additional features. A major thrust was multifunctionality, or products that combined many features into the same product. Japanese companies also offered a steady stream of new models over time, dramatically shortening the product life cycle.

• *Lean production*
The lean production system[1] played a central role in the Japanese corporate model. Pioneered by Toyota, lean production treats product development, production, and purchasing as a total system. By optimizing the system, Toyota achieved high levels of quality, productivity, timely delivery, and flexibility simultaneously. The origins of the lean production system date back to the beginning of the Toyota Motor Company in the 1930s, when the founder, Kiichiro Toyoda, stressed the concept of 'just in

time.' In the late 1940s, Taiichi Ohno, then a Toyota production supervisor, combined elements of the Ford and Taylor approaches, such as work standardization and a craft-type system that allowed workers to develop multiple skills. Toyota continuously improved this hybrid system, which many other Japanese companies then adopted.[2]

The components of lean production, an internally consistent system, include:

- *Total quality control.* All Japanese workers were guardians of the quality of the product and consequently had the authority to stop the entire manufacturing process to remedy production problems. Workers were trained in standardized problem-solving processes to improve quality;
- *Continuous improvement,* otherwise known as *kaizen.* Improvements were often suggested by workers and implemented before being officially proposed. Approaches that revealed problems before they became serious, such as monitoring stocks of inventory, stopping the assembly line when defects were found, and cleaning factory floors to detect minor abnormalities in machines were key elements of *kaizen*;
- *Just-in-time (JIT) manufacturing,* or manufacturing to demand rather than to inventory. JIT was implemented through the *kanban*[3] or 'supermarket' system in which the downstream production station obtained just the quantity of parts needed, while the upstream production station produced just enough to replenish what was taken;
- *Design for manufacturability.* Engineers worked on the assembly floor to determine how product designs could be modified to make them less expensive or easier to manufacture;
- *Close supplier relationships* encouraged joint development of improved products and components by suppliers as well as loyalty between the parties. Among the key practices were frequent information exchanges from the very beginning of the development process, personnel rotation, long-term relationships with a small number of first-tier suppliers, and incentives to suppliers for improvements in efficiency;[4]
- *Flexible manufacturing,* in which firms attempted to reduce production lot sizes and increase production line flexibility in order to accommodate wide product lines and rapid model changes. Flexible manufacturing involved machines that were adaptable to design changes, work standardization and multitasking, and a shop floor design that enabled the process layout to change easily. It thereby expanded the ability to

tailor products to specific market segments and cut the time needed to introduce new products; and

- *Rapid cycle time*. To support fast product life cycles, new products were developed and introduced rapidly through parallel rather than sequential development processes, multiskilled engineers, rapid production of prototypes, and the active participation of suppliers in development. Powerful product managers coordinated the effort.[5]

- **Employees as assets**

The Japanese corporate model emphasizes a set of human resource policies intended to create a strong sense of community within the company, employee loyalty, and a long-term orientation in managerial decision making.[6] Highly selective recruiting to limit the number of employees hired, bonuses based on overall corporate performance, and participatory management styles are all thought to have contributed to a sense of community. This system was widely adopted by large Japanese corporations in the 1950s and 60s, and it spread to smaller companies in the 1970s.[7]

- **Permanent employment**

At the center of the Japanese human resource system was lifetime employment, which guaranteed full-time, male employees a position for the extent of their careers. This commitment aligned the incentives of the employee with those of the company.[8] Furthermore, employee identification shifted to the company and away from the specific job or task such as welding or lathe operating. As a result, employees were much less resistant to change. Lifetime employment also encouraged on-the-job training and created generalist, multiskilled, and adaptable workers.[9]

Although lifetime employment made controlling the size of the workforce difficult in the short term, it diminished some of the destabilizing factors found in the United States, such as high turnover, recruitment and termination costs, and worker alienation.[10] If lifetime employment sometimes resulted in too many workers allocated to a given activity, the cost was thought to be more than offset by the efficiencies that came from increased worker trust and cooperation.

Lifetime employment led Japanese managers to emphasize career development.[11] The personnel department in a Japanese company was highly respected,[12] and a system of rotation throughout the company developed managers who were generalists and well versed in all aspects of the business.[13] Because Japanese managers knew that they would hold many different positions over the course of their careers, they were less resistant to change and more loyal to their companies than most Western managers.[14]

Promotion and pay based on seniority also aimed to improve long-term company performance by decreasing competition among individuals, fostering group cohesion, and allowing managers to be judged on long-term performance.[15] It is worth noting that seniority-based compensation means that young workers are prone to be underpaid relative to their contributions, a situation that is sustainable only when the secondary job market is underdeveloped and there is little possibility that young workers will be attracted by higher compensation elsewhere.[16]

Company unions were characterized by close relationships between union leaders and middle management. Company unions reinforced the Japanese human resource system and helped companies avoid many of the West's labor problems.[17] The union structure also helped to make workers more receptive to innovation because the union was attuned to the company's particular needs and workers would readily switch tasks within the company. This system aligned employee goals more closely with corporate priorities than Western approaches.[18] Active participation by employees in management and in process improvement has also been linked to lifetime employment, promotion and pay based on seniority, and union structure.

● *Leadership by consensus*
The leadership process in the Japanese corporate model is characterized by a search for consensus. The so-called *ringisho* decision-making process built consensus and smoothed implementation by allowing all managers to express opinions about proposals under consideration.[19] Informal groups within the formal organizational structure encouraged discussions that served as the basis for decision making.[20] Although there was a clear hierarchy within each group corresponding closely with age, responsibility for actions was spread out in an informal group structure that did not correspond to seniority. Ezra Vogel argues that these informal group dynamics had more to do with Japanese managerial success than the more frequently stressed *ringisho* decision-making system, lifetime employment, and seniority-based promotion.[21]

Quality circles and TQM also fostered consensus building and a company orientation. A host of formal and informal participatory management processes contributed to the companies' ability to achieve high-quality standards and introduce gradual innovation on the shop floor.[22]

Because of the seniority system, promotion to senior management was usually slow, after many years of rotating through various positions.

However, in the immediate post-World War II period and up to the 1970s, a management vacuum allowed individuals to become CEOs at a relatively young age. Akio Morita at Sony and Soichiro Honda at Honda were two such leaders. After the 1970s, the average age of CEOs rose and their average tenure shortened to give more individuals an opportunity to hold this position at the end of their careers. Given these circumstances, it is not surprising that most of the current generation of senior management is highly sensitive to the harmony of the workplace.

● **Strong intercorporate networks**

An important part of the Japanese corporate model is an intricate web of relationships among banks, suppliers, and companies in related fields. These relationships were ubiquitous in Japan but were best known within the industrial groups known as *keiretsu*. Japanese companies historically financed 80% to 90% of their assets with bank loans, often from their *keiretsu* bank affiliate. Much equity was usually held in friendly hands through cross-ownership arrangements. Such arrangements, in which companies hold equity in one another, created a stable, long-term ownership structure and removed pressure from the stock market to achieve short-term results.[23] Shareholders were rewarded in the form of business relationships and capital gains due to sustained growth. Although *keiretsu* companies managed their affairs quite autonomously, there was a strong presumption to buy (and hence sell) goods and services within the group when possible. The *keiretsu* structure, then, created a built-in network of suppliers and customers that was seen as highly beneficial to collaboration and competitive success.

● **Long-term goals**

The combined effects of stable ownership and policies such as lifetime employment led Japanese managers to make decisions based on a very long time horizon compared with Western executives, who focused more heavily on near-term profitability. Japanese managers ranked pursuit of market share as their number one priority, while the number one priority for US managers was attaining an attractive return on investment.[24]

The importance of growth and market share in Japan was tied directly to the need to keep plants running at full capacity to maintain employment. Under a lifetime employment and seniority system, for example, rapid growth meant greater chances for promotion and pay increases.

Many consider this difference between Japanese and US corporate goals to be central to Japan's success in international markets, especially in industries such as semiconductors, which require years of investment before a return is achieved. Because US firms tended to set higher return on investment hurdles, Japanese firms could enter markets, price aggressively to build market share, drive down return on investment, and count on their US competitors to disinvest or leave the market.

- **Internal diversification into high-growth industries**

The strong growth orientation also encouraged diversification, especially into high-growth industries. Doing so would extend the life of the company and provide opportunities to redeploy workers freed up by the maturing of established businesses. Relative to Western firms, Japanese diversification tended to occur through internal development and in related industries. This pattern developed because acquisitions were not an accepted and feasible management practice, in part because of cross stock holdings and permanent share ownership. The desire to redeploy employees also led companies to favor related industries where the same skills could be applied.

An Internally Consistent System

The elements of the Japanese corporate model were internally consistent. The simultaneous pursuit of quality and cost demanded a culture of continuous improvement in which everyone's ideas were solicited and integrated. Human resource and leadership practices fostered just such a culture. The focus on market share and growth led to wide product lines, frequent product introductions, and related diversification. Wide and rapidly changing product lines, in turn, required flexible production, cycle time reduction, and generalist, multiskilled workers who could and would respond to changing needs. Human resource practices such as lifetime employment aligned employee incentives with this behavior. The stability of corporate networks allowed managers to focus on the long-term horizon needed to build share and grow rather than short-term profits, which could also threaten employee jobs. These networks also fostered the relationships with suppliers that boosted efficiency and accelerated product development.

Not only was the corporate model internally consistent, but it was in close alignment with the government model. For example, a long time horizon was nurtured by benign antitrust policies, weak corporate governance, and protection from international competition. Cooperative R&D and targeting fostered corporate growth through internal development while maintaining lifetime employment. Tight control of financial markets allowed Japanese financial institutions to gather the low-cost capital required for aggressive investments in new products and new capacity. The system of minimal corporate governance mitigated shareholder pressure for profitability that might stand in the way of growth and employment.

The internal consistency of the Japanese model amplified its success by making the various practices mutually reinforcing. However, that same internal consistency created a vulnerability. A system so oriented to one type of progress limits others and hampers its extension to new dimensions of competition and to new fields. Moreover, if individual elements of the model are flawed or the system needs to change, the challenge of reinventing the whole model will be daunting.

Warning Signals

In the mid-1980s, Japanese companies' results were so stunning that many Western companies believed that they were competing unfairly, pricing below cost. For the most part, however, the companies were simply incredibly productive. Exports grew rapidly, and Japanese manufacturers took world market share in an array of important industries. Because labor productivity was rising so dramatically in these industries, the model supported strong growth in Japanese wages and *per capita* income. Clearly, the Japanese corporate model was working.

Even before the difficulties of the early 1990s, however, there were signs that the Japanese corporate model was not the universal prescription it was thought to be. As we discussed in Chapter 1, many industries and companies remained uncompetitive throughout the post-World War II period, even though they followed the same practices. Hence, something else must have also been decisive in determining productivity growth and competitive success.

More troubling than the existence of uncompetitive industries, however, is the fact that even successful Japanese companies earned persistently low

Table 3-1   Return on sales of leading tire manufacturers, 1994–98 (%)

	1994	1995	1996	1997	1998
Bridgestone	2.0	3.2	3.6	1.8	4.7
Michelin	2.0	4.5	4.4	5.2	4.6
Goodyear	4.6	4.6	0.8	4.2	5.4
Continental	0.7	1.6	1.9	2.5	3.1
Sumitomo	2.1	0.0	0.8	0.9	0.8
Yokohama	0.6	0.6	0.9	0.4	0.8

Source: Company reports, *Tire Nenkan*

returns on investment. While periods of low profits would have been expected as companies pursued long-term competitive advantage, low profitability was a chronic condition. Many companies seem to have gained market share by sacrificing long-term profits rather than by offering truly superior quality or attaining a fundamentally lower total cost position – especially during the last decade.

Consider tires. Table 3-1 shows the after-tax return on sales of the six leading tire manufacturers between 1994 and 1998. The three Japanese firms have an average ROS of 1.55%, compared with 3.34% for the non-Japanese producers. Even Bridgestone, the world market share leader that owns the major American producer Firestone, has been less profitable (3.06%) than Goodyear and Michelin (which averaged 4.03%). This same phenomenon occurs over and over again in other industries.

Because they face little pressure from shareholders, large Japanese companies tended to maintain unprofitable businesses indefinitely instead of redeploying capital to more productive uses. Japanese executives euphemistically called their poorly performing businesses 'healthy red divisions.' The persistent inability to produce a good return on investment is the most fundamental sign of the flaws in the Japanese system.

The second most important sign was the concentration of Japanese success to a limited array of fields and industries for a nation of its size. As described in Chapter 1, the Japanese model worked only in certain fields. These were enough to boost the nation's productivity and standard of living for a time, but the limits eventually became compelling. Clearly, the Japanese corporate model was incomplete.

The fact that Japanese market positions in many competitive industries peaked in the 1980s was another warning signal. Since that time, a wide range of formerly successful industries, ranging from semiconductors to shipbuilding, have experienced declines in their international positions. Even those industries where the Japanese competitive approach had been successful were showing its limitations.

Finally, precious few new Japanese success stories have emerged in the last decade. There are exceptions, and we will discuss some of them later in this chapter. But the *keiretsu* that were once the principal drivers of new business growth now seem to be in retreat.

There is evidence that *keiretsu* firms tend to overinvest and overproduce relative to independent firms.[25] Another study found that *keiretsu*-affiliated firms registered significantly lower returns on assets between 1971 and 1982 than independent firms.[26] Chronic underperformance, then, was more prevalent in the very type of company that was most identified with the nation's competitive success. Many of the companies that led Japan's success have faltered, then, and the Japanese model has held back others from taking their place.

Competing on Operational Effectiveness

How can we reconcile Japan's apparent competitive success on the one hand, with its low profitability, limited array of competitive industries, and inability to sustain competitiveness on the other? The answer lies in making an important distinction between approaches to competition.

In the 1970s and 80s, the Japanese set the world standard for operational effectiveness – that is, for improving quality and lowering cost in ways that were widely applicable to many fields. Japanese companies taught the world an array of approaches, such as total quality management, just-in-time inventory management, lean production, cycle time reduction, and others we described earlier, that improve productivity in nearly every company in every industry.

Indications that Japanese companies were becoming leaders in operational effectiveness were already evident in the motorcycle industry as early as the 1960s. After saturating the large domestic market, four Japanese manufacturers – Honda, Yamaha, Kawasaki, and Suzuki – established a huge cost advantage over Harley-Davidson, BMW, and other Western manufacturers and started penetrating global markets. The Japanese manufacturers pursued lean production, cycle time reduction, and zero defects by investing aggressively in large automated facilities equipped with highly mechanized machining and assembly lines. Advanced production techniques such as high-pressure die casting and hot and cold forging and sintering reduced processing costs and metal wastage. Close connections were maintained with suppliers.

Japanese motorcycle companies continuously added new features, such as electric starters, four-cylinder engines, disk brakes, and five-speed transmissions. They upgraded their models and introduced annual model changes. By the mid-1970s, Japanese companies were outperforming their Western rivals, offering lower cost as well as superior quality.

Japanese videocassette recorder (VCR) manufacturers achieved a similar feat. The unit production cost of a VCR dropped from ¥127,000 in 1980 to ¥62,000 in 1985, according to the Electronic Industries Association of Japan. Japanese manufacturers lowered costs by standardizing parts and processes, utilizing integrated circuits, and introducing automatic parts-insertion machines. They also improved products by making them lighter and more compact, enhancing sound quality, and increasing picture

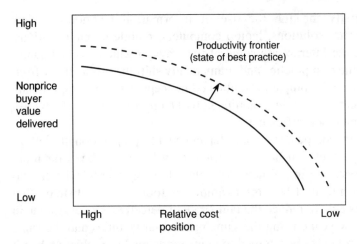

Figure 3-2   Japanese companies shifted the productivity frontier

sharpness. Operational innovations such as these diffused quickly throughout Japanese industry.

Japanese companies were so far ahead on operational effectiveness that they defined the frontier of productivity (see Figure 3-2).[27] We can think of this frontier as the maximum buyer value that a company can deliver at a given cost, using the best available technologies, skills, management techniques, and purchased inputs. In essence, the productivity frontier is the sum of all the best practices existing in an industry at any given time.

In the 1970s and 80s, Japanese companies pushed the productivity frontier well beyond the capabilities of many Western companies. Far more operationally effective, they could beat Western competitors on both cost and differentiation. In the successful industries, numerous Japanese rivals competed fiercely, rapidly matching one another's moves and driving operational improvement even faster. Even when Japanese competitors started out with different product varieties (as was the case in fax machines, for example), product lines eventually converged. As a result, each company offered full product lines with all the same features.

Initially, there was room for all to grow. Although one Japanese company rarely stayed ahead of the others, as a group they gained share in international markets – at least during the decade it took for the rest of the world to catch up.

Starting in the mid- to late 1980s, however, the gap in operational effectiveness between Japanese and Western companies began to narrow. Then, having successfully emulated Japanese operational practices, US companies in particular began to push the productivity frontier outward themselves, especially through the use of information technology. New packaged-software solutions, laptop computers, mobile communications, and the use of the Internet are some of the ways in which US companies began to redefine best practice and dramatically shift the productivity frontier. In addition, US companies embraced concepts such as supply chain management and outsourcing, facilitated by IT improvements, which radically transformed their efficiency.

Not only have companies outside Japan caught up operationally but, as international competition has intensified, they have also been far more aggressive in restructuring. When Motorola sold its Quasar television division to Matsushita in 1974, for example, it found, to its dismay, that Matsushita was able to reduce the unit's rate of defective TV sets to one in 100 in just a few years, using the same production facilities and the same workers. Motorola also was forced to confront its quality problem when it faced stiff competition from the Japanese in portable telephones. Chairman Robert Galvin's lament in 1979 that the quality of Motorola products 'stunk' precipitated a sweeping quality movement within the company.

In 1980, Motorola named a senior executive to lead a five-year effort to improve quality tenfold. In the mid-1980s, the company embarked on its famous Six Sigma program, whose objective was to achieve virtually flawless manufacturing. The company realized cost savings of $2.2 billion over five years from these efforts. In 1988, Motorola became the first recipient of the US Malcolm Baldrige Award for quality.

By the early 1990s, then, Motorola had caught up with the Japanese by emulating their operational practices. Then Motorola went several important steps further. It raised the bar even higher on quality and brought customer focus into all of its processes instead of limiting it to the factory, as was customary in Japan. Motorola's Total Customer Satisfaction effort began in 1991.

Hewlett-Packard (HP) is another example. In 1987, its then-CEO, John Young, became a believer in the TQM movement when he saw the improvements realized by Yokogawa Hewlett-Packard, HP's Japanese subsidiary. Yokogawa products outperformed others in the HP family because of manufacturing cost reductions and quality improvements. Yokogawa adopted quality circles in 1979 and won the coveted Japanese Deming Award for quality in 1982. Seeing the TQM movement's potential, Young called for a tenfold improvement in quality within ten years. HP took the process even further by establishing what is known in the company as QMS (Quality Maturity System). Each division underwent a QMS review in five areas: strategic focus, business planning, process management, *kaizen* projects, and leadership. HP also established the President's Quality Award, to be given to the division with the best track record on quality.

Even companies in more mature industries responded. In motorcycles, for example, Harley-Davidson was driven by Japanese competition to seek government protection in 1981. It used the subsequent five-year 'grace' period to come back with a vengeance by improving operational effectiveness. It emulated Japanese practices by investing heavily in factory automation and worker empowerment programs, which reduced unit costs and raised productivity. Harley also incorporated more electronics into its bikes and embarked on a TQM program. By the early 1990s, Harley-Davidson could boast of a productivity level on a par with its Japanese competitors and a backlog of orders from around the world. What Harley-Davidson also had – and what Japanese companies lacked – was a unique strategic position, which we will discuss further.

As Japanese companies have discovered, then, sooner or later competitors can imitate best practices. The most generic operational improvements – that is, those involving widely applicable management techniques, process technologies, and input improvements – diffuse the fastest.

There is a deeper problem with the Japanese approach to competing, however. Relentless and single-minded efforts to achieve best practice tend to lead to *competitive convergence*, which means that all the competitors in an industry compete on the same dimensions. The more rivals source from world-class suppliers, often the same ones, the more similar they become. As rivals imitate one another's improvements in quality, cycle time, or supplier partnerships, competition becomes a series of unwinnable races down identical paths. Because Japanese companies think of competition only in terms of operational effectiveness – improving quality and cost simultaneously – they have made it almost impossible to be enduringly successful. The more benchmarking companies do, the more they look alike. Little real innovation occurred.

Consider the Japanese PC industry. The major players are competing head to head, serving all types of customers, offering the same array of technologies, investing heavily in the same new manufacturing equipment, running their production lines faster, and trying to reduce head count. But the resulting productivity gains are being captured by customers and suppliers, not retained in superior profitability for the industry. Unlike in the United States, where Dell, Gateway, and Apple have each had distinctive strategies and been highly profitable in most years, no PC company in Japan has registered attractive financial performance.

Having lost their decisive lead in operational effectiveness, slower growth and competitive convergence have become a painful combination for Japanese companies. Competition based on operational effectiveness alone is mutually destructive, leading to wars of attrition. Absolute improvement in operational effectiveness does not translate into relative improvement for anyone. If every company offers more or less the same mix of value, customers are forced to choose on price. This inevitably undermines price levels – and devastates profitability. At the same time, competitive convergence leads to duplicate investments and a strong tendency toward overcapacity. In early 1999, for example, Japanese over-capacity in steel was estimated at 39%, automobiles at 26%, synthetic fiber at 33%, and shipbuilding at 22%.[28] By competing on operational effective-ness alone, then, many Japanese companies have been caught in a trap of their own making.

Competing on operational effectiveness alone has another, more subtle, consequence. The profitability of any company is partly the result of the structure of its industry, which determines the average return of all industry participants. Industry structure consists of five basic competitive forces: the power of customers, the power of suppliers, the threat of new entry, the pressure from substitutes, and the nature of rivalry.[29] The Japanese approach to competing not only eliminates differences between competitors but also undermines the entire industry. Competition gravi-tates to price, power shifts to the buyer, and homogenization lowers the barriers to entry both in Japan and for me-too Asian rivals. Profit pressures become even greater.

The Japanese government model, with its widespread protection and distortion of financial markets, allowed the flaws in the corporate model to persist. Intervention, cheap capital, and the lack of shareholder pressure meant that companies could cross-subsidize using domestic profits and keep investing aggressively despite low profits.

Competing Without Strategy

Continuous incremental improvement is not strategy. Neither is imitating and emulating competitors. When rivals offer most (if not all) of the same product varieties, features, and services, employ the same distribution channels, and match one another's production processes, none has a distinctive competitive position. The Japanese approach to competition, and the dangers that the absence of strategy lead to, are vividly illustrated by cases from some representative industries.

Table 3-2   Ranking of world semiconductor companies
in terms of sales, revenue, selected years

Ranking	1988	1992	1998	1998 market share
1	NEC	Intel	Intel	16.4
2	Toshiba	NEC	NEC	6.0
3	Hitachi	Motorola	Motorola	5.0
4	Motorola	Toshiba	Toshiba	4.4
5	Texas Instruments	Hitachi	Texas Instruments	4.3
6	Fujitsu	Texas Instruments	Samsung	3.4
7	Intel	Fujitsu	Hitachi	3.4
8	Mitsubishi Electric	Mitsubishi Electric	Philips	3.3
9	Matsushita Electric	Philips	ST Micro Electronics	3.1
10	Philips	Matsushita Electric	Fujitsu / Siemens	2.8

Source: Dataquest (*Nikkei Business*, February 22, 1999, p. 25)

Semiconductors

The penchant of Japanese companies for symmetric strategies is virtually universal. Consider semiconductors, an industry in which Japanese manufacturers held the top position in world market share for seven consecutive years beginning in the 1980s.[30] In 1988, six of the world's top ten semiconductor companies were based in Japan. NEC, Toshiba, and Hitachi held the top three positions. By 1992, Intel was the world leader, and by 1993, Japanese companies no longer held the largest share. In 1998, only four Japanese companies ranked among the top ten, and only one ranked in the top three (see Table 3-2).

The consequences of the Japanese approach to competition have not only been losses in market share but a chronic lack of profitability. In 1999, none of the Japanese competitors was expected to make a profit in semiconductors.[31] All the major Japanese producers had posted losses for at least the previous three years, in stark contrast to US producers.

What explains Japan's loss of ground? In brief, the Japanese producers all fell prey to the perils of competing solely on operational effectiveness. A mutually destructive war of attrition is still unfolding. As Table 3-3 indicates, all the Japanese semiconductor manufacturers offer a full line of products, ranging from transistors to microprocessors. In comparison, US semiconductor manufacturers have been much clearer about what *not* to do. By 1995, for example, all the companies but Texas Instruments had withdrawn from memory chips.[32]

Table 3-3 Symmetric strategies of Japanese semiconductor manufacturers

Segments	Japanese Companies						Non-Japanese Companies			
	NEC	Toshiba	Hitachi	Fujitsu	Mitsubishi	Matsushita	Intel	TI	Motorola	Philips
Diodes	×	×	×	×	×	×				×
Transistors	×	×	×	×	×	×				×
Rectifiers	×	×	×	×	×	×				×
Thyristors	×	×	×	×	×	×				×
Opto-electronic devices	×	×	×	×	×	×				
Hall elements	×	×	×	×	×	×				
Thermoelectric/pressure sensors	×	×	×	×	×	×				
Thermistors	×	×	×	×	×	×				
Varistors	×	×	×	×	×	×		×		×
CCDs (image sensors)	×	×	×	×	×	×		×		×
Integrated circuits	×	×	×	×	×	×		×	×	×
Microprocessors/microcontrollers	×	×	×	×	×	×	×	×	×	
Gate array/cell-based ICs	×	×	×	×	×	×	×			
Memory devices	×	×	×	×	×	×	×			
Solar cells	×	×	×	×	×	×		×	×	
Display devices	×	×	×	×						
Photomasks/mask blanks		×				×				
Package		×			×	×				
Lead frames		×	×		×	×				
Electronic components and others		×	×	×	×	×				

Note: Entries in the table refer to producer offerings in the home market, with Europe as Philips' home market.

Open up a PC today and the contrast between US and Japanese semiconductor makers is evident. The higher priced, branded chips (including microprocessors, chip sets, graphic accelerators, hard-disk controls, and others) are all made in the United States. A Japanese imprint appears only on memory chips. Surprisingly, this situation prevails not just in PCs made by IBM, Compaq, Dell, and other US producers but also in PCs made in Japan for Japanese customers by Japanese manufacturers.

US companies focus on much narrower customer groups than Japanese companies. Take Texas Instruments (TI). Until the mid-1980s, TI was the world's largest semiconductor producer, serving a broad range of customers including the defense and military segment. Today it specializes in the cellular telephone market, having sold its defense division to Raytheon, its mobile PC division to Acer, and its memory chip division to Micron Technology. Western companies also vary in production approaches. Many companies do not fabricate semiconductors at all; they outsource the production of chips based on their own unique design to fabricators.

Japanese companies, in contrast, do not have distinctive strategies. In addition to each offering a full line of products and serving all types of customers, they all employ the same vertically integrated business model. They all conduct virtually all R&D work internally, operate their own automated production facilities, and rely on in-house staffs to carry out marketing, sales, and customer service activities. Focused on reducing manufacturing cost, Japanese companies all invest heavily in the latest plant and equipment to make the same products, which has led to chronic overcapacity in the Japanese industry.

Japanese semiconductor manufacturers, then, have a self-defeating approach to competition. When they were superior in operational effectiveness, symmetric strategies were offset by the ability to gain share against Western producers. Today, however, operational advantages are largely absent. Industry structure has been undermined. Producers from other Asian countries have been able to readily imitate Japanese operational practices in commodity items. With every company offering the same things, customers are led to choose on the basis on price, which inevitably undermines profits.

Faced with poor performance, Japanese companies are beginning to retreat from general purpose DRAMs. Oki Electric and Matsushita Electronics have decided to withdraw from the next-generation 256 megabit DRAM market, and Fujitsu, Hitachi, Matsushita Electronics, Mitsubishi Electric, and Oki have closed DRAM factories. So far, these cutbacks are modest. No Japanese company shows real signs of committing to a truly distinctive positioning.

Apparel

Japanese are avid consumers of apparel and are willing to pay some of the highest prices in the world. Yet none of the leading Japanese apparel companies – Onward Kashiyama, Renown, World, Itokin, or Sanyo – is internationally competitive or has any significant market position internationally. Why not? Once again the answer centers on me-too strategies. The apparel case also illustrates some of the unexpected consequences of Japan's protected domestic sectors.

Historically, Japanese apparel companies contracted out most of their production to small, domestic sewing firms that they keep under considerable cost pressure. With no direct involvement in actual production, however, apparel companies have not achieved the kind of process innovations that are the hallmark of Japan's manufacturing successes. Instead, they have concentrated on securing retail space from department stores, extending their product lines, and licensing high-quality imported brands.

In the early 1970s, the apparel companies began to establish increasingly tight relationships with department stores, which had emerged as the premier urban retail fashion outlets. Onward Kashiyama pioneered the 'Onward Way,' under which its employees actually worked in department stores as sales clerks responsible for display, pricing, and inventory control. Merchandise was sold to the store on consignment and could be returned if unsold.

Rivals quickly copied Onward's practices, which became the *de facto* industry standard. The Onward Way system enabled apparel companies to eliminate discounts, gather hands-on customer information, conduct on-site market testing, and make fast changes to merchandise mix, style, and colors. At the same time, however, this cozy relationship deterred the apparel companies from developing new or captive sales channels and from venturing outside of Japan. Because every company was doing the same thing, moreover, no company developed a distinctive positioning.

In the late 1970s, the focus shifted to increasing market share through multiple branding. Companies began to introduce lower quality, slightly outdated versions of their products under different brands through general merchandise stores, supermarkets, and other mass-market outlets. New brand names were required so as not to upset the apparel companies' major department store customers. Renown pioneered this practice, but rivals followed suit almost immediately. The result was brand proliferation, but no company had a distinctive positioning.

The problem of brand proliferation was exacerbated by the practice of rapid introduction of new styles, which the Onward Way system encouraged. Japanese consumers became accustomed to seeing new items every time they visited the store. Companies became preoccupied trying to match one another in introducing continuous streams of new products as rapidly as possible.

Busy with managing multiple brands and styles at home, apparel companies ignored the prospect of developing brands outside of Japan. Moreover, to offset the costs of producing multiple brands and styles, all the major companies reduced, almost simultaneously, the number of sizes offered per line. This practice was acceptable in Japan, where consumers are more alike in size and shape and tolerate poorer fit. But it undercut Japan's ability to compete in the United States and other markets that are more size and fit sensitive.

In the 1980s and the early 1990s, apparel companies once again competed by racing down an identical path, this time licensing European and US brands. In 1988 alone, more than 50 license agreements were signed, mostly with foreign companies competing in the premium-quality fashion segment. In addition to the large apparel companies, Japanese trading companies such as C. Itoh and Mitsui became aggressive licensors of imported brands. Because of fierce competition for the same group of licenses, Japanese companies agreed to overly generous minimum purchase quantities and long-term agreements, and guaranteed local brand marketing support. Table 3-4 lists some of the brands licensed by just one Japanese company, C. Itoh, during the 10-year period between 1982 and 1991.

Table 3-4　Foreign brands licensed by C. Itoh

Year	Brand
1982	Mila Schon (Italy)
1983	Dunhill (UK)
1985	Chester Barry (UK)
1986	Trussardi (Italy)
1987	Giorgio Armani (Italy)
	Emporio Armani (Italy)
1988	Enrico Coveri (Italy)
1989	GFT (Italy; dissolved in 1991)
1990	Serene (Italy)
	Nazareno Gabrieri (Italy)
1991	Bulgari (Italy)
	Mario Valentino (Italy)

The more agreements the Japanese rivals signed, frequently with licensors based in the same countries, especially Italy, the more similar they became. As a flood of imported brands hit the Japanese market, their appeal waned. In addition, the unprecedented boom in licensed imports coincided with the peak of the bubble economy. The result: the race to sign licensing agreements ultimately destroyed industry profitability. Licensing also meant that, once again, no company developed the unique styles and brand strength required to penetrate international markets.

Chocolate

Finally, consider chocolate, a favorite sweet throughout the world. While foreign chocolate manufacturers such as Mars, Hershey, Suchard, Nestlé Mackintosh (merged in 1989), Lindt, and Godiva have made sustained efforts to penetrate the Japanese market, the reverse has never been true. Despite the fact that Japan is a substantial producer of chocolate, no Japanese manufacturer has ventured abroad in any significant way, through exports, joint ventures, or direct foreign investments in the United States and Europe.

The leading Japanese chocolate manufacturers – including Morinaga, Meiji, Lotte, Glico, and Fujiya – inundate the domestic market with a multitude of similar products, each of which possesses an insignificant market share. Companies operate in every segment, and none has a distinctive product line or market positioning. Competition is based on minor modifications of existing products – shape, name, packaging, and additives – and rarely incorporates real changes in taste or quality. At the peak of the bubble economy in 1991, for instance, Morinaga alone introduced 32 new chocolate items and deleted 42; its total line numbered 89. Other companies' practices are similar. The product changes, though minor, drive up cost. The desire to phase out old products rapidly has also given rise to another costly practice, producers' willingness to accept returned chocolate.

Although the industry began to address product proliferation in 1992, companies still maintain huge product lines. Compare Morinaga, which has 60 brands (after cutting more than 100), with its successful foreign rival Mars. Mars competes in 120 countries with only 40 brands. Japanese manufacturers still introduce between 100 and 120 new items every year. One of the drivers of this meaningless product proliferation is Japan's peculiar distribution channels, which expect each company to introduce a fresh lineup of products almost every month to maintain its shelf space allocation.

All the leading Japanese chocolate manufacturers rely on the same complex distribution system. Chocolate is sold to large wholesalers, which in turn involve local wholesalers. Separate wholesalers are used to reach supermarkets, department stores, and hundreds of thousands of small retailers. A separate distribution system serves the Tokyo area, where the density of retail outlets is significantly higher.[33]

Japanese chocolate manufacturers imitate not only one another but also Western companies. For example, Lotte, the leading Japanese chocolate manufacturer, formed a joint venture with Nestlé in Japan in 1973 and licensed the Swiss company's technology to produce Nestlé's Crunch bar. To Nestlé's dismay, Lotte introduced an imitation product called Crunky the same year. Lotte sold 300 tons of Nestlé's Crunch and 3,000 tons of its own Crunky bar in 1973. After Mars introduced M&Ms to Japan in 1973 through a 100%-owned subsidiary, 25 imitation products appeared on the Japanese market within six months.

In essence, trying to be all things to all customers is the antithesis of strategy. The symmetric and imitative strategies of Japanese chocolate manufacturers have not only undermined domestic profitability but have also precluded any international competitive advantage.

Competing on Strategy

Operational effectiveness is just one of two ways a company pursues superior performance. The other is through strategy, or competing on the basis of a unique positioning involving a distinctive product or service offering. For example, Harley-Davidson's distinct positioning focusing on big bikes, a macho image, and customer loyalty programs. While Harley strives continuously to improve its operational effectiveness, it also has a clear strategy.

Operational effectiveness is concerned with performing the same or similar activities better than competitors. The essence of strategy is to perform the activities involved in competing in the business *differently* from rivals. If the same set of activities are the best ones to produce all varieties, meet all needs, and access all customers, operational effectiveness will determine performance. However, tailoring activities often allows a company to achieve unique cost or customer value in its chosen positioning. Harley-Davidson, for instance, has a different approach to product design and marketing than BMW and other rivals, which is fundamental to its competitive advantage. Strategies without significant differences in activities are rarely sustainable.

Strategy, then, requires real innovation. Companies must devise new product concepts, new services, and new ways of conducting activities that set them apart from rivals. Incremental improvement along an established path is insufficient for strategy.

Strategy is not only about choosing a unique position and tailoring activities but also about making *trade-offs* in how a company delivers value to its customers. Trade-offs occur when strategic positions and the resulting activities are incompatible – when offering more of one thing necessitates less of another. Trade-offs therefore limit the likelihood and ease of imitation. An airline, for example, can choose to serve meals, adding cost and slowing turnaround time at the gate. Or it can choose not to, as Southwest Airlines has done, successfully targeting budget-sensitive US travelers. But it cannot do both without bearing major inefficiencies. Similarly, a cosmetics company can decide to advertise, as Estée Lauder does, or it can decide to forego media advertising in favor of other means of communication, as the Body Shop does.[34] But it cannot do both.

The choice of what *not* to do is thus central to strategy. Deciding which target group of customers, varieties, and needs a company should serve is essential to developing a strategy. But so is deciding not to serve other customers, meet other needs, or offer other features or services. Without trade-offs, competition degenerates to mutually destructive battles on the same dimensions of value, and success rests wholly on operational effectiveness.

Thus, strategy requires constant discipline and clear communication. Indeed, one of the most important functions of an explicit, communicated strategy is to guide employees in making the right choices when trade-offs arise in the course of their individual day-to-day activities.

Choosing not to do something is particularly difficult because it appears to constrain growth. Excluding one group of customers to serve another, for instance, places a real or imagined limit on revenue. Strategies emphasizing low cost and low price result in lost sales from customers sensitive to features or service. Differentiators lose sales to price-sensitive customers.

Managers are constantly tempted to take incremental steps that will relax these limits but blur a company's strategic position. Eventually, pressures to grow market share or apparent saturation of the target market lead companies to broaden their position. They succumb to the temptation to chase 'easy' growth by adding popular features and taking on product lines or services that do not fit their strategy. Or they target new customers or market segments in which the company offers nothing unique. Worse yet, they start imitating competitors' popular products or services, matching their production processes and even making parallel acquisitions.

Compromises and inconsistencies required to pursue market share and growth run a grave risk of eroding whatever competitive advantages a company originally had. Attempting to compete in several ways at once creates confusion and undermines organizational motivation and focus. Profits fall, so more revenue is seen as the answer. With managers unable or unwilling to make choices, the company embarks on a new round of broadening and compromises. Often rivals continue to match one another's moves until desperation breaks the cycle. In the West, this means merging or downsizing.

Strategy and operational effectiveness are both necessary for sustained, superior performance. The rapid diffusion of best practices throughout the world has made the pursuit of operational effectiveness a given. However, superior performance cannot be achieved through operational effectiveness alone. Strategy is what sets high performers apart from low performers. Distinctive strategies are also much harder to imitate.

Competing on strategy has another important benefit. A more positive-sum form of competition is created in which customers gain real choice, rivals become superior in serving their chosen segments, and the overall market can expand. Industry structure often improves in the process.

Japanese Exceptions that Prove the Rule

Few Japanese companies have strategies, as our earlier examples amply illustrate. Instead of choosing distinctive ways of competing, tailoring activities, and making trade-offs, Japanese companies tend to proliferate products and features, serve all market segments, sell through multiple channels, and emulate one another's production approaches. Continuous operational improvement is confused with strategy.

The lack of strategy is reinforced by many aspects of the Japanese corporate model. The penchant to pursue growth and ignore profitability drives imitation and broadening. Common Japanese practices such as wide product lines, multifunctionality, and rapid product turnover blur strategic positioning. At the same time, strong organizational forces and cultural norms make it extremely difficult for Japanese companies to make strategic choices, a subject we will explore in Chapter 6.

Although most Japanese companies lack distinctive strategies, there are some notable exceptions. A handful of the most celebrated and successful companies in Japan *do* have clear strategies, though they are not widely appreciated as what sets them apart. Sony did not win because it was better at *kanban* or TQM. It won because it had a distinctive strategy: producing differentiated consumer electronics that sold at premium prices and marketing them in unique ways. From the beginning, Sony emphasized originality – no matter what the cost. The company's positioning was evident when it created the Trinitron television picture tube instead of copying the shadow mask system, and when Sony became one of the first Japanese companies to sell directly in the American market.[35] It is telling that Japan considers some of its most successful companies such as Sony – those with unique strategies – to be mavericks.

When Japanese companies compete with distinctive strategies, they have remained highly competitive and profitable, despite the fact that Western firms have reached comparable levels of operational effectiveness and despite the problems in the general economy. Here we examine several Japanese companies with clear strategies: Honda – in automobiles – and Nintendo, Sega, and Sony – the three leading video game producers. The striking contrast to semiconductors, apparel, and chocolate will be evident. That these large, established Japanese companies have strategies is a clear indication that the problem lies more in mind-set than in unchangeable local circumstances.

Honda

Honda Motor became Japan's number two automaker in 1999 (surpassing Nissan for the first time). Revenues in 1998 were $54 billion, with earnings of $2.4 billion. Though a late entrant into automobiles and small relative to some of its global competitors, Honda has outperformed its rivals. Its share among Japanese automakers had increased from 5.9% in 1975 to 14.4% in 1998. Honda has also registered a superior profitability, with a five-year average after-tax return on sales of 2.8%, versus the Japanese average of 1.7%. Only Toyota, with a much larger proportion of its sales in the nearly captive Japanese market, has been more profitable, though Honda surpassed Toyota in profitability by a comfortable margin in fiscal 1998 (4.6% versus 3.6%). Other Japanese auto companies have suffered yearly losses and earned chronically low returns.

From its early years, Honda has carved out a distinctive competitive position. In 1999, a survey by Nikkei and the Nikkei Sangyo Shouhi Research Center ranked Honda first as the company with the most unique personality (Toyota ranked 453).

Honda began as a motorcycle producer. The company was founded by Soichiro Honda in 1946 as Honda Technical Research Institute in Hamamatsu. Mr. Honda (who died in 1991) was interested in mechanical technology and dreamed of building his own automobile. The company has been dominated by engineers ever since.

In motorcycles, Honda sought to offer highly engineered machines at lower prices, based on unique, easy-to-manufacture designs and efficient manufacturing processes. It was committed to quiet but powerful four-stroke engines, which gave Honda particular strength in the on-road segment, while its rivals (Yamaha, Kawasaki, and Suzuki) targeted the off-road segment.

Honda ventured internationally in motorcycles early, establishing the American Honda Motor Company in Los Angeles in 1959. The company started selling its 50cc Super Cub in a market that was dominated by large machines at the time. Lower production costs helped fund Honda's heavy investment in marketing and distribution. It targeted new customers and used advertising, promotions, and trade shows to convince the public that its bikes were affordable, reliable, easy to use, and light. The 1962 advertising slogan, 'You meet the nicest people on a Honda,' helped to distinguish its target audience from the black leather jacket-clad bikers exemplified by Marlon Brando in the movie *The Wild One*.

Honda established a broad dealer network including sporting goods stores and hobby shops and emphasized service (for example, generous warranty terms and quick spare-parts availability). Honda improved its models continually and widened its line to include larger bikes – providing a way for customers to trade up after experiencing the pleasure of motorcycle riding.

Honda's penchant for being different was backed up by an almost fanatical devotion to independence and a maverick disregard for conventional wisdom. This is illustrated vividly by Honda's entry into the automobile industry. If the Japanese government had had its way, Honda would never have built cars. In the early 1960s, the Ministry of International Trade and Industry tried to discourage Soichiro Honda from creating new competition for Toyota, Nissan, and other Japanese automobile makers. Honda ignored MITI and forged ahead, knowing that such resistance would mean no official support in the business.

Honda has always followed a distinctive strategy in automobiles. It makes no trucks, only passenger cars. It seeks to build higher performance vehicles, based on superior engineering and innovative features. The company spends 5% of revenue on R&D, a higher percentage than virtually all other automobile companies and a much

higher percentage than its Japanese rivals. Soichiro Honda broke with
Japanese tradition by luring top talent from competitors. He was fond of
saying, 'Challenge conventional wisdom,' 'Don't be afraid to make
mistakes,' and 'Don't imitate others.'

Engines are the cornerstone of Honda's product differentiation. In 1973,
Honda introduced the innovative Compound Vortex Controlled Combustion (CVCC) engine. Unlike competitors' engines, Honda's engine ran on
cheaper, leaded fuel, but it was more powerful and fuel efficient. The
CVCC, in the Civic model, was launched in the US market in 1974, just
after the Oil Shock. It became an instant hit. The vehicle met the requirements of the US Clean Air Act even though it ran on leaded fuel.

Honda's major commitment to racing since 1954 has nurtured the
company's innovative engineering. Racing played an important role in
fostering Honda's drive to develop something new and different since the
motorcycling days. Honda considers the race track its 'mobile laboratory'
that tests the company's ability to meet technological challenges and
address competitive developments. Honda has supplied engines for
Formula 1 cars for many years. As former chairman Hideo Sugiura put it,
'The race track is an effective training ground for young engineers. It is
also a showroom for our latest technology. Besides, it pulls everyone in the
company together. We all have a race bug in our blood.' In 1991, Honda
introduced the lean-burning VTEC-E engine into its 1992 Civic models,
attaining the best gas mileage of any four-cylinder car in the United States,
and superior environmental performance. The technology developed
through Honda's involvement in car races and sports cars made the breakthrough possible.

A second pillar of Honda's distinctive strategy is styling. Honda
pioneered the practice of putting the engine into its Civic sideways,
creating more room for passengers. Its models have clean but contemporary shapes, offer excellent visibility, and have roomy interiors. Recently,
Honda's line of sporty station wagons, minivans, and sport utility vehicles
have taken the market by storm. They are lighter, nimbler, and more fuel
efficient than competitors', and they include creative accessories such as
wire mesh headlight guards and built-in picnic tables. The StepWGN and
S-MX have striking, postmodern designs that are especially appealing to
younger buyers.

Honda has long been an innovative marketer, using creative advertising
campaigns to set itself apart. The company is alone among the major
automakers because it refuses to offer cash rebates or sell cars to rental
fleets at wholesale prices in the US market.

Another distinctive aspect of Honda's strategy was to become a global competitor long before its rivals. Honda was the first Japanese auto manufacturer to build passenger cars in the United States. Commercial production commenced in the Marysville, Ohio plant on November 1, 1982. The move proved prescient since it enabled Honda to avoid the voluntary import quotas that were enacted soon after. By 1995, Honda was building more cars overseas than in Japan (50.8%), a far greater proportion than its Japanese rivals.

Honda's president, Hiroyuki Yoshino, reaffirmed in 1999 Honda's intention to pursue a distinctive positioning. The company is to remain independent, and not search for partners as had become the norm in the industry. Yoshino, an engineer, has committed the company to a revolutionary new manufacturing method designed to cut by half the cost of making a car.

Video Games

The video game industry is an even more striking exception to the Japanese norm. Here, all three significant competitors – Nintendo, Sega, and Sony – have pursued distinctive strategies. The result is not only profitability for each company but expansion of the entire industry.

Nintendo became a major player in the video game industry when it released Donkey Kong in 1981, but its real takeoff occurred in 1983 when it introduced an 8-bit video game system called the 'Famicon' (for Family Computer) in the Japanese market. The product was launched in the United States under the name Nintendo Entertainment System (NES) in 1986. By 1990, Nintendo held more than 90% of the US home video game market.

Famicon, which consists of a console and controllers, enables players to enjoy the 'feel' of an arcade game at home. Games such as the megahit *Super Mario Brothers* are sold as individual cartridges that plug into the console. Only Nintendo cartridges can be played on the system. The company decided to target the 7- to 14-year-old segment, believing that older children had too many interests competing for their time. Nintendo judged that 'playability' (the ease of setting up and running the system as well as the speed of retrieving images to produce fast-moving action) was more important to their target audience than enhanced graphical images. Partly as a result, Nintendo was slower than Sega in introducing a 16-bit system that offered better graphics.

Nintendo's approach has been to produce one or two hit games of exceptional quality each year and promote them with large-scale advertising, rather than many games that are modest successes. Nintendo withdraws games as soon as interest wanes. The company intentionally has not kept all of the retail demand and kept more than half its game library inactive.

The company originally designed all of its own games, pitting its engineers against one another in an internal competition uncharacteristic of Japanese companies. To improve the chances of developing truly fresh game concepts, the R&D group was isolated from the marketing department. Later, Nintendo outsourced some of its software development to independent software companies. However, it offered licenses to only a limited number of developers over whom it maintained strict control. Developers were charged a steep 20% royalty on every cartridge sold and were required to contract with Nintendo for manufacturing. Nintendo, in turn, outsourced all cartridge manufacturing.

Sega chose a different positioning. Founded in Tokyo by two Americans in 1951, Sega began as an operator of entertainment arcades in Japan. By the early 1980s, it had become the market leader. Sega transformed the image of arcades as dirty, dingy, and seamy by building spacious, brightly lit facilities in popular shopping areas that the whole family could enjoy.

Sega's arcade experience shaped its strategy in the home video game industry. Sega targeted the over-14-year-old segment. After an initial entry into 8-bit games, Sega launched a 16-bit system with enhanced graphics capability known as Mega Drive in Japan and Genesis in the United States. Adapted from Sega's arcade machines, the Mega Drive boasted 512 colors, high-quality sound, and an ability to display several layers of background. Sega traded off speed and playability (emphasized by Nintendo) for enhanced graphics capability. Mega Drive was designed to expand into a home office processor via such add-ons as a keyboard, printer, and modem. Overall, Sega sought to be the company with superior technology.

In 1992, true to its philosophy, Sega moved quickly into CD-ROM technology when it introduced Sega CD, a $300 CD-ROM add-on to the Genesis. CD-ROM had the advantage of offering enhanced graphics, but it was slower to play than cartridges because information could not be retrieved as quickly. This trade-off fit Sega's positioning. Sega followed with other high performance games, including the 32-bit Sega Saturn. In 1996, Sega began offering a 28.8-baud modem called Net Link that allowed Saturn owners to browse the Internet on a television screen.

To become a technology leader, Sega invested heavily to recruit software developers, breaking Japanese tradition by paying headhunters to hire the best and brightest from Japan's top technology companies. High salaries and generous development budgets were offered as incentives. Sega relied heavily on third-party software houses to develop games for its new 16-bit system, competing against Nintendo by initially charging lower royalties and giving developers the right to manufacture their own software and to design games for other manufacturers.

Sega also offered generous terms to retailers, which were eager to carry an alternative to Nintendo. It ensured that retail inventories were adequate and took advantage of retailer ill-will toward Nintendo to cultivate strong retailer relations. Sega also engaged in heavy advertising and aggressive introductory pricing. In June 1991, it launched to the slogan 'Genesis does what Nintendon't.' Sega worked hard in other ways to be a 'cool' company, one that teenagers could identify with. However, Sega failed to deliver on its philosophy toward retailers when it introduced its 32-bit machine. Retailer dissatisfaction was an important contributor to the Saturn's poor performance.

The third major player – Sony – also had a distinctive strategy. Sony had followed the video game market for years but did not enter until late 1995 when the market began to gravitate toward CD-ROM technology, where Sony had considerable strengths. Sony had pioneered both audio CD and CD-ROM hardware.

Sony entered video games with a 32-bit CD-ROM machine called PlayStation. Where Nintendo focused on playability and Sega on graphics, Sony focused on providing good quality at a low price, especially on software. Sony saw an opportunity to distinguish itself by establishing a cost leadership position. Nintendo, for example, maintained the costly cartridge system because of its superior playing performance. Sony enjoyed advantages due to its wide array of other consumer electronic products and components.

Sony offered a large number of games. Unlike Nintendo and Sega, Sony did not develop software internally, enticing third-party developers with low licensing fees. It benefited from the fact that many developers had gained experience by developing CD-ROM software for Sega. Sony also sold software directly to its established network of retailers, bypassing the wholesalers used by other companies for 80% of its sales volume.

With three distinct positionings, it is not uncommon for a video game aficionado to own a Sega Genesis, a Super Nintendo Entertainment System, a Sony PlayStation, and now a Nintendo N64. This positive-sum competition is helping to fuel a boom in the $15 billion video game market, which some analysts had written off due to the rising popularity of home PCs. All three companies have been highly profitable. Nintendo recorded an average ROE of 25% from 1986 to 1996, while Sega had an average ROE of 15% over the same period, although it has stumbled recently due to the failure of the Sega Saturn. Both Nintendo's and Sega's long-term average ROEs are far above the Japanese average. PlayStation generated 41% of Sony's total operating profit in 1997, and the estimated after-tax ROS of Sony's game business is 9.6%.

Summary

Competing on strategy is not a zero-sum game. As the video game industry demonstrates, competition on strategy can expand the total market and allow many companies to prosper simultaneously. Japan's strengths in operational improvement remain important, but without strategy, the Japanese approach to competing is dangerously incomplete.

Japanese companies remain highly successful when they have strategies. The challenge is that only a handful of large, established Japanese companies have one. Moreover, both the Japanese government model and the Japanese corporate model work against a strategic approach to competing.

The large Japanese companies with clear strategies prove that it can be done. The problem is more in mind-set than in unchangeable circumstances in Japan. Moreover, a cadre of emerging Japanese companies that are much less well known are prospering based on competing with unique strategies. These companies also represent exceptions to the rule that Japan is spawning few new businesses. Interestingly, many of the emerging companies are based in the Kyoto area and other locations outside Osaka and Tokyo. We will examine Kyoto and some of the new companies in Chapters 5 and 6, because they point the way to what Japanese economic policy and corporate strategy must become.

Notes

1. As it was dubbed by the International Motor Vehicle Program at MIT (Womack et al., 1990).
2. Fujimoto (1997, 1999).
3. Kanban is the name of reusable slips attached to standardized reusable containers that linked the upstream and downstream stations.
4. Fujimoto (1997).
5. Clark and Fujimoto (1991); Takeuchi and Nonaka (1995).
6. Ballon (1969); Drucker (1971); Yoshino (1968); Furstenburg (1974); and Ouchi (1981).
7. Imai and Komiya (1989).
8. Ballon (1969).
9. Drucker (1971).
10. Cole (1972); Dore (1973, 1986).

11. Drucker (1971); Cole (1979); Ouchi (1981); Itami (1987).
12. Gibney (1979).
13. Ouchi (1981).
14. Itami (1987).
15. Ballon (1969); Yoshino (1968); Furstenburg (1974); Gibney (1979); Ouchi (1981) and Koike (1981).
16. Ito (1995).
17. Cole (1971); Dore (1986); Kanamori (1984); Uchino (1988) and Itami (1990).
18. Whitehill and Takezawa (1978).
19. Yoshino (1968); Glazer (1969).
20. Tracy and Azumi (1976); Ouchi (1981); Yoshino (1968); Ballon (1968); Rohlen (1975) and Nakane (1970).
21. Vogel (1975).
22. Schonberger (1982); Alexander (1981); Sasaki (1988) and Kagono (1988).
23. Abegglen and Rapp (1970); Barret and Gehrke (1974); Dore (1986, 1987) and Dertouzos, Lester and Solow (1989).
24. Abegglen and Stalk (1985).
25. Weinstein and Yafeh (1995).
26. Nakatani (1984).
27. See Porter (1996), also reprinted in Porter (1998b).
28. *Nikkei Business*, March 9, 1999.
29. Industry structure and its role in profitability are discussed in Porter (1980). For recent evidence of the influence of industry structure on profitability, see Porter and McGahan (1997).
30. Naono (1996).
31. 'Intensifying Survival Competition of Semiconductor Manufacturers', *Nikkei Business*, October 12, 1998, p. 42.
32. However, the memory chips produced by TI were made in Japan (KTI Semiconductor, a joint venture with Kobe Steel) and Singapore (TECH Semiconductor, a joint venture).
33. The distribution channels for most imported chocolate were different from domestically made chocolate. As most foreign manufacturers did not have their own sales subsidiaries in Japan, they relied on Japanese chocolate companies and agents to carry out the necessary importing and storage selectively to high-class grocery stores specializing in imported food items as well as to department stores. Thus, the number of retailers carrying imported chocolate was limited.
34. The Body Shop relies on its salespeople to provide in-depth product information, distribute brochures publicizing its societal and environmental policies, encourage sampling, and create a vibrant and friendly store atmosphere.
35. Nathan (1999).

CHAPTER 4

What Does Explain Japanese Competitiveness?

As we seek to understand the roots of Japan's past performance, we face a paradox: the government practices that are widely believed to explain Japan's success – practices that limit competition in myriad ways – have, in fact, inflicted great economic costs. A set of Japanese industries prospered *in spite* of these policies, not *because* of them. What, then, does explain Japan's competitive success and failure? What should a new model for Japan look like?

Our study of Japan's competitive and uncompetitive industries has generated findings that are consistent with what we know to be universally true about the competitiveness of nations: vigorous competition in a supportive business environment, free of government direction, is the only path to economic vitality. Japan is not a special case after all.

Prosperity and Productivity

Ultimately, a nation's wealth depends on the productivity with which its firms compete.[1] The productivity of a nation's economy is measured by the value of the goods and services (products) produced per unit of the nation's human, capital, and physical resources. The revenue produced per unit of labor or capital sets the wages a nation can sustain, the returns earned on invested capital, and the surplus (after costs) generated by its physical resources. These are the primary determinants of national per capita income.

Productivity, then, defines competitiveness for a nation.[2] Productivity, rightly understood, encompasses both the value (prices) that a nation's products command in the marketplace and the efficiency with which they are produced. Improving efficiency alone, or producing more units per unit of labor or capital, does not necessarily elevate wages and profits unless the prices of the products or services are stable or rising. As global competition places greater pressure on the prices of standard goods, efficiency alone is insufficient. Advanced nations improve their standard of living more by driving up the value of their products and services (because of better technology, marketing, and associated services, for example) and moving into new fields through innovation than by producing standardized products at lower cost.

The central issue in economic development, then, is how to create the conditions for rapid and sustained productivity growth. A nation's productivity is the sum of the productivity of all its companies. The productivity and prosperity of a location rest not on the industries in which its firms compete but on *how* they compete. Firms can be more productive in any industry – shoes, agriculture, or semiconductors – if they employ sophisticated methods, use advanced technology, and offer unique products and services. *All* industries can employ high technology; all industries can be knowledge intensive. Targeting 'desirable industries' is based on a flawed view of competitiveness, in which economies of scale determine success and domestic competition is seen as wasteful. As we discussed in Chapter 2, Japanese targeting did not work. Government policy should instead focus on removing constraints to productivity.

Efforts to improve productivity growth must encompass local industries, because they affect not only the cost of living but also the cost of doing business for internationally traded industries. Japan's current situation illustrates the dangers of thinking that competitiveness is necessary only for traded industries, and redressing this mistake is one of the nation's central challenges.

The productivity imperative means that a nation's wealth is principally of its own collective choosing. Geographic location, natural resources, and even military power are no longer decisive. Instead, national prosperity depends on how a nation and its citizens organize and manage their economy, the institutions they establish, and the types of investments they make, both individually and collectively.

Sound macroeconomic policies and stable political and legal institutions create the potential for improving national prosperity. But wealth is actually generated at the microeconomic level – in the ability of firms to create valuable goods and services productively that will support high wages and high returns to capital. Prosperity depends, then, on improving a nation's capabilities at the microeconomic level. This can be understood only by examining the way in which productivity increases at the firm, industry, and cluster levels. (We will define clusters later in this chapter.) Here, public policy and private business practice intersect.

Until recently, Japan has had a largely sound set of macroeconomic policies, and it has enjoyed macroeconomic stability. Japan's real problems are rooted in the microeconomics of competition and will not be addressed even with unprecedented macroeconomic stimulation. The microeconomic foundations of productivity rest on two interrelated areas: the sophistication of company operations and strategy, and the quality of the microeconomic business environment. The sophistication with which a nation's companies compete (for example, their technology and marketing approaches) ultimately determines its productivity. Unless a country's companies become more productive, its economy cannot become more productive.

Company sophistication in competing can be thought of in two parts, drawing on the ideas presented in Chapter 3. The first is *operational effectiveness*, or the extent to which companies in a nation approach world best practices in areas such as production processes, technologies, marketing methods, and management techniques.[3] The other aspect of company sophistication, more fundamental to success in an advanced economy, is the degree to which companies have *distinctive strategies*.

If there is to be rising prosperity, companies must transform their ways of competing. The basis for competition must shift from comparative advantage (low-cost labor or natural resources) to competitive advantages created by unique products and processes guided by distinctive strategies. Company operations and strategies, then, are directly linked to a nation's competitiveness because they determine productivity.

Yet the sophistication with which companies compete is not solely of their own making. It is strongly influenced by the quality of the national business environment in which companies operate. The business environment has much to do with the levels of operational effectiveness that companies can attain as well as the types of strategies they can choose. Operational effectiveness is unattainable, for example, if regulatory red tape is onerous, logistics are unreliable, or firms cannot get timely supplies of components or high-quality service for their production machinery. Similarly, firms have a hard time competing with differentiation strategies if they cannot find well-educated staff, if marketing channels are poorly developed, or if local customers are unsophisticated.

Improvements in the national business environment and the upgrading of individual companies are inextricably intertwined. A national business environment with better quality inputs, improved infrastructure, and more advanced educational and other institutions fosters more sophisticated company strategies. At the same time, company upgrading can directly contribute to improving the business environment (more sophisticated corporate buyers, for example, will create demand for higher quality suppliers), and raise the standards that have to be met on the part of the government and other institutions.

The relationship between company performance and the microeconomic business environment was evident in every one of our case studies. Japanese companies were internationally competitive if they had significant advantages in operational effectiveness. However, their competitiveness was especially robust if they competed with distinctive strategies, as some companies did in video games, automobiles, and robotics. Competitiveness arose and was sustained when the Japanese business environment in the industry was dynamic, stimulating, and intensely competitive.

Japanese companies and industries were uncompetitive if the local business environment detracted from innovation and productivity. In uncompetitive industries, Japanese firms imitated one another, competed in ways that created little value in international markets, or faced impediments to operational effectiveness improvement.

Competitiveness and the Japanese Business Environment

Every nation's business environment is shaped by four distinct but related influences. These can be depicted graphically as a diamond, as shown in Figure 4-1.[4] Japanese competitiveness depends on Japan's circumstances in

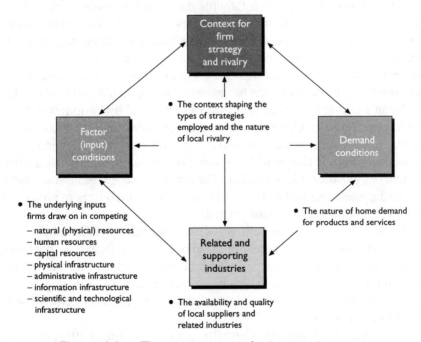

Figure 4-1   The microeconomic business environment

Source: Porter, 1990

these areas compared with other nations. In our case studies, those industries where Japan had favorable factor conditions, sophisticated home demand, a cluster of competitive supporting industries, and intense home rivalry flourished. In contrast, those industries where critical inputs were unavailable or of poor quality, local customer needs were misaligned with international needs, critical supporting industries were weak or nonexistent, and/or no effective home market competition existed were invariably uncompetitive.

Tables 4-1 and 4-2 (at the end of the chapter) summarize the business environment for the industries and sectors we studied. In the following pages, we compare the circumstances of some competitive and uncompetitive industries in each area of the diamond to illustrate our overall findings.

The Cost, Quality, and Specialization of Factor Inputs
(Factor Conditions)

Factor conditions refer to the inputs that allow competition to take place, such as human resources and the local scientific base. Companies must be able to access such inputs at competitive prices and qualities to attain high levels of productivity. Factor inputs range from tangible assets, such as physical infrastructure, to less tangible ones, such as pools of information and university research institutes. Inputs that are generic across many industries rarely constitute a competitive advantage because they tend to be available in many nations; they can be a source of disadvantage. To increase productivity, factor inputs must improve in efficiency, quality and, ultimately, their specialization to the needs of a particular industry cluster.

Japan's failure industries typically were plagued by basic factor disadvantages. Consider chocolate, where government trade barriers caused Japanese companies to pay excessive prices for imported sugar and cocoa. This contrasted markedly with the situation in internationally competitive Japanese industries, like soy sauce. Perhaps because soy beans are a staple of the Japanese diet and there have been few local producers to protect, no import restraints on soy beans existed.

Japan also was not competitive where essential specialized infrastructure was missing. Development of the civil aircraft industry was hampered by the lack of specialized experimental facilities, such as wind tunnels and test flight runways. In contrast, the existence of a well-developed local communication infrastructure aided the competitive development of facsimile machines.

Competitive advantages normally arise from pools of specialized personnel. Japan's supply of highly trained electrical engineers, for example, has clearly given Japan an edge in a host of industries such as fax machines, robotics, and consumer electronics. Employees' experiences in seemingly unrelated industries can create transferable skills that give rise to competitive advantage. Japan's large, well-developed comic book industry produced an ample supply of artists and animators for video games.

Conversely, we noted in Chapter 2 that Japan was often uncompetitive in industries in which there was a dearth of specialized personnel. Japan's weak chemical sector has long suffered from a shortage of chemists and chemical engineers, a problem related to weaknesses in Japan's university system and in its research institutions. Similar shortages of specialized skills have undermined competitiveness in the securities, software, and aircraft industries.

Pools of inputs created in one industry can be redeployed in others. For example, the early entrants in sewing machines immediately after World War II were former machine-gun manufacturers. Because the Allies initially prohibited aircraft production, aircraft engineers were redeployed in automobiles. The decline of synthetic fibers, once a prestigious, major industry, freed up well-trained specialized talent to carbon fibers.

Japan's successes occurred where there was a local capability in science and technology. In optics and electronics, for example, corporate laboratories assembled talented professionals who researched such areas as galium-arsenide material, optical lithography, and optical communication. These corporate labs were the driving forces in semiconductors and opto-electronics.[5] In contrast, competitive failures occurred in software, chemicals, pharmaceuticals, and biotechnology, where domestic research capability, especially in basic science, is weak.

Selective disadvantages in the more basic factor inputs, such as rising wages, local raw material shortages, and resource depletion, can trigger innovation and foster successive waves of productivity growth, provided other favorable microeconomic conditions are present. In automobiles, for example, labor disputes in the 1950s led manufacturers to minimize the hiring of full-time workers. Companies were pushed instead to increase productivity by introducing new production equipment and management techniques such as total quality control and multiskilling. Rapid growth of domestic demand in the 1960s and export growth in the 1970s further accelerated efforts to enhance the productivity of workers.[6]

In the area of capital, patient, low-cost capital from main banks as well as internal funding within diversified companies allowed large-scale investments and quick expansion in semiconductors, carbon fibers, VCRs, and facsimile. However, the lack of risk capital in Japan hampered the development of software and biotechnology, where the combination of high risks with the absence of hard assets to collateralize made the industries unsuited to traditional bank financing.

The Availability and Competitiveness of Local Clusters: Suppliers, Related Industries, and Supporting Institutions

Rising levels of productivity and more advanced strategies cannot be achieved without efficient access to sophisticated suppliers of materials, components, machinery, services, and information. Although some of these items are provided by government, universities, and other institutions, most are produced by firms. And while international sourcing is possible, local sourcing from capable suppliers is highly preferable because it can enhance productivity and improve the capacity for innovation and the rate of productivity improvement.[7] Local access to related industries – industries that share technology, channels, or customers – can offer similar benefits. Clusters create efficiencies and other advantages that cut *across* industries – what economists term externalities.

Clusters are geographic concentrations of interconnected companies, specialized suppliers, service providers, firms in related industries, and associated institutions (such as universities, standards agencies, and trade associations) in particular fields. Clusters arise in nations, states, and even cities. When interconnected companies and institutions in a given field cluster in one location – Silicon Valley, for example – all of its members benefit from the ease of pursuing relationships and from the ability to source specialized components, personnel, and services efficiently. Access to specialized know-how and personnel, which enables companies to boost productivity and pursue more sophisticated strategies, is another important cluster benefit. Indeed, clustering is especially critical in more advanced forms of competition because it provides local companies with efficient access to the most sophisticated information, people, suppliers, and partners that more distant rivals are hard pressed to match. Companies do not have to pay the cost of creating such assets internally, but can access them at low cost.

Competitive Japanese industries invariably benefited from a strong base of specialized local suppliers. Consider robotics. It is no accident that Japan has also been a world leader in a host of related and supporting industries: numerical controls, machine tools, optical sensors, and motors. In home air conditioners, Japan is a world leader in components such as converters, compressors, small motors, and radiators, all of which have contributed to the industry's success. In the fax machine industry, Japan's success grew out of a powerful cluster of related industries in cameras, optics, electronics, and small motors. Similarly, forklift trucks benefited from the existence of the strong Japanese automotive suppliers; continuous synthetic weaves and carbon fibers drew heavily on Japan's competitive synthetic fiber producers.

Some clusters formed out of necessity. In automobiles, rapid growth and product proliferation in the 1960s pressured auto assemblers to expand outsourcing in both production and product development, leading to the establishment of deep supplier networks. Suppliers were commonly located near the assembly company. The cluster not only boosted productivity but also allowed automakers to weather demand fluctuations.[8]

In contrast, the chocolate industry has suffered from cluster weaknesses, in areas such as food processing machinery and in related industries such as dairy products and other packaged foods. Likewise, detergents suffered from the absence of competitive related and supporting industries in Japan, including chemicals, advertising agencies, and washing machines. In software, Japan's weakness in microprocessors and PCs further impeded software development, which requires detailed knowledge of hardware architecture.

Striking competitive success often occurs where several clusters overlap and where the fusion of related technologies drives innovation. In cameras, entrants from the strong optical and electronic industries spurred the development of the auto-focus single-lens reflex camera. The typewriter industry benefited from the juxtaposition of electronics and precision mechanical parts suppliers. The typewriter industry, in turn, served as the foundation for the printer industry.

Japan has been particularly competitive where overlapping clusters led multiple firms to enter new fields, drawing on differing backgrounds and approaches. In facsimile, Canon spearheaded the development of a new optical scanner based on its experience in copiers, leading to an extremely compact fax machine. Taking advantage of its expertise in consumer electronics and personal computers, Sharp introduced high-performance facsimile machines at the price of medium-level machines.[9]

Clusters cannot foster competitiveness, however, when the boundaries of related industries are frozen by regulation. In securities and banking, the Ministry of Finance determined the product segments each type of financial institution could serve, blocking new products that crossed these artificial boundaries. The result was an almost complete absence of both product innovation and competitiveness.

The Sophistication of Local Customers (*Demand Conditions*)

The process of economic upgrading requires that firms develop the capacity to improve product quality, offer up-to-date features and, ultimately, create unique products and services. In advanced economies, firms do not just respond to international markets but lead them. Demand conditions at home – local customer needs and buying behavior – strongly influence the upgrading process. Sophisticated customers press firms to improve and offer insights into existing and future needs that are hard to gain in foreign markets. Local demand also reveals segments of the market where firms can differentiate themselves.

Sophisticated home demand spurs companies to compete more productively. When local customers are knowledgeable and demanding, companies must work harder and smarter to satisfy them. Stringent quality, safety, health, and environmental standards often enhance the sophistication of local demand by pushing companies to employ more advanced technologies and to make higher value products.

In robotics, for example, Japanese manufacturers moved to large-scale robot use much faster than producers in other countries because of their highly sophisticated manufacturing practices, shortages of skilled workers, and caution in hiring due to lifetime employment. In fax machines, the unavailability of the Japanese language typewriters and telex machines coupled with tight office space constraints, large time differences with foreign markets, and expensive telephone charges created a very demanding local market.

The contrast between demand conditions in the air conditioner and detergent industries has much to do with their striking difference in competitive performance. Japan is a nation of small, closely packed houses and hot, muggy summers, so there is a large local market for compact, quiet air conditioners. Demanding consumers have continually pushed manufacturers to upgrade their products through improved performance and additional features. Following the oil crisis of the 1970s, the government set stringent energy standards that triggered further innovations in energy efficiency.

In detergents, by contrast, the Japanese market is so unique that home demand distracts Japanese companies from becoming globally competitive. Some of the same energy and space constraints that led to success in air conditioning resulted in small washing machines and the practice of frequent washing of small loads of laundry. This, coupled with softer water, led to detergents with performance qualities less stringent than those required by foreign customers.

Demand conditions peculiar to Japan hampered some industries and helped others. Japanese customers' unwillingness to pay for intangibles was an obstacle for software.[10] In contrast, Japanese are willing to pay a premium for high-performance golf clubs, fishing rods, and tennis rackets to make the most of their limited leisure time. This speeded the early growth of the carbon fiber industry. In packaged foods, Japanese customers can detect subtle differences among soy sauce brands, pushing makers to produce high-quality sauces. In chocolate, however, Japanese consumers have only recently come to appreciate the taste of high-quality chocolates; in the past, they preferred idiosyncratic Japanese candies that held no appeal for foreign customers. Also, Japan's distribution channels for chocolate are fragmented and complex; they operate very differently from channels in the rest of the world. As we noted in Chapter 3, this has encouraged excessive product proliferation and other practices that detracted from Japan's competitiveness in chocolate and other packaged-food industries.

Sometimes sophisticated demand is the result of customers' experiences and learning in related industries. Consider the car audio industry. Because most Japanese households own high-quality audio systems, customers demanded the same sound quality in their cars. Even though the car units had to operate under tougher conditions including vibration, high temperature and humidity, low available electric voltage, and limited space, manufacturers simply had to deliver the same quality sound. Meeting these challenges made Japanese car audio manufacturers internationally competitive.

Government's affect on demand conditions can be conscious or unwitting. The policy of offering sewing classes in public schools created a large demand for sewing machines in the early postwar period. In the case of civil aircraft, government promoted public ground transportation and suppressed the demand for air travel, not recognizing that this policy confounded its parallel efforts to build a competitive Japanese aircraft industry. When the YS-11, the first domestically developed transport aircraft, was introduced in the 1960s, it was good enough for inexperienced domestic customers, but American passengers complained about its noisy flaps and landing gear.[11] Japanese aircraft makers had never before been forced to address passenger comfort.

Intense Local Rivalry

Of the four aspects of a nation's microeconomic business environment, the extent of local rivalry is perhaps the most powerful predictor of global competitiveness. It drives innovation and continual improvement in productivity. Without competition at home, firms will never be competitive abroad.

Part of the context for local rivalry is the climate for investment in the forms necessary to support sophisticated competition and higher levels of productivity in an industry. The structure of the tax system, the corporate governance system, labor market policies affecting workforce development, intellectual property rules and their enforcement: all these things, among others, affect the rate of investment in R&D, training, and capital equipment.

The nature and intensity of local rivalry is also governed by policies, incentives, and local norms. An open trade policy, a policy of welcoming foreign investment, and a strict antitrust policy are all essential to ensuring healthy domestic competition.

In virtually all the Japanese failure cases we studied, domestic rivalry was constrained in some way, often by the government. In chemicals, for example, the government controlled production levels and industry capacity. In securities, intrusive government regulation and fixed commissions created a comfortable oligopoly of just four (now three) players. In detergents, the government protected the home industry from foreign competition, effectively giving two domestic players control of the market. In civil aircraft, essentially all development projects were conducted jointly.

When we did observe local competition in the failure cases, it was on dimensions distorted by the peculiar Japanese context. In apparel, the major rivals competed to acquire licensing rights to overseas brands and often overpaid, leading to brand proliferation and customer confusion. In detergents, Kao and Lion fought to control Japanese channels that are far more complex and fragmented than those in major international markets. The only notable innovation in detergents was Kao's introduction of the highly concentrated detergent 'Attack,' which required less detergent per load. This product met the needs of Japanese buyers, who typically go shopping on foot or by bicycle and carry their own groceries. Concentrated detergents had less of an impact overseas, however, where light, compact detergents were much less needed.

In contrast to the blunted competition in the failure cases, we found vigorous local competition in all of Japan's internationally successful industries. In air conditioners, more than a dozen rivals competed aggressively. There were well over 100 robotics companies, twenty domestic sewing machine manufacturers, and more than fifteen Japanese producers of fax machines. Table 4-3 shows the number of Japanese rivals in the competitive industries we studied in selected years.

Table 4-3   Estimated number of Japanese rivals in selected industries

Industry	Estimated number of Japanese rivals, 1997	Estimated number of Japanese rivals, 1987
Air conditioners	20	13
Audio equipment	14	25
Automobiles	9	9
Cameras	13	15
Car audio	8	12
Carbon fibers[1]	13	7
Construction equipment	30	20[4]
Copiers	15	14
Facsimile machines	20	10
Large computers	5	6
Lift truck	15	8
Machine tools[2]	93	112
Microwave equipment	7	5
Motorcycle	4	4
Musical instruments (pianos)	5	4
Personal computers	9	16
Robotics	190	280
Semiconductors[3]	15	34
Sewing machines	20	20
Shipbuilding	7	33
Steel[5]	8	5
Synthetic fibers	10	8
Television sets	11	15
Truck and bus tires	6	5
Trucks	11	11
Typewriters	8	14
Videocassette recorders	9	10

Notes
1. Yano Research Institute estimates that three major players lead the industry.
2. According to the Japan Machine Tool Builders Association, some industry experts say that there are more than 200 small companies in the industry.
3. Definition of semiconductors follows EIAJ's official definition.
4. The number of firms varies by product area. The smallest number, ten, produced bulldozers. Fifteen firms produce shovel trucks, truck cranes, and asphalt paving equipment. There are twenty companies in hydraulic excavators, a product in which Japan is particularly strong.
5. Number of integrated companies.

Sources: Nippon Kogyo Shinbu, Nippon Kogyo Nenkan, 1987; Yano Research Institute, Market Share Book 99; and field interviews

Overall, the strong link between domestic rivalry and international success was one of our most striking findings. Some Japanese say that local competition is excessive; we believe that any excess exists only because of Japan's flawed approach to strategy, the lack of focus by

Japanese companies on profitability, pervasive imitation, and the absence of distinctive positioning.

VCRs present a particularly striking example of competition-led upgrading. Sony and JVC fought fiercely over the Beta and VHS standards, and even MITI failed to impose a unified standard. While Sony kept its technology to itself, JVC, the latecomer, actively shared its technology with other producers to increase the installed base and become the *de facto* standard. JVC eventually won this 'war,' as rivalry among VHS suppliers pressured faster improvement and greater availability of software. However, fierce competition between the camps on additional features and superior product quality was a crucial factor in the rate of innovation.

Statistical Findings on Japanese Competitiveness

Statistical analysis confirms the findings from our case studies. Using a sample that included every Japanese industry for which comparable data are available, we tested the relationship between Japan's world export share and the traditional explanations for trade competitiveness, such as labor intensity, human capital intensity, physical capital intensity, and the size of the home market. However, we also included a measure of the intensity of local rivalry among the leading companies in each industry by tracking fluctuations in market share over an eighteen-year period. Where market share among leading competitors fluctuates a lot, this is a reliable sign that rivalry is fierce.

Our results were unequivocal: the intensity of local rivalry was by far the dominant factor explaining the international success of Japanese industries.[12] Conversely, the presence of trade protection or the existence of a cartel worked against international competitiveness. Traditional comparative advantage variables, such as capital and labor intensity, had a weak or nonexistent relationship with export share. The size of the home market was also insignificant, suggesting that economies of scale per se is not an important factor in determining competitiveness.

Figures 4-2 and 4-3 are illustrative of the Japanese industries in the statistical sample. Contrast the domestic market share fluctuations in the highly competitive camera and integrated circuit industries with the stability in the uncompetitive chocolate and polyethylene film industries. Time and time again, the vitality of rivalry is manifested in international competitiveness.

Recent comparative data also allow us to assess the Japanese business environment relative to a large sample of other nations. Since 1998, the

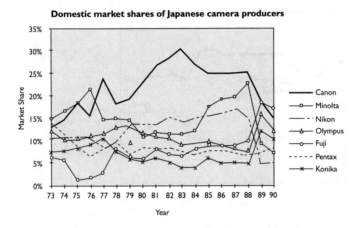

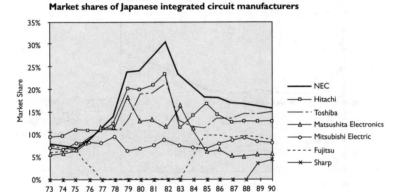

Figure 4-2   Domestic market share fluctuations, selected competitive industries

Source: Yano Research Institute, *Market Share Encyclopedia,* various years

Global Competitiveness Report has included a ranking of the quality of the microeconomic business environment based on the diamond theory.[13] Data are drawn from a survey of more than 3,000 business and government leaders in 55 countries; the responses of executives in multinational companies that have a comparative perspective are heavily weighted. Common factor analysis is used to construct an index of microeconomic competitiveness. Japan's ranking has fluctuated from 18 to 14, well below Japan's ranking in terms of GDP *per capita* adjusted for purchasing power. This means that Japan's current level of GDP *per capita* is higher than justified by the quality of its business environment – a danger sign. Preliminary statistical evidence suggests that nations with incomes that are ahead

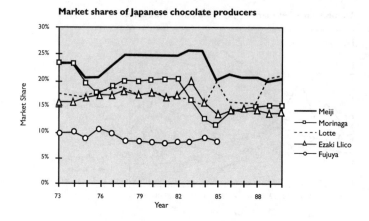

Market shares of Japanese chocolate producers

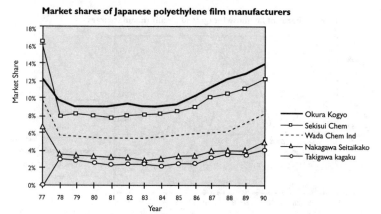

Market shares of Japanese polyethylene film manufacturers

Figure 4-3   Domestic market fluctuations, selected uncompetitive industries

Source: Yano Research Institute, *Market Share Encyclopedia*, various years

of their microeconomic circumstances will fall in relative income level over time.

The microeconomic competitiveness model allows us to assess those aspects of the overall business environment where Japan is strong or weak relative to its current level of GDP *per capita*. Table 4-4 shows these areas for 1999. The rankings listed on Table 4-4 refer to Japan's standing relative to all other countries.

Japan enjoys a generally strong supplier base, sophisticated customers, excellent railroad infrastructure, adequate schooling, high-quality engineers, substantial public investment in R&D, demanding regulatory standards, and numerous local competitors, among other strengths. These overall strengths are consistent with our findings in the case studies.

Table 4-4   Quality of the Japanese business environment relative to other nations, adjusted for *per capita* income (1999 data)

	Rank[1]
ADVANTAGES	
Railroad infrastructure development	3
Domestic supplier quantity	3
Public investment in nonmilitary R&D	3
Domestic supplier quality	4
Adequacy of average years of schooling	4
Buyer sophistication	7
Quality of scientists and engineers	4
Quality of science research institutions	8
Extent of locally based competitors	6
Demanding regulatory standards	9
Intensity of local competition	8
DISADVANTAGES	
Hidden trade barrier liberalization	45
Computer utilization	26
Legal barriers to entry	39
Ease of access to loans	31
Venture capital availability	42
Quality of business schools	50
Difficulty of financing start-ups	35
Air transport infrastructure quality	29
Openness of public sector contracts	56
Stock market access	30
Financial market sophistication	26
Financial disclosure requirements	25
Tariff liberalization	24
Business information availability	19
Adequacy of private sector legal recourse	26
Administrative burden for start-ups	37
Port infrastructure quality	18
Bureaucratic red tape	20
Road infrastructure quality	17
Effectiveness of antitrust policy	17
International direct dial communications costs	17

1. Rank refers to Japan's ranking on each measure compared to the 58 nations surveyed.
Source: Authors' calculations based on data and models from *The Global Competitiveness Report* 1999

Notably, however, Japan registers more microeconomic weaknesses than strengths when its current *per capita* income in taken into account. There are numerous unproductive government interventions in competition, from hidden trade barriers to legal barriers to entry to closed public sector contracts. Antitrust policy is ineffective. Japan also registers weaknesses in its financial markets, especially access to capital for start-ups. Information and disclosure is a disadvantage, as is the administrative burden on companies, the amount of red tape, and the inadequacy of private sector legal recourse. Management education is poorly developed. Road and airport infrastructures are weak, and communications costs are high. These weaknesses, again consistent with our case study evidence and the discussion in previous chapters, are a legacy of a flawed economic model.

The Role of Government in Competitiveness

Because government affects so many aspects of the business environment, it has an inevitable role in economic development. But government's role should be to improve the environment for productivity and competition, not to get directly involved in the competitive process. Our theory highlights the ways in which government policy works for or against competitiveness. Government can shape factor conditions, for example, through its training and infrastructure policies. Regulatory standards and processes, government purchasing, and openness to imports influence the sophistication of home demand. Similar influences are present in every part of the diamond. Distinct roles for government exist at the national, state, and local levels. A concerted effort to improve the microeconomic environment must ideally occur at all three levels.

In addition to government, universities, schools, infrastructure providers, standard-setting agencies, and myriad other institutions also contribute to the business environment. Such institutions must proliferate and improve in quality to support more productive modes of competition.

Finally, the private sector itself is more than just a consumer of the business environment. It can and must help shape it. Individual firms can take steps such as working with local universities, attracting suppliers, or defining standards that benefit not only them but the overall competitive context. Collective industry bodies, such as trade associations and chambers of commerce, also play important roles in improving infrastructure, upgrading training institutions, and the like that are often overlooked.

Our theory makes clear why many aspects of the Japanese government model were counterproductive. By attempting to become directly involved in the competitive process, the Japanese government violated the most basic tenet of effective policy. Many government practices limited domestic rivalry and distorted the nature of competition away from forms that were valued in foreign markets. Weak antitrust enforcement, legalized cartels, subsidies, protection, and cooperative R&D all blunted innovation and sapped competitive vitality. Weaknesses in educational policy reduced the supply of specialized personnel. Trade barriers drove up the cost of inputs. Intervention in competition in domestic industries such as retailing and transportation made them costly and uncompetitive, and it distorted the demand conditions facing many other Japanese industries. Government – through guidance, subsidies, approval requirements, and other means – inserted itself in corporate decisions instead of trusting the process of competition to sort them out.

The diamond theory also helps us understand why certain government activities (identified in Chapter 2) were so beneficial. Where government stimulated the demand for new or advanced products, it improved demand conditions, and with them, competitiveness. The same thing happened when government set stringent regulatory standards. When government expanded university programs in electrical and mechanical engineering in the 1960s and 70s, it expanded the supply of specialized talent for affected industries, thereby improving factor conditions.

Some Japanese corporate practices also fit the new model of competitiveness particularly well. For example, a system that emphasized tight linkages with nearby local suppliers allowed Japanese firms to gain advantages missed by Western companies that treated their suppliers as adversaries. The Japanese propensity to diversify through internal development into related industries was also good for the economy because it leveraged and extended clusters.

Japan did well where a cluster was present and where companies reinforced cluster development. In video games, for example, we have described how Nintendo subcontracted manufacturing for the Famicon. Specialized chips were sourced from Ricoh and other leading Japanese chip makers. Nintendo worked closely with outside game cartridge manufacturers and with independent game developers such as Namco, Hudson (a computer software maker), Taito, Konami (computers and coin-op games), and Bandai (Japan's largest toy maker). In the process, a cluster was developed. When Sony entered, it could draw on Japan's strong cadre of game developers. Sony leveraged the cluster by offering some 4,000 game development tools to make it easy for developers to come up with new titles quickly.

The video game case also shows that Japanese competitiveness is extraordinary where clusters are broad and deep. The well-developed Japanese comic book (*manga*) and animation industries, among others, have numerous linkages to video games. Japan thus had a large pool of artists who excelled in developing both stories and cartoon characters (artists such as Osamu Tezuka, Ikki Kajiwara, and Katsuhiro Otomo are household names in Japan). The huge sophisticated Japanese home market for comics and animation was readily transferable to games. More than 200 comic book publishers competed fiercely, coming up with new products with breathtaking speed. Japanese print-publishing and film-developing firms, with the world's most advanced machinery, offered world-leading turnaround times. All of these interconnected industries played a significant role in the vitality of Japan's video game producers.

Conclusion

While no theory explains everything, and there is always room for interpretation in case studies, the diamond theory offers a compelling explanation for Japan's competitiveness. Unlike the old Japanese government model, it discriminates between competitive and uncompetitive industries.

The Japanese economy is not a special case after all. The microeconomic foundations that drive competitive performance in the rest of the world are just as decisive in Japan. Understanding this reality is essential in order to chart an accurate course for the nation's future.

Notes

1. A microeconomic theory of economic development is described in Porter (1998a).
2. Competitiveness of a nation is different than competitiveness for an individual firm. A firm many gain market share through means such as cutting wages and exploiting workers that lower the standard of living.
3. See Porter (1996).
4. The diamond theory is described in detail in Porter (1990).
5. High-Tech Strategy Research Committee (1990).
6. Fujimoto (1999).
7. For a detailed treatment, see Porter (1998a).
8. Fujimoto (1999).
9. Enright(1991).
10. *Datamation*, April 1, 1987.
11. The Society of Japanese Aerospace Companies (1987).
12. A more complete discussion of the methods and results can be found in Sakakibara and Porter (2000).
13. *Global Competitiveness Report*, 1998 and 1999.

Table 4-1 Diamond conditions in uncompetitive Japanese industries

	Access to specialized inputs (factors)	Japanese home demand	Local Japanese rivalry	Related and supporting industries
Apparel	• Dearth of local apparel design schools • Low status of fashion designers until recently	• Demand for Western-style ready-to-wear clothing is comparatively recent (last 40 years) • Japanese customers were picky about stitching but unsophisticated with respect to fit, comfort, and color • Small number of sizes needed in Japan was a constraint to penetrating overseas markets • Apparel companies competed to acquire desirable floor space in department stores and solidify department store relationships. The 'Onward Way' system of working with stores was not transferable overseas • Lack of professional buyers within department stores to pressure apparel innovation	• Major rivals competed to acquire licensing rights of overseas brands, foregoing the development of new designs and new fashion concepts • Brand identification was linked to foreign brands and the retail store, rather than company brands that could be developed internationally • The tendency to copy designs and concepts precluded differentiation • Channels were protected from competition by the Large-scale Retail Store Act, limiting rivalry • Strategies involving ownership of channels were limited by department store linkages	• Apparel companies did not develop linkages with the synthetic fiber industry. Japan was weak in dying, fabric production, and design • Apparel manufacturing was outsourced to small, inefficient manufacturers with few specialized skills and little innovative process technology • Strength in industrial sewing machines and mass-production technologies did not translate into apparel manufacturing

(cont'd)

Table 4-1 Diamond conditions in uncompetitive Japanese industries (cont'd)

	Access to specialized inputs (factors)	Japanese home demand	Local Japanese rivalry	Related and supporting industries
Chemicals	• Limited advanced education programs in chemistry • Chemical engineers had less prestige than electronic engineers • Research was focused on catching up with the West, not innovation • Research within companies was limited because patents failed to protect product innovations until 1975 • Research programs in universities were underfunded and highly bureaucratic • National research institutes never played an important role in chemical sector research	• Unsophisticated buyers, except for the automobile and consumer electronics industries where Japan has some areas of strength in chemicals • The most advanced customers demanded many different grades, which misaligned Japanese company product lines with global needs • Demand primarily for bulk chemicals. Not enough pressure to move into fine chemicals	• Government intervened heavily in the development of the chemical sector • The intensity of rivalry limited by government influence on production levels and capacity • Cartels formed repeatedly to weather recessions and scrap excess capacity. This allowed weak companies to survive, maintained industry fragmentation, and limited pressure to upgrade • Major competitors earned acceptable returns in the home market with basic products, deterring movement into fine chemicals or overseas markets • Underdeveloped research and marketing capabilities led to me-too strategies	• Japan's process equipment and engineering industries were strong, but their service capabilities are not as sophisticated as those offered by Western suppliers • The oil refining industry is inefficient, and rivalry was restrained by government

| Civil aircraft | • Limited supply of university degree programs in aeronautical engineering
• Limited research facilities
• Limited supply of well-trained aircraft production workers
• Research within aircraft-producing companies was focused on developing general engineering expertise in diversified heavy machinery rather than aircraft
• The absence of a defense industry limited skills and experience in large-scale systems integration
• Sourced all important technologies from overseas (especially from Boeing) through international R&D consortia | • Lower demand for air travel in Japan because of convenient substitutes (public ground transportation) and high prices resulting from stifling regulations of airlines
• Japanese customers were not experienced in air travel
• Most traffic occurs between Tokyo and Osaka; the area is served by an efficient train system
• Limits to flight scheduling because of noise concerns and limited airport capacity
• Modest military demand
• General aviation demand severely limited
• The airline industry was regulated to limit competition that might otherwise have stimulated aircraft innovation | • Heavy intervention by government to limit entry and competition in aircraft
• No rivalry among Japanese companies that would promote upgrading. Virtually all projects were joint efforts
• Major players not focused on ways to develop unique skills and strategies (e.g. timely new product introduction, timely delivery, marketing, service) | • Lack of a defense industry that could share technologies and develop engineers for the aircraft industry
• Lack of a home-based capability in specialized CAD/CAM systems and types of machine tools, which were important to aircraft production |

(cont'd)

Table 4-1 Diamond conditions in uncompetitive Japanese industries (cont'd)

	Access to specialized inputs (factors)	Japanese home demand	Local Japanese rivalry	Related and supporting industries
Chocolate	• All important raw materials were either imported or produced by protected, high-cost local producers. Government frequently changed its policy on import restrictions and tariff rates, forcing chocolate manufacturers to constantly adjust their recipes to accommodate shifting ingredient prices • Strong government price controls and high import barriers on basic ingredients • No specialized expertise in chocolate product development and production; everything was imported and copied	• Unsophisticated local buyers, who preferred chocolate snacks peculiar to Japan • Loose regulatory standards for chocolate led to inferior quality • Many conventional Japanese snacks are cheaper substitutes for chocolate • Fragmented and complex distribution channels were different from those in international markets, hindering customer learning and fostering idiosyncratic Japanese business practices	• Government protected the domestic market until the late 1980s through import quotas and high tariffs. Foreign competitors that could have helped upgrade the industry were kept out • Very little differentiation among the leading competitors, which constantly imitated one another's products • Rivalry based on product proliferation to secure shelf space	• Weak supporting industries in food-processing machinery • Weak related industries, including dairy and packaged foods

| **Detergents** | • Little university research and development in detergent chemistry

• No specialized local expertise in chemical engineering related to detergent production | • Unusual home market conditions – including soft water (which contains less calcium), smaller capacity washing machines, frequent washing of small loads, and low water temperature – were not transferable to other markets

• Soft water and frequent washing did not demand advanced detergents, discouraging innovation

• No standards were set by the government for product type, quality, or environmental impact

• Slow diffusion of washing machines in the 1960s led to low demand

• Distribution skills developed for Japanese market were not transferable overseas | • Government protected the industry from foreign competition until 1970

• Competition was limited primarily to two Japanese companies

• The complex distribution system worked as a barrier to entry

• Patent laws failed to protect products until 1975, discouraging innovation

• Detergents were positioned as loss leaders, limiting incentives for investment by Kao and Lion | • Related and supporting industries were not competitive, including chemicals, washing machines, advertising, consumer-packaged goods, and retailing |

(cont'd)

Table 4-1 Diamond conditions in uncompetitive Japanese industries (cont'd)

	Access to specialized inputs (factors)	Japanese home demand	Local Japanese rivalry	Related and supporting industries
Securities	• No strong finance programs in universities • No theoretical finance research in universities • The separation between universities and business inhibited flow of new products • Slow adoption of computers in securities firms • Incentive systems within firms inhibited the development of specialists	• The strength of commercial banking as the primary lending and savings institution limited demand for sophisticated financing • Cross-shareholdings limited the float of securities traded in the market, making markets subject to speculation • Unsophisticated customers sought guaranteed returns. Securities firms turned to unfair manipulation of the market • Limited local market for merger and acquisition-related services due to cross-shareholdings and less developed regulations	• Entry restrictions and other regulations by the government limited firms' ability to innovate and upgrade • Fixed brokerage and underwriting commissions limited rivalry • A comfortable oligopoly of four (now three) powerful firms was encouraged • Government encouraged copycat strategies to avoid 'excess competition.' There were virtually no differences in strategy among the big four • All competition in the domestic market centered on market share instead of innovative products. Competition was oriented toward seeking stable relationship with customers • Virtually all innovations came through alliances with foreign firms	• The banking industry was separated from securities through regulation, blocking new products that crossed regulatory boundaries • Investment management firms were late arrivals to Japan • Poorly developed database industry

Software			
• Limited software curriculum in universities • Lack of software-related research in national labs and universities • Insufficient supply of software engineers • Lack of venture capital for software start-ups • Lack of large-scale R&D projects by the government (unlike in the US) to build skills and technology	• Multiple operating systems existed in mainframe computers and, historically, in PCs. Incompatible platforms made it difficult for packaged software to be profitable • Slow penetration in Japan of packaged software and distributed processing in companies • Customer resistance to pay separately for software • Very slow penetration of computers in schools led to low level of computer literacy • Use of English language alphabet made keyboard and software operation more difficult for users and contributed to the slow penetration of computers • The Japanese language acted as an obstacle to develop and market products for the global market	• Very few significant competitors in applications software except in video games, the one segment where Japan is competitive • Hardware manufacturers that dominated the software industry until recently bundled software and hardware, treating software as a give-away • Software companies competed largely on unit price per man-month for custom software development instead of packaged products • Government subsidies for packaged software invited moral hazard by software makers. Companies took advantage of the subsidies but were not serious about commercialization	• Incompatible platforms used by hardware manufacturers hampered the market growth of software • Absence of significant defense and aeronautical sectors after WWII lowered the priority of software development • Japan is relatively weak in microprocessors, PCs, and workstations

Table 4-2 Diamond conditions in competitive Japanese industries

	Access to specialized inputs (factors)	Japanese home demand	Local Japanese rivalry	Related and supporting industries
Automobiles	• Wartime aircraft engineers switched to the automotive sector, transferring technology and project management skills • Shortages of skilled workers and labor disputes in the 1950s forced automakers to increase productivity	• Japanese customers are very sensitive to fit and finishes • Customers desire latest models and features • Japanese market needs led to emphasis on compact vehicles, fuel efficiency, and small trucks • Demand fluctuations led Toyota to adopt the lean production system and to minimize the number of full-time workers, creating flexibility and a low cost structure. This approach spread throughout the industry	• Nine automakers competed vigorously across multiple product segments • Intense battle for home market share spilled over into international markets • Many process innovations including JIT, *kanban*, multitask workers, *kaizen*, and TQC were pioneered by auto companies	• Technology transfer occurred from the weaving machine industry including multitasking, work standardization, and benchmarking • Rapid growth of domestic demand and the shortage of capital during the early postwar period led auto assemblers to delegate more tasks to suppliers than in other countries. This resulted in the establishment of deep supplier networks • Japan is highly competitive in robotics, machine tools, car audio, consumer electronics, and control systems
Cameras	• Abundant supply of electrical and mechanical engineers	• Large, sophisticated home demand due to Japanese obsession with taking photos • Japanese love exchanging photos as well as taking group photos • Japanese customers are often early adopters for new models and features that become widespread	• Many Japanese competitors (15 in 1987 and 13 in 1997) • Fluctuations of market share among leading firms signal aggressive local rivalry • New entrants came into the camera industry from other industries (for example, film makers such as Fuji Film and Konica entered the compact camera segment, and	• Strong electronics and equipment industries • Developments in electronics feed product innovation in cameras (for example, auto-focus single-lens reflex cameras) • Strong Japanese optical lens industry • Strong geographical cluster in the Suwa district of Nagano

Car audio	• Large pool of talented electrical engineers • Expertise in miniaturization developed in other electronic products that proved to be an essential strength due to limited space in a car	• Most households owned high-quality home audio systems and wanted the same quality for their cars, forcing manufacturers to constantly invest in R&D • Sophisticated, powerful, and demanding automakers were the primary immediate customer. Close working relationships in product development • Expensive car audio systems are a status symbol among customers in their 20s, who comprise close to two-thirds of the Japanese customer base • Sophisticated users prompted the development of features such as remote control	• Numerous independent car audio manufacturers (12 in 1987 and 8 in 1997) from various backgrounds and with varying strengths led to innovation • Vigorous rivalry in the home market signaled by large market share fluctuations	• Capable small- and medium-sized electronics parts suppliers • Highly competitive in radios and home audio
		consumer electronics companies such as Sony, Sanyo, Epson, and Toshiba entered the digital camera segment) • Intense local competition led camera manufacturers to move early to compete in global markets		where Olympus, Chinon, Epson, and other precision instrument makers are headquartered

(cont'd)

Table 4-2 Diamond conditions in competitive Japanese industries (cont'd)

	Access to specialized inputs (factors)	Japanese home demand	Local Japanese rivalry	Related and supporting industries
Carbon fibers	• Technical expertise in spinning technology and quality control was drawn from the synthetic fiber industry • The synthetic fiber industry attracted top students at universities in the 1960s • Government research institute, under the leadership of Dr Shindo, developed important basic technology • R&D investments by Toray preceded market demand • Internal funding by synthetic fiber companies and loans from banks allowed large-scale investment	• Lack of home demand in cost-plus aerospace and military applications • Early home demand in golf clubs, fishing rods, and tennis rackets, where cost and performance pressures are greater • Light and flexible quality of carbon fiber fit well with physical characteristics of Japanese buyers • Japanese customers were willing to pay premiums for high-performance golf clubs and other products to make the most of their limited leisure time • Limits on local demand forced Japanese producers to move early to international markets	• Intense local rivalry among seven Japanese rivals • Toray took a large risk and bet on carbon fiber, helping to create the market through mass producing carbon fiber early • Japanese companies moved early to compete globally, while Western competitors focused on their local aerospace and defense markets	• Japan had an early lead in the development and production of synthetic fibers • Synthetic fiber makers entered carbon fibers seeking new opportunities in the face of declining demand • Japanese trading companies were important in international marketing

| **Continuous synthetic weaves** | • Ample supply of skilled workers
• Farmers participated in the textile industry as a second occupation, providing a buffer during recessions | • Popularity of high-quality, silk-like fabrics in the Japanese market due to the traditional kimono garments
• Local demand for small lot sizes, subtle differences in shades, and flawless fabrics | • More than 5,000 Japanese producers in 1986
• Fierce competition on price, innovation, specialized skills, and turnaround time | • The traditional silk textile cluster has been in northern Japan for over 1,000 years
• Japan is highly competitive in water jet looms, used for synthetic weave production
• Japan is competitive in synthetic fibers
• General trading companies helped establish licensing agreements in synthesizing nylon and polyester fibers in the 1950s, and became financiers and exporters |

(cont'd)

Table 4-2   Diamond conditions in competitive Japanese industries (cont'd)

	Access to specialized inputs (factors)	Japanese home demand	Local Japanese rivalry	Related and supporting industries
Facsimile machines	• Large pool of electrical engineers	• High cost of long-distance telephone charges stimulated demand for fax machines	• Intense local rivalry among 13 Japanese competitors (as of 1976) resulted in improved product quality and falling prices	• New entrants from the telecommunication, office equipment, and consumer electronics industries brought complementary technologies and stimulated innovation
	• Applied technology developed in the electronics, optics, and office equipment industries	• Government agencies were early adopters of facsimile machines	• Japan was early to adopt international product standards	• Japanese components suppliers are competitive in all important areas
	• Well-developed communication infrastructure	• Reduction in the depreciable life of facsimile machines stimulated demand and encouraged upgrading to higher value products	• Competition was based on technology, features, and compactness	• World-class Japanese supporting industries, including semiconductors, lenses, thermal paper, machine tools, and robotics
	• Nippon Telephone and Telegraph (NTT) conducted basic research related to facsimile in its Musashino Communication Research Center	• Government sanctioned fax copies as legal documents, stimulating demand	• There was a strong export drive due to early saturation of the home market	
	• A cooperative, private sector association, the Institute of Image Electronic Engineers of Japan, studied aspects of facsimile technology	• Use of *kanji* and hand-written memos for communication led to the need to improve the quality of images and fineness of resolution		
		• Early saturation of the Japanese market led to continued innovation and upgrading		
		• Japanese multinationals provide an early market for fax machines to overcome international time zone differences		
		• The Japanese language hindered the use of telex		

Forklift trucks	• Complementary advanced technologies were developed by the automobile industry	• Local demand for small, versatile forklifts that could be used both indoors and outdoors facilitated product standardization and mass production • The decline of domestic demand due to the Oil Shock spurred exports	• Intense domestic rivalry among eight Japanese rivals spurred efforts for constant cost reduction, product improvement, and export • Major competitors came from different industries including autos and construction machinery. Rivals brought complementary skills which fostered innovation	• Suppliers to forklift truck assemblers are also auto parts suppliers • Japan is competitive in automobiles, trucks, engines, hydraulics, bearings, tires, and construction machinery
Home air conditioners	• Large pool of talented electrical engineers	• Muggy, hot weather in the summer stimulated large home demand • Home demand for compact, noise-free, energy-efficient air conditioners due to small, closely packed homes and high energy prices. This drove technical development in the Japanese industry • Customers demanded features that enhanced convenience and operational efficiency • Government set stringent energy standards after the Oil Shock	• Intense rivalry among manufacturers to develop separate units • High levels of competition among 13 key players forced constant product upgrading • Every competitive move was copied immediately, intensifying competition to develop new features • Aggressive use of electronics technology to upgrade models and features	• Japan was the world leader in compressors • Japan was the world leader in freezing, air equalizing, and condensing • Japan led the world in components industries such as converters, motors, and radiators

(cont'd)

Table 4-2   Diamond conditions in competitive Japanese industries (cont'd)

	Access to specialized inputs (factors)	Japanese home demand	Local Japanese rivalry	Related and supporting industries
Home audio equipment	• Pool of talented electrical engineers	• Demanding and trend-sensitive buyers pressed manufacturers to add advanced features • Tight Japanese living conditions led to an intense concern with compactness and multifunctionality	• Intense rivalry among 25 Japanese firms produced branded audio equipment	• Access to sophisticated, high-quality components at low cost due to the strong electronics industry
Microwave and satellite communications equipment	• Microwave communication network technology developed through joint research with NTT	• Japanese geography, with its many islands and mountains, was more suited to microwave than cable communication • NTT and other government agencies were early adopters of microwave and satellite communication • Sophisticated buyers forced manufacturers to innovate and upgrade	• Local rivalry among five Japanese companies • NEC was the first company in the world to incorporate solid-state technology, which enhanced reliability and energy efficiency. Others followed rapidly	• Japanese competitiveness in semiconductors, microwave generators, high-speed common circuitry, antennas, and other electronics
Musical instruments (piano)	• Availability of high-quality wood suited for pianos along the Tenryu River in Hamamatsu • Expertise in wood-drying technology • Pool of talented electronic engineers who incorporated the latest electronic technology	• Yamaha stimulated home demand by operating piano schools. Today, both Yamaha and Kawai operate a total of 25,000 piano schools throughout Japan. Piano lessons are seen as a tool for parents to instill discipline in children • The piano became a symbol of	• Yamaha and Kawai, both of which are headquartered in Hamamatsu, competed fiercely with each other • To catch up with Steinway, both players invited world-famous pianists to Japan and actively sought their endorsement and advice	• Strong electronic components industry • Competitive in home audit and electronic musical instruments

	affluence and prestige • Music instruction at elementary schools created early postwar demand • Japanese living conditions created anticipatory demand for silent pianos and compact pianos		
Robotics	• Large pool of well-trained electronics and mechanical design engineers • Japanese manufacturers had expertise in mechanical and electronic technologies through experience in electrical appliances, machinery, and transportation equipment	• Car companies, consumer electronics companies, and other Japanese manufacturers were among the most sophisticated buyers in the world • Shortage of skilled labor in auto and electronics industries in the 1970s fostered demand for robots, including in small- and medium-sized firms • Early Japanese market evolution and saturation triggered upgrading and exports	• Intense local competition among nearly 300 producers (in 1987) • Some competitors are also sophisticated users of robotics in electronics and machinery industries	• Japan was world leader in numerical controls, machine tools, motors, and optical sensors, among other supporting industries

(cont'd)

Table 4-2   Diamond conditions in competitive Japanese industries (cont'd)

	Access to specialized inputs (factors)	Japanese home demand	Local Japanese rivalry	Related and supporting industries
Semiconductors	• Abundant supply of electrical engineers. In the peak year (1977), the number of college graduates with EE degrees was 1.8 times that of the US • Strong research capability in corporate labs in electronics, optics, and new materials • Internal funding within diversified companies and bank loans allowed large-scale investments	• Sophisticated home demand for semiconductors in consumer electronics, communications, and computers, especially for memory and simple logic chips • Early semiconductor demand for use in electronic calculators in the late 1960s led to an orientation toward mass production at low cost	• Many Japanese rivals competed fiercely • Major competitors were diversified electronics companies, able to finance large-scale investment even in down cycles	• Strong optical industry helped the development of process technology • Strong base of semiconductor equipment manufacturers including Nikon, Canon, Tokyo Electron, and Advantest • Presence of many competitive related industries including measurement equipment, precision instruments, and abrasives
Sewing machines	• Sophisticated technologies for producing weapons, including precision engineering and manufacturing expertise, were transferred to the machine tool industry, enabling the increased efficiency and modernization of the sewing-machine manufacturing process during the immediate postwar period • Machine gun manufacturers (notably Juki) applied their expertise to sewing-machine production • Electro-mechanical technology and manufacturing know-how from other wartime industries	• Home sewing was a major source of clothing in the early post-World War II period • Strong postwar demand for clothing, combined with the fragmentation of the apparel industry, increased demand • Fixed monthly payment plans on the part of sewing machine companies stimulated demand • Public schools (which offered sewing courses for girls) and sewing schools served as large, demanding customers stimulating quality improvement	• Intense rivalry among numerous Japanese competitors (20 in home sewing machines alone) • Early push to export on the part of the government and industry • Continuous improvement of cost and quality	• Intense rivalry among competitive components suppliers in Tokyo, Osaka and Nagano (needle-related components), and Niigata (bobbin-related components) • Manufacturers had multiple available suppliers • Standards set by the government enabled the growth of components industries • Worldwide distribution capabilities of Japanese trading companies provided extensive overseas sales networks

	• Government eliminated taxes on industrial sewing machines in 1948 and household machines in 1951, stimulating home demand • Leading companies upgraded from the in-home segment to the more sophisticated industrial segments as home demand waned • Industrial demand took off and surpassed household demand due to the surge of ready-to-wear apparel in the 1960s	• Intense rivalry among trading companies in the 1950s and 60s to handle exports	• Competitive supporting industries in machine tools, motors, and later robotics
Soy sauce	• Unrestricted soy bean imports • Expertise in fermentation technology dated back to the early eighth century when soy paste (miso) was first introduced from China	• Soy sauce integral to national cuisine. Japanese restaurants and sushi bars carry soy sauce as a staple • Demanding local customers • Export of Japanese food stimulated overseas demand	• Intense local rivalry among thousands of Japanese soy sauce companies (2,500), encouraged continuous product and process upgrading • Firms created cooperative associations to produce soy sauce more efficiently using larger scale production facilities	• Trading companies were instrumental in developing overseas markets for soy sauce • Strong processing equipment industries involving fermentation technology, including steam boilers, temperature control equipment, and pressure regulators

(cont'd)

Table 4-2 Diamond conditions in competitive Japanese industries (cont'd)

	Access to specialized inputs (factors)	Japanese home demand	Local Japanese rivalry	Related and supporting industries
Tires for trucks and buses	• Low labor cost until the early 1970s	• Poor road conditions created demand for tires that could withstand wear and tear • Japanese customers changed their tires more frequently than their Western counterparts (four times more than UK drivers, twice as frequently as US consumers) • New products were introduced annually	• Fierce domestic competition among five Japanese companies • Competitive pressure led to an early move to the most advanced technologies, especially radial tires	• Internationally competitive car and truck industries • Trading companies were important to penetrating the export markets • Competitive mass production technology suppliers helped advanced technology to a labor-intensive industry • Raw materials, which accounted for 60% of total manufacturing cost, were mostly purchased from domestic firms, some are affiliated companies
Trucks	• Skilled knowledge base (especially mass production) from the automobile industry • Abundant supply of mechanical engineers	• Mountainous terrain and narrow roads created demand for small trucks in Japan, the segment where Japanese companies are competitive	• Intense domestic competition among 11 Japanese rivals	• Process and product technologies migrated from the passenger car industry • Japan was competitive in automobile parts, tires for trucks, machine tools, and robotics
Typewriters	• Japanese manufacturers had prior expertise in manufacturing precision mechanics through the production of sewing machines and knitting machines	• Home demand for typewriters was small, but local production was the only way to satisfy local demand due to import barriers	• Intense domestic rivalry with the advent of electronic typewriters	• Japanese competitiveness in semiconductors and other electronic components benefited Japanese manufacturers in electronic typewriters

VCRs	• Japanese manufacturers had prior expertise in audio and video technologies through the production of home audio equipment, tape recorders, and TVs • Pool of talented electrical engineers • Internal funding within diversified companies and low-cost loans from banks allowed large-scale capital investment	• High demand for compact, high-performance units from sophisticated domestic buyers	• Fierce domestic competition between the VHS and Beta camps led to constant innovation and upgrading	• VCR makers worked closely with parts makers to develop high-precision, high-performance parts • Competitive Japanese suppliers of magnetic heads, tuners, tape decks, volume regulators, other electronic parts, machine tools, and robotics
Video games (software)	• Large pool of skilled cartoon artists and game developers	• Demanding home customers who were constantly looking for new versions or new genres • High penetration of video games in the Japanese market (*Final Fantasy VII* sold 2 million copies in a year)	• Intense local rivalry among many Japanese developers (more than 500 third-party software developers provide game software to Sony) • Intense rivalry in video game hardware	• Japanese comic book and animation industries are world leaders • Competitive semiconductor and electronic products industries • Strong cluster involving comic books, animation, games, TV shows, and character-based consumer products

CHAPTER 5

How Japan Can Move Forward: The Agenda for Government

What really ails Japan has to do with the nation's deeply ingrained attitudes toward competition. The government mistrusts competition and therefore is prone to intervene in ways that harm the nation's productivity and prosperity. Japan's corporate problems are also rooted in the approach that Japanese companies take to competing. Guided by the wrong model, companies engage in destructive competition that undermines their own profitability.

How can Japan move forward? Armed with a better understanding of past competitive successes and failures, it is easier to see why piecemeal solutions and quick fixes – bailing out financial institutions, lowering consumption taxes, issuing merchandise vouchers – will not work. To address the nation's extensive structural problems, Japan's policy makers and business leaders must embrace – in parallel and interdependent ways – a more effective form of competition. What is needed is nothing short of a new economic strategy, one that builds on the true bases of Japan's past success, recognizes the differences between the country's rebuilding challenges and its present circumstances, and addresses the realities of modern global competition. Unfortunately, there is a grave danger that the current sense of urgency and the mounting calls for decisive action will drive both policy makers and business leaders to attempt to solve the wrong problems.

In this chapter, we focus on the agenda for the Japanese government. Essential reforms in the corporate sector are the subject of Chapter 6.

Priorities for Policy Makers

Policy makers will have to abandon approaches that are a source of great national pride in favor of those that have actually proved successful and fit today's competitive realities. Public policy did play some important roles in Japan's postwar success, but less obvious ones than usually thought.

Japan will also have to address certain deep-seated weaknesses that heretofore have been avoided.

In February 1999, the Economic Strategy Council, a private council established by Prime Minister Obuchi to transform Japan into 'a competitive society with soundness and creativity', recommended a set of regulatory reforms. The recommendations included the establishment of a smaller and more efficient government, greater local sovereignty, tax reform to create a fairer and more rewarding system, and educational reform to enhance employees' creativity.

Although these institutional reforms are a step in the right direction, they will fall far short of achieving their goal. Japan's approach to competition, its business environment, and the mind-set of Japanese companies and citizens must change if the nation is to move to the next stage of competitiveness.

Continuing What Works

An important first priority is to recognize and continue the practices that have worked in the past. High standards in basic education, policies to encourage savings and investment, a stable macroeconomic policy, the collection and dissemination of extensive business information, and continual upgrading of physical infrastructure have all enhanced Japan's productivity. These should be continued.[1] In this light, current macroeconomic policies raise serious concerns. Large government budget deficits, together with huge government guarantees of bank loans, threaten Japanese macroeconomic stability in the long run. These dubious efforts to bolster demand and bail out financial institutions are treating symptoms rather than the underlying problem.

While Japan is indeed over-regulated, and the pace of regulatory reform must be greatly accelerated, it is overly simplistic to think that all regulation is bad. High standards in the areas of energy usage, safety, quality, and noise have encouraged innovation and productivity growth. Our case studies revealed many instances where stringent regulatory standards were beneficial, and Japan should continue to enforce and even raise such standards. Regulation in unnecessary areas and the cumbersome process of administering regulations are the problems, not high standards per se.

Japan has also benefited from regulatory choices that stimulated early demand for new products. These policies encourage sophisticated local demand and enhance competitiveness. Similarly beneficial is the process of seeking timely consensus on product standards to foster industry growth and encourage the development of suppliers. All these practices should be continued and even widened to new fields.

The New Economic Policy Agenda

There are, however, important priorities for change. Although there is room for improvement in macroeconomic policy, the most fundamental problems are microeconomic.

Trust Japan's Ability to Compete

We have shown that Japan has prospered where competition has been allowed to flourish and failed where it has not. The single biggest lesson from Japan's failures is that the government should abandon its prevalent anticompetitive policies. Japanese policy makers need to rethink their approach to antitrust policy, cartels, consortia, government guidance, and regulatory barriers to competition. Enhancing competition, not just deregulation, must be the goal of regulatory reform efforts. This means, for example, that privatization must be accompanied by opening the market to competition, not just turning a public monopoly into a private monopoly.

Aversion to competition has deep roots in Japanese policy thinking. There has been a long-standing view that unbridled competition is too disruptive; it runs the risk of hurting workers, harming small companies, and degrading valuable corporate assets. But our evidence attests that this view is obsolete. Japanese companies today are fully capable of competing. Moreover, efforts by government to protect companies from competition have failed and have hurt not only consumers but also the companies themselves as well as other businesses that must deal with them. Unless Japan embraces competition, the productivity growth and innovation that is so essential to prosperity in the modern global economy will not occur.

Japanese citizens, who are also wary of 'free competition', must begin to understand that competition is a much more egalitarian system than one in which market distortions allow some Japanese to prosper at the expense of many others. Competition is also a necessity for improving productivity in the long run, the only way to bring down the high cost of living. Citizens must learn to see the connection between government's distortion of competition and their everyday lives. Japan can enhance its innovative capacity by unleashing its energetic and effective people and by removing government-enforced barriers to competition.

The policy agenda to unleash competition involves a wide array of areas. Antitrust laws should be strengthened, and meaningful penalties instituted. The enforcement of antitrust laws, heretofore nonexistent, must be stepped up. This will require greater resources and more autonomy for the FTC. The arguments for legal cartels are obsolete, and the enabling legislation needs to be reformed. Countless other laws, rules, and permitting requirements should be reexamined with a view to reducing the many subtle competitive barriers they present. Rescues of troubled companies and industries must be replaced by transitional assistance to encourage workers and capital to flow to more productive uses. The failed policy of targeting must be replaced with an orientation to improve the business environment for all Japanese industries.

There are some encouraging signs of progress. Many of the industry-specific laws allowing legal cartels were abolished in 1997, and remaining cartel laws are under review with the goal of abolishing them.[2] In addition, MITI published the skeleton of a 'Twenty-first century vision' in June 1999, which recognized the importance of creating of new businesses, deregulation, greater transparency of rules, and supporting innovation.

The question is, How? MITI still seeks to minimize the risks of competitive failure. For example, the Special Law for Industrial Revitalization, enacted in August 1999, allows companies that obtain government approval of restructuring plans to carry losses forward for seven years, up from five. Some suspect that this law, designed chiefly to help steelmakers, may be implemented via new cartel-like arrangements.[3] Fear of competition is so deeply entrenched in the mind-set of Japanese policy makers that only a concerted effort will change it.

Recognize that Open Trade Will Make Japanese Companies More Competitive and Prosperous, Not Less So

Restraints on imports and foreign investment have actually crippled many of the industries they aimed to protect. Trade restraints do more than hurt consumers through higher prices or poor quality. They almost guarantee that protected firms will be neither dynamic nor innovative enough to compete. Trade and investment barriers also devastated other Japanese producers by driving up the cost of inputs they depend on, stunting their ability to compete.

The consequences of high input costs and inefficient local suppliers are evident in our case studies. Chocolate producers, for example, faced large disadvantages in the cost of cocoa beans, sugar, and dairy products;

chemical manufacturers had to use expensive feedstocks produced by heavily protected domestic petroleum refineries. Similarly, restraining foreign investment also undermines competitiveness by denying Japanese firms access to efficient international suppliers that would otherwise establish operations in Japan, inhibiting cluster development. Finally, trade restraints lower the rate of innovation in an economy by reducing the flow of ideas, technologies, and the stimulus of rivalry.[4] In the global economy, restraining trade and investment has had a negative, boomerang effect on domestic producers that was neither understood nor anticipated. It is one important reason why Japan's range of competitive industries was narrow and why virtually no new export industries have developed since the 1980s.

The Japanese government has only to look to its own agricultural sector to see evidence that open trade will make its companies more prosperous. Seeds are one of the few segments of Japanese agriculture that is not highly protected and regulated. Yet Sakata Seed Corporation has captured 70% of the world pansy seed market and 80% of the US broccoli seed market. Unlike protected firms, Sakata ventured abroad early. It first gained worldwide recognition in the 1930s by winning awards at an international flower show held in the United States. Continually upgrading its product line, Sakata moved into fruit and vegetable seeds. Today it produces 60% of its seeds overseas and exports to 130 countries. It is virtually the only internationally competitive Japanese agricultural company.

Where protection has been reduced, there are already signs of progress. Consider cellular phones.[5] Prior to 1994, Japanese citizens were not even allowed to own cellular phones; they could only rent them from NTT. Here the government's policies retarded the quality and sophistication of the home market. Government's policy of establishing two cellular phone formats – one based on Motorola technology and the other based on NTT and limited to Japan – effectively kept out foreign manufacturers. As a result, Japanese-made cell phones were second-rate and expensive.

After opening the market in 1994 under intense pressure from US and European firms and governments, Japan has become the world's leading market for cellular phones. With 50 million cellular phones in use in a nation of 126 million people, Japan now has a higher concentration of cellular telephones than the United States.

Japanese-made phones have already caught up with the European models that were the pacesetters in the industry. In response to customer and competitive pressure, cellular phones have been transformed into devices to buy and sell stocks, reserve tickets for trains and airplanes, transfer funds between bank accounts, and send and receive text messages and simple drawings. In 2001, Japanese firms will introduce third-generation cellular technology, which promises greater voice quality and the ability to transmit data and video. One company, Kyocera Corporation, has brought out an early version already. This case is a vivid reminder that Japanese firms can succeed when they are motivated by intense competition and demanding customers, and they operate in an environment free from trade protection or other distortions.

It is time for Japan to have the confidence to embrace free trade. Doing so will reduce input costs, stimulate innovation, and enhance competitiveness across many industries. Self-sufficiency may have made sense 40 years ago, but changes in Japan and in the world economy have made such thinking obsolete. The rationale of nurturing struggling companies has long since disappeared in such a large and advanced economy. Statistical evidence has accumulated that openness to trade and foreign investment is strongly associated with economic growth and a rising standard of living.[6]

The large trade surplus that many Japanese still see as a source of pride is, in fact, a staggering disadvantage because it is caused by restraining foreign competition that would dramatically enhance productivity in the Japanese economy. And, ironically, trade protection is driving Japanese companies out of Japan both to source inputs more efficiently and to deal with the trade friction induced by the nation's lingering protectionism.

Embracing free trade means that both direct and indirect trade and investment barriers must come down. It is important to establish a system in which Japanese customers have fair choices between domestic and foreign goods. In the trade dispute over flat glass, for example, a number of practices discouraging the use of imported glass (such as each Japanese manufacturer using exclusive dealers) operated as subtle entry barriers to foreign firms.[7] Strengthening antitrust enforcement practices will also help to open the distribution system to competitive foreign companies that will, in turn, foster the competitiveness of Japanese companies. The advent of e-commerce is raising the awareness of Japanese consumers of the price differentials between domestic and foreign markets and creating opportunities to deal with foreign sellers directly. This should accelerate the market opening process.

Build a World-class University System

The university system has become an increasingly important ingredient for competitiveness in an advanced industrial economy. The role of universities in a nation's innovation system goes far beyond the research conducted there. First, research in universities is open and tends to diffuse more rapidly than corporate R&D or research conducted in government laboratories. Second, research at universities is valuable in training the next generation of scientists and engineers. Third, research in the university setting is a powerful mechanism for spawning new companies. Between 1980 and 1997, for example, just three US universities (MIT, Stanford, and the University of California) were responsible for at least 245 spin-off companies.[8] Finally, the university is an important link between a nation's basic scientific capability and the private sector. Porter et al.'s 1999 study of national innovative capacity has demonstrated that the proportion of national research conducted in universities has a significant influence on national innovative output.

The roots of Japan's uncompetitive industries can often be traced back to its universities, as we described in Chapter 2. To be sure, the nation's basic education system is anchored in high standards and has been a source of strength. However, we agree with those who believe it now needs significant reform.

An educational system based on rote memory alone is no longer sufficient. Japan must place more emphasis on creative problem solving, measuring student skills, and responding to student preferences, and move away from a totally uniform curriculum set by the Ministry of Education.

Because of growing weaknesses in basic education, universities such as Tokyo University have to offer remedial courses in math, physics, and chemistry for incoming students. In a recent large-scale survey of college freshmen, for example, more than 10% of students in liberal arts could not solve simple calculations involving fractions.[9] Students seeking admission to university must be expected to demonstrate competence in all foundation subjects, not just those directly tied to their major.

Japan's advanced education system has long left much to be desired. Not only is university and graduate-level training uneven in quality, but Japanese universities also fail to produce enough students in important disciplines, such as computer software and biotechnology. The number of Japanese college graduates who majored in biology-related subjects was 1,875 in 1996, versus 62,081 in the United States.[10] The number of graduate students per 1,000 population was 1.3 students for Japan in 1996 compared with 7.7 in the United States (1994) and 3.5 in France (1995). The percentage of graduate students relative to undergraduate students in the same years was 6.9% in Japan, 16.4% in the United States, 21.3% in the United Kingdom, and 17.7% in France.[11]

Chronic shortages in specialized skills have held back productivity growth in a range of important industries, as Chapter 2 illustrated. A recent example is lawyers. Japan in often cited as benefiting from a less litigious approach than the United States, but lawyers are still needed in any complex economy. A shortage of lawyers is delaying business transactions, and there is a critical shortage of lawyers capable in technical fields.

Japanese productivity and innovation will not rise unless its population acquires advanced and specialized skills in a full range of academic disciplines. Company training programs are a strength, but they cover only the small fraction of the workforce that is employed in large corporations. Company training cannot substitute for first-rate university education. Moreover, company training tends to produce generalists, while the modern knowledge economy requires more specialists. Even the celebrated Japanese corporate approach to human resource development is in need of change.

Tough entrance exams make getting into the best universities in Japan difficult, but getting out is easy. Many students think of their college years as four years of vacation, or 'moratorium.' Students have had little incentive to study, since companies have relied on in-house training and have not been concerned with students' grades when hiring. Companies will benefit from a greater emphasis on university training as part of their human resource development systems, and from closer ties with universities to ensure that universities are delivering the types of skills needed.

Part of the problem with Japanese universities is tight control and micromanagement by the government bureaucracies. For example, professors at most of the prestigious universities such as the University of Tokyo, which are state run, are not allowed to join corporate boards or work with companies. Recently, a leading academic economist resigned his full-time position because the National Personnel Authority would not permit him to join Sony's board, despite the personal intervention of Prime Minister Obuchi. Extensive interactions between universities and companies should be encouraged, not discouraged.

Of course, part of the problem lies with the universities themselves. They have been content to exist in a highly regulated system and have exerted little pressure on students. Most classes are large lecture sessions, where students often engage in private conversation. Professors do not think twice about canceling class since there are almost no student evaluation systems in place. Japanese universities have been slow to change, resisting new departments and specialties. A system to tie the funding of university programs to performance evaluation is needed, as is the development of greater competition among universities through the support of new schools and the expansion of successful existing schools.

As noted earlier, university research is the bedrock of a nation's basic research system and is fundamental to innovation. Yet because of limited funds and antiquated research facilities, Japanese universities lack strong research programs in many important fields. Their focus is in applied work rather than original science. With faculty promotion based on seniority and homogeneous backgrounds, incentives to conduct innovative work in new fields have been minimal. Japan has won just five Nobel Prizes in science in the last century, compared with more than 180 by the United States, 60 by Germany, and 9 each by the tiny countries of Denmark and Austria.

The core of Japanese research effort resides in companies and, to a far lesser extent, government laboratories. Historically, the private sector was not allowed to invest in university research. It was not until 1998, for example, that the Ministry of Education abolished regulations preventing academics from accepting corporate funds.

Lacking a vibrant university system, Japan has tried to compensate through intervention and subsidies. The Japanese practice of granting R&D subsidies to individual companies distorts market outcomes, and government-sponsored cooperative R&D projects are cumbersome and encourage homogeneity of strategies.[12] As we discussed in Chapter 2, cooperative R&D is a second-best solution, and has had only limited influence on Japanese competitiveness. The use of cooperative R&D should be selective, and limited to research projects that are distant from commercialization and do not threaten competition. Projects should be organized to facilitate knowledge spillovers among the participants.

In September 1999, the Ministry of Education (MOE) announced sweeping reforms affecting the 99 state-run universities and colleges. MOE plans to reclassify schools as independent administrative agencies in order to artificially meet the goal of reducing the number of central government employees by 25% over a decade. However, independent administrative status will not give universities the freedom to operate more independently. For example, MOE plans to appoint university presidents who are now elected internally. The bureaucratic processes involved in modifying university programs remains deadening.

The current policy debate lacks any sort of strategic framework for how the universities should be operated. MOE argues that making universities 'independent' will match the US private system but maintains tight regulatory control over the system.

Funding for university research in Japan should be substantially increased. In 1996, Japan allocated 0.7% of GDP to university-based research and education, which is substantially less than 1.1% in the United

States and 1.5% in Germany.[13] Research funding should also be allocated by independent, merit-based peer review along the lines of the US National Science Foundation and National Institutes of Health.

Some encouraging signs are just beginning to appear. Although national university professors in the social sciences are still not allowed to serve on the boards of private companies, national university professors in the natural sciences may now launch venture companies that use technology developed at universities or national research centers. In April 1999, a biotech venture company was established in Yokohama with a professor of a national university, Nara Institute of Science and Technology, as president. Researchers at the Institute of Industrial Science at the University of Tokyo established a venture company to produce silicon for solar cells, and professors at Osaka University have teamed with a private university to set up a venture company to design system chips.[14]

The Ministry of Education has given the go ahead to open professional graduate schools in Japan. The first to open is Hitotsubashi University's Graduate School of International Corporate Strategy, a business school offering an MBA and a financial engineering program. The daytime MBA program at Hitotsubashi will be taught entirely in English and will accommodate students from around the world. The Ministry of Education hopes that the establishment of business schools, law schools, and other professional schools geared toward students with several years of work experience will foster more active interactions between universities and companies.

Modernize Archaic, Inefficient Domestic Sectors

It is ironic that the nation that taught the world operational effectiveness does not practice it at home in large parts of the economy. Many of Japan's failures can be traced to fragmented, inefficient, and anachronistic domestic sectors such as retailing, wholesaling, logistics, financial services, health care, energy, truck transportation, telecommunications, construction, housing, and agriculture. By design, government policies over the years have created two Japans, one composed of highly productive export industries, the other containing the 'domestic' sectors. Inefficiency in the domestic sectors has been all but guaranteed by a huge array of rules and policies that raised costs, limited competition, and held back consolidation.

Japan's retail sector, for example, is highly fragmented because of restrictions on competition. The Large-scale Retail Store Law remains onerous even though it has been relaxed in the last few years. Opening a store of more than 1,000 square meters (10,760 square feet) requires *de facto* approval by a prefectural government charged with minimizing the effect on local shop owners. Then the average large retailer must file over 150 documents to gain permission to sell everyday items like meat, tofu, electronic appliances, and dry-cleaning services.[15]

The Japanese construction industry, another example of a highly fragmented, inefficient, and uncompetitive domestic industry, has been known for bid-rigging, corrupt links between the industry and public officials, and strong protection from foreign competition. Since public works spending has accounted for a substantial portion of industry revenues, politicians and bureaucrats from the Construction Ministry have wielded enormous power through the awarding of public contracts. When public works projects are put out for tender, the ministry typically decides in advance on a limited number of companies that are allowed to bid. It has become normal practice for designated bidders to get together and decide whose turn it is to 'win' the competitive bid, and then set their respective bids to ensure attractive profit margins – a practice termed *dango*.

The rationale behind the creation of the two Japans, and this tolerance of a lack of competition, seemed plausible: the efficient Japan would carry the rest of the economy, and the inefficient Japan would provide stability, jobs, self-sufficiency, and an implicit retirement system of small family businesses. Construction, for example, employed 6.8 million in 1999 (about 10 percent of the entire workforce) and provided jobs in rural areas which lacked other industries. The cost of the inefficient Japan was to be borne by Japanese consumers in the form of higher prices for everything. Indeed, the effect on the cost of living and the quality of life of Japanese citizens has been substantial, as the figures in Chapter 1 illustrate.

Yet policy makers failed to anticipate two devastating consequences of this approach. First, the local 'domestic' industries affect the export industries. The inefficient Japan drives up not only living costs but also business costs, thus weakening the competitiveness of the export industries. Construction costs, for example are estimated to be at least one-third higher than in the United States.

The second consequence of the unproductive domestic sectors is more subtle but, in the long run, potentially more important. The inefficient Japan inhibits the formation of new internationally competitive industries in huge parts of the economy. Because Japan's domestic sectors are so unproductive and structured so differently from most of the rest of the world's, Japanese firms that sell through them (for example, consumer packaged good and food producers) or to them are forced to meet needs or adopt operating practices that do not work in foreign markets. Because

Japan's circumstances are so idiosyncratic, it is virtually impossible for such companies to compete internationally. The net result is an almost total absence of new Japanese export industries.

Consider how Japan's policy of protecting small shops and the established department stores from new forms of competition has backfired. Because of the department stores' power and dominance, Japanese apparel companies have become skilled at operating dedicated in-store boutiques. With their outlets secure, they did not have to develop design or brand marketing skills and were content to license foreign products. Similarly, because of the need to compete for shelf space in highly fragmented outlets, Japanese chocolate manufacturers focused on marketing gimmicks and the proliferation of new products geared toward children that had little potential in export markets. Japanese companies in these and other domestic industries were deprived of the opportunity to learn world-class marketing at home.

The pervasive distortions in Japan's service sector mean that Japan is uncompetitive – and worker productivity is low – in virtually every service industry. The productivity gap with the United States has been estimated to be as high as 40% in industries such as airlines, telecommunications, retail banking, general merchandise, retailing, and restaurants.[16] Japanese department stores, specialty retail shops, and banks retain personnel long ago replaced by self-service outlets or technology in the West; in addition, they provide personal services never found in other countries.

In today's economy, Japan's service gap has become a serious drag on the country's performance. In all advanced nations, services are a rapidly growing part of the economy, and they are increasingly traded internationally. Japan is virtually out of the game in this important area.

Recently, there have been some tentative signs of progress, although much remains to be done. In telecommunications, the high cost of access has stunted use of the Internet. Without a competitive local phone service market which would have pushed Nippon Telephone and Telegraph (NTT) to reduce its exorbitant line charges, the Ministry of Post and Telecommunications (MPT) belatedly had to call on NTT to offer a fixed monthly telephone charge for domestic users. NTT launched a test service at ¥8,000 a month in limited areas of Tokyo and Osaka starting in November 1999 and announced that it would reduce the monthly rate to ¥4,000 in the future. But even the prospective rate is much higher than those in the United States. This example illustrates how the Japanese government still cannot resist intervening directly in company behavior rather than encouraging competition.

In gasoline retailing, the government only allowed self-service stations in 1997. Traditionally, Japan's 60,000 or so stations employed large numbers of people to provide 'full service', including throwing away trash, emptying ashtrays, and helping customers cope with traffic as they leave the station. The opportunity to operate self-service stations will allow Japanese customers to choose the level of service they are willing to pay for and should substantially boost productivity.

In construction, the bidding system for public works became the subject of a US–Japan trade dispute in the late 1980s (notably around the huge Kansai airport project). There have been some efforts to open public works projects to foreign firms. However, the cozy structure of the construction industry is still largely intact.

To deal with anachronistic and unproductive domestic sectors, Japan must open up competition, and cartels, and remove all restraints to entry and company operating practices that are not directly tied to health and safety. The government will be tempted to attempt to direct restructuring through new regulations or guidance (as in telecommunications), but such efforts will fail.

Opening domestic sectors to foreign competitors will accelerate the restructuring process. The entry of Toys R Us into Japan in 1991 shook up the toy-retailing industry. It gave consumers a choice of shopping at a small, convenient, neighborhood, family-oriented store or patronizing a larger, no-frills store with lower prices and a wider selection.

Measures that improve, for example, the efficiency of the transportation and distribution systems will lower both the costs facing Japanese companies and the cost of living. Rationalization of transportation and distribution will also stimulate greater trade, because high logistical costs and multilayer wholesale markups disadvantage imported goods.

If the government is willing to address the problems in Japan's domestic sectors, there is no reason why the nation cannot simultaneously lower the cost of living, reduce business costs, expand home demand for goods and services, and grow many new exporting companies. Any loss of jobs will be temporary, and outweighed in the long run by the new job opportunities created.

Create a True System of Corporate Accountability

In postwar Japan, companies were accountable principally to government ministries and to banks. Ministry bureaucrats, not elected politicians, have been the actual policy makers in Japan. As we have seen, bureaucratic guidance and regulation have been central to the corporate governance system. Banks have acted both as major lenders and as the centers of the cross-holding system known as *keiretsu*. However, banks have not exercised day-to-day monitoring, neither did they step in unless companies faced financial distress.

The system of cross-share ownership favored stability rather than corporate accountability. Most company shares were held for very long-term appreciation and rarely traded. There was virtually no threat of takeover. Outside shareholders exercised little or no influence. Boards of directors have been composed solely of insiders. Accounting rules have been flexible, giving companies wide latitude in reported earnings. Disclosure requirements have been limited.

The Japanese corporate governance structure encouraged long-term investment, which was sometimes a strength. But it often led to overinvestment, a lack of attention to productivity, and the practice of maintaining unprofitable products and businesses indefinitely. In industries where there was fierce local competition and pressure from sophisticated customers, these governance problems were compensated for and did not matter. Elsewhere, however, weak accountability helped create and perpetuate many of Japan's failures.

In recent years, even the modicum of corporate accountability that was present has been diminishing. The prestige and influence of bureaucrats have been eroded by scandals and by the growing backlash against regulation. At the same time, banks have lost influence over companies that no longer carry high levels of debt. Lately, banks have been preoccupied with the task of dealing with problem loans.

Japan needs a new corporate governance system that will hold companies accountable for their use of resources. Without the pressure to use capital efficiently and earn decent profitability, Japanese companies will not address their fundamental competitiveness problems.

Japan must introduce more transparency into corporate decisions and financial results, establish standards making boards of directors more independent, and provide shareholders with more influence. The tools to reorient the corporate governance system include corporation law, standards for boards and disclosure established by securities regulators, rules for reporting established by accounting standards bodies, and policies of the stock exchanges.

We do not advocate that Japan imitate the Anglo-Saxon system, which has it own shortcomings. Japan should seek to preserve its longer investment time horizons, not replicate the frenzied trading and near-term earnings fixation of the Anglo-Saxon system. It should avoid US-style tax and accounting policies, such as pooling of interest and recurring restructuring charges, that encourage uneconomic mergers and obscure true corporate performance.

Instead, Japan should reinforce its strengths by creating tax incentives for long-term holding and devising accounting approaches that treat investments in employees and technology as assets rather than expenses.

A recent move to enact new disclosure rules is a step in the right direction. The Japanese government is considering amendments to the securities laws that will radically change the way companies report earnings, report on pension plan funding, and value their stock portfolios. New Japanese accounting standards were set to be implemented between 1999 and 2001. Until now, parent companies had to consolidate subsidiaries only if they had more than 50% ownership. Under the new rules, the parent must consolidate a minority affiliate if the parent company finances the affiliate's debt or appoints a member to the affiliate's board. In the past, it was typical for a parent company to move excess employees to affiliates or shift losses to affiliates' books, obscuring true profitability. Companies will also have to disclose pension plan-funding liabilities and value investments in other tradable securities (including investments in other companies) at market instead of historical cost. Gaining the benefits of this change will require new rules for corporate tax consolidation. Foot dragging by government puts into question its ability to meet its own deadline, another indication of the ambivalence about true reform.

Create a New Model of Innovation and Entrepreneurship

Japan has made considerable progress in enhancing its national innovative capacity over the past three decades. Porter *et al.* (1999) found that Japan has registered major increases in *per capita* international patenting since the early 1970s relative to other nations.[17] This good performance reflects strength in some key innovation fundamentals revealed by Porter *et al.* Overall, Japan spends heavily on R&D and on secondary and tertiary education. Much R&D is funded by companies, which fosters commercialization.

However, weaknesses in the Japanese innovation system are now becoming more apparent. Japanese economic policy has relied heavily on large companies and the *keiretsu* as the engines of innovation and new business formation. Government has been actively involved in identifying important technologies, and government-sponsored cooperative R&D projects have been the most prominent technology policy. This approach has produced some major successes, but it also has limits.

In 1999, MITI announced that it would publish an Industrial Technology Strategy in 2000. It plans to identify target technology areas in which the private sector should concentrate its efforts. This approach still reflects the old mind-set. MITI needs to realize that the government's job is not to identify promising technologies but to improve the overall environment for innovation.

Japan needs a new national innovation strategy that maintains its commitment to R&D and education while substantially changing the structure through which innovation occurs. First, the Japanese government must remove itself from the role of directing the innovation efforts of companies. It should concentrate instead on improving the incentives for innovation, upgrading the quality of scientific and technical personnel, strengthening the nation's scientific infrastructure, and removing distortions to home demand from unnecessary regulations and protected domestic sectors.

Second, small- and medium-sized companies must be seen as an important force for innovation and growth, alongside large companies. New companies often spin out of universities. They grow up within clusters of related firms and industries concentrated in particular geographic regions. Nurturing them will require a new mind-set and new policies.

Third, Japan must make universities the center of its innovation strategy. Public investment in research should be channeled primarily through universities, for reasons discussed earlier. Japan must also better connect its universities (and government laboratories) to companies and to the process of entrepreneurship. This will require putting in place the flexibility, technology-licensing rules, and supporting infrastructure (for example, incubators and steps to ease administrative burdens on start-ups) that encourage the movement of university and laboratory research into new and established companies.

Fourth, Japan must base its innovation strategy on competition rather than on collaboration. While cooperative projects can play a role in innovation, the actual driver of Japan's past innovation success has been fierce rivalry. The fields where innovation has been the greatest are those with the most intense competition. Japan needs to expand competition to more fields and further open the Japanese market to trade and investment. Porter *et al.* (1999) have shown that international openness is beneficial to a nation's rate of innovation by exposing the economy to new ideas and new companies while increasing competitive pressure.

Fifth, intellectual property protection needs to be strengthened. While there have been efforts to harmonize the Japanese patent system with that of other industrialized countries, there is little evidence that the reforms have been meaningful enough to induce more innovation.[18] Further steps are necessary, especially in speeding up the process of deciding patent infringement cases. It takes four years to obtain a decision in Japan versus one year in the United States.[19] By the time a suit is settled in Japan, the technology has often become obsolete. In fact, Japanese firms have begun to bring suits against other Japanese firms in US courts in order to obtain a speedy resolution.

Moreover, the penalties for patent infringers need to be stiffened. Until 1998, a convicted patent infringer had to pay only the equivalent of a typical licensing fee to the patent holder and a fine of only ¥5 million ($50,000). Since 1998, the penalty has been increased to the amount of the patent holder's lost profits and the fine has been increased to as much as ¥150 million ($1.5 million). Although this represents progress, the penalties should be made even stronger to act as a real deterrent.

Sixth, Japan's environment, safety, quality, and other regulations must become consistently pro-innovation. While strict standards in some areas have been a strength (as discussed in Chapter 2), too often regulations have retarded the move to new products and technologies.

Finally, Japan needs to mount a concerted effort to foster the start-up and growth of new companies. Approvals, reporting requirements, and other regulatory barriers to starting or growing companies must be dramatically reduced. Regulatory costs always fall disproportionately on smaller companies because they are calculated independent of sales volume. Lighter paperwork and approval requirements should apply to companies below a certain size threshold, and periodic inspections should replace ongoing requirements that require substantial management time and cost.

Powerful incentives for entrepreneurship need to be established, such as lower long-term capital gains tax rates that reward company building, rules that encourage stock ownership and options, and liberal policies allowing tax losses to carry forward. Until 1997, for example, stock options were banned except at small venture companies.

Japan must also take steps to move from a financing model for smaller enterprises based on collateralized loans and guarantees to a model that encourages investments in risk capital. Japan needs a plan to provide easier access to public capital markets to fund start-up companies and to provide greater liquidity for investments in new businesses. In the past, Japanese companies that wanted to go public have had to jump huge hurdles. They were required to start on one of the country's eight local exchanges, the over-the-counter market, or the Tokyo Stock Exchange's less efficient second section. It could take a company as long as twenty years to make it to the Tokyo Stock Exchange's first section, the best platform for raising capital.

There have been some positive steps to open the supply of risk capital in Japan. The New York Stock Exchange established a Tokyo office in March

1999, and Japan's Softbank announced that it would team up with Nasdaq to establish Nasdaq-Japan by 2001. This competition is pressuring the Tokyo Stock Exchange to respond. TSE established its own market for fast-growing start-ups in November 1999. It also plans to begin waiving the requirement that applicants post earnings for at least three years, which has hindered the listing of new companies. Other hurdles to entry, such as a rule requiring that companies issue at least 100 million shares, have also been eased.

Encourage Decentralization, Regional Specialization, and Cluster Development

The Japanese government model has tended to centralize economic activity in and around Tokyo and Osaka. These two cities account for nearly 50% of Japan's total manufacturing shipments. This level of concentration is striking for a highly advanced economy; it is more characteristic of developing countries. Geographic concentration in Japan has been due less to inadequate infrastructure in outlying areas, which is typical in developing countries, than to a powerful and intrusive central government, with its centralizing bias in policies and institutions. Centralization then carries over to the private sector; virtually all major trade associations are located in Tokyo.

Concentration of economic activity has created debilitating congestion. It introduces delays, drives up costs, and reduces productivity. For example, 25% of commuters to central Tokyo spend three hours per day commuting. The average traveling speed on highways in Tokyo is 18 miles per hour, slowing to 11 miles per hour during rush hour. Concentration of activity also drags down the quality of life. Greater Tokyo has 4.5 square meters of green tracts of land per capita, compared with 29.1 square meters in New York (1997), 25.3 square meters in London (1994), and 11.8 square meters in Paris (1994).

The concentration of economic activity has also worked against the productivity benefits of geographic specialization and cluster formation. Retarded development of clusters, in turn, hampers innovation and the growth of new companies. The number of new companies formed in Japan as a percentage of total companies peaked at 7.0% in 1972 and declined to about half that rate in 1996, as shown in Table 5-1. The 3.7% figure for Japan in 1996 is only about one-fourth the rate of new company formation in the United States, which has maintained a 12%–14% level since 1983.

Along with centralization has come nationwide standardization of rules and policies, which work against regional specialization. This hurts Japan

Table 5-1   New company formation as a percentage of total companies*

	1969	1972	1975	1978	1981	1984	1987	1990	1993	1996
Japan	6.5	7.0	6.1	6.2	6.1	4.7	4.2	4.7	4.7	3.7
US	NA	NA	NA	NA	NA	14.3	14.8	13.8	13.5	13.7

Note: *Excludes primary industries such as agriculture and mining.
Source: White Papers on Small- and Medium-sized Companies (Chushou Kigyo Cho, 1997 and 1999)

in advanced competition, where many of the drivers of competitiveness are quite local – for example, linkages with suppliers, specialized skill pools, and unique, cluster-specific institutions. Specialization at the regional level fuels productivity improvement and fosters innovation. For example, in California, which is approximately the size of Japan, there are vibrant clusters in microelectronics and biotechnology in Silicon Valley, multimedia in San Francisco, entertainment and defense/aerospace in Los Angeles, and pharmaceuticals and analytical instruments in San Diego.

In Japan, the modicum of regional specialization and cluster formation that existed in the past – motorcycles in Hamamatsu, for example, and synthetic fibers in the Hokuriku area – is on the decline. Today, many regions are attempting to become more and more like Tokyo by trying to recruit large companies, broadening the industrial base, and pumping up public-works spending.

Government needs to free up control, decentralizing many choices about what infrastructure to develop, how to enhance educational institutions and tie them to industry, and how to regulate economic activity. At the same time, the central government must encourage and even mandate the development of competitiveness programs at the prefectural and local levels. Prefectural and local leaders, in turn, need to take more initiative and establish their own distinctive economic development plans.

Another powerful form of economic decentralization is the cluster development process. Clusters include not only companies but also suppliers, service providers, university researchers, financial institutions, and regulatory bodies. They provide a forum for dialogue between business, government, and other institutions about such things as developing needed specialized skills in the workforce, improving specialized infrastructure, streamlining regulations, and building needed technological capabilities in universities. Many US states and regions, for example, have used cluster development initiatives as a tool for enhancing innovation and competitiveness.[20]

The case of Kyoto illustrates the vitality that is triggered when regions specialize, take economic initiative, and encourage clusters. As noted in Chapter 3, many of the nation's new entrepreneurial companies are located in the Kyoto area, together with some of Japan's most vibrant established companies such as Kyocera, Nintendo, Omron, and Sanyo Chemical. Kyoto companies account for four of the top twenty Japanese companies in terms of the increase in market capitalization since their CEOs took office. The city has a distinctive character of independence and freedom, which may explain why four of Japan's five Nobel laureates hail from Kyoto. Its entrepreneurial culture and scientific and technological sophistication are especially attractive for technology companies.

The clusters of information technology, materials business, and precision electrical products in Kyoto have deep local roots. One is the area's 1,200-year history in ceramics, fine arts, and design. Kyoto is also the home of world-famous gardens, castles, temples, and shrines. Tea ceremonies, flower arrangements, Noh dancing, and other arts originated in Kyoto. Kyoto is known for Japan's most advanced level of *shinbigan*, which literally translates as 'eye to judge beauty.' It is home to renowned artisan companies such as Kyo-yaki and Kiyomizu-yaki in ceramics and Kyo-Yuzen and Nishijin-ori in fabrics. Hundreds of kimono manufacturers and woodblock printers are also based there. Traditional crafts proved a good apprenticeship for the painstaking detail of software engineering, chip design and fabrication, and game design.

The Kyoto region also boasts Japan's greatest concentration of higher education institutions; it has 33 universities and eleven colleges. One out of every ten inhabitants in Kyoto is said to be a college or graduate student. Kyoto is also believed to have the largest number of foreign students on a *per capita* basis. Talented foreign students flock to Kyoto, enhancing its environment for originality and creativity.

Local economic initiative, most of it private, is also much in evidence. The city makes a concerted effort to encourage new business formation. Kyoto has one of Japan's first business 'incubators' for small venture-based businesses. Thanks to an investment by a local utility, Kyoto is one of Japan's few cities with a private technology park (Kyoto Research Park) in its downtown corridor. Kyoto Enterprise Development Committee, a private group, was formed to evaluate and support venture projects. Kyoto's universities have established one of the first technology-licensing activities in Japan to speed the transfer of technology from research labs to business start-ups. Kyoto University has a laboratory for venture businesses. Ristumeikan University offers management courses for scientists and engineers. Local government and private initiatives, not the central government bureaucracy, have built a highly supportive business environment.

How has Kyoto done it? The city has been relatively isolated, and it is modest in size (1.5 million people, or about one-eighth the size of Tokyo).

It was the only city spared from bombing in World War II, which left an established base of small businesses. The absence of large, dominant firms and industries allowed smaller firms to prosper. MITI's large cooperative R&D efforts ignored Kyoto companies. Religious organizations, academics, and artisans hold as much power in Kyoto as government officials and business leaders. This dispersion of power has forestalled rigid hierarchies and encouraged the creation of networks where introductions are made on a who-knows-whom basis.

Small Kyoto businesses, unable to penetrate the closed *keiretsu* networks, were forced to identify and market to foreign customers. Kyoto companies have avoided what is known in Japan as 'big company disease', an obsession with size and market share in the domestic market. Instead, they have focused on core businesses where they compete globally. Since Japanese banks were unwilling to lend to small firms with no collateral or *keiretsu* affiliation, Kyoto-based firms tended to raise capital through equity markets.[21]

The case of Kyoto illustrates a recurrent theme in our research. Competitive pressure, in a business environment that contains high-quality inputs and institutions and is open to innovation and dynamism, is the real path to economic progress.

A New Role for the Government

In the past, the Japanese government has seen its role as guiding, controlling, and constraining competition in the name of improving efficiency and stability. Clearly, a new conception of government's role is needed. Now government must work to improve the inputs available to business, facilitate competition, and encourage innovation. Improving the quality and dynamism of the business environment, not managing the competitive process, should be the government's new goal.

The Japanese government must stop limiting competition and start mounting a serious antitrust policy. It needs to stop limiting trade and investment and start encouraging specialization, innovation, and productivity. Government needs to stop holding back the restructuring of Japanese industries and attempting to spread the pain of restructuring across all companies. Instead, it should free market forces so that only the most productive companies remain in the market, and it should build a safety net to ease the effects of restructuring on workers and mechanisms to facilitate the redeployment of freed-up resources to other sectors. Government needs to stop restricting competition in domestic sectors and holding back their restructuring; it should accept the fact that adjustments in domestic sectors are essential to the nation's long-term competitiveness.

Government needs to stop trying to manage the financial markets and acting as the corporate governance system for firms. Instead, it should substitute an effective system of private corporate governance coupled with strict disclosure and securities regulations. Finally, government needs to stop trying to manage economic policy at every level and start relinquishing responsibility to local citizens and their leaders.

In modern competition, government must also invest in improving the assets companies draw on in competing, and build the institutions required for advanced competition. In Japan, for example, there is a need for heavy investment in the university system and for restructuring the style of basic education. There is a pressing need to bring the nation to the forefront of information technology in all parts of society (see Chapter 6). There is a need to invest in programs to encourage new business formation and entrepreneurship. Finally, government must not waver from its positive regulatory roles, including strict quality and safety standards and raising expectations about environmental impacts.

This new role for the Japanese government is neither a diminished nor a less important one. It is a different role, one better suited both to Japan's status as an advanced economy and to the realities of modern competition.

In order to play the new role, the process of government decision making will need to change as well. Because of a tradition of collective decision making and the frequent rotation of the key positions in the bureaucracy, no one is held accountable when the government sets a bad policy. More accountability will be fostered by greater involvement by elected representatives in the policy-making process. The policy process must become more open and public so that think tanks, business groups, and the media, among others, can offer competing points of view. Independent review of government decisions by watchdog organizations should be encouraged.

Utilizing Japan's Human Potential

Progress toward this new agenda is necessary not just to restore Japan's competitive vitality but also to allow the nation to grow and maintain its standard of living. It is well known that Japan has an aging population, a reality with important implications for the nation and its economy. What is less widely understood is that the reality of an aging population brings a greater urgency to the changes we have outlined. Unless Japan becomes more productive and utilizes its labor force in new and better ways, the nation's standard of living cannot be sustained.

Three things determine a nation's rate of economic growth: its work-force growth, growth in the supply of capital, and productivity growth. Japan's rate of savings is already high, and its natural workforce growth will be slow or even negative. The only way that Japan can grow is to find new ways to expand the workforce and dramatically increase productivity.

In the short term, unemployment appears to be the problem. In a few years, however, it will become clear that worker shortages are the real problem. Japan will no longer be able to afford to have workers tied up in inefficient domestic sectors or unproductive industries that survive because of trade barriers. Freeing up labor from these sectors becomes a necessity. Japan will also need to increase the equal participation of women in the workforce. Tapping this new pool of employees will require changes not only in mind-set but also in support structures, such as increasing the number of affordable day care facilities. Creating a more flexible labor market will also become a necessity, but not only for efficiency reasons. New labor market structures will be needed to allow citizens to work part time and make it possible for older citizens to remain in the workforce. Without such changes, healthy rates of economic growth will be almost impossible.

Conclusion

The Japanese government accomplished a remarkable process of economic rebuilding in the post-World War II period. However, yesterday's policies – policies that had a place in the 1950s, 60s, 70s, and 80s – are no longer appropriate. Government continued too long to set policies as if Japan was still a poor country and failed to adapt to the realities of modern competition. The so-called 'convoy system', in which government attempts to manage and protect the interest of a limited number of companies, is obsolete in a global economy where government has lost the power to control competition and where new companies and industries are created every day.

As Japan moves into the twenty-first century, the government must fundamentally change its approach to competition and redefine its role in the economy. There is still an important role for government in modern global competition, but a different one than in the past. Although there are calls for change in Japan, proposals for reform have been piecemeal. What is needed is nothing short of a systemic change in which a whole array of new policies are pursued together that will be mutually reinforcing. Opening up trade will speed the restructuring of inefficient domestic sectors, for example, which will help Japanese companies deal with more vigorous local competition. A new governance system will elevate the importance of profit and encourage more distinctive strategies, while improvements in universities and incentives will allow Japanese companies to be more innovative and foster new export industries. We have no doubt that progress across these areas will be uneven. With an overall understanding of direction, however, Japan can overcome the doubts and indecision that have made reforms so halting.

Notes

1. Patrick and Rosovsky (1976); Eads and Yamamura (1987) and Porter (1990), Chapter 8.
2. Koshiro (1999).
3. *Asahi Shimbun*, July 28, 1999.
4. Porter, Stern and Council on Competitiveness (1999) and Stern, Porter and Furman (1999).
5. *New York Times*, July 27, 1999, and *NTT Multimedia Mobile Forum*, November 19, 1998 and February 2, 1999.
6. Porter (1999); Porter and Bond (1999) and Sachs and Warner (1995).
7. Japan Fair Trade Commission (1993).
8. AUTM Licensing Survey, reported in Chikamoto Hodo and Hiroyuki Suzuki, 'Sangaku Renkei, Seiko niwa Mittsu no Joaken' ('Three Conditions for a Successful Alliance between Industry and Academia'), *Nikkei Business*, May 31, 1999, p. 53.
9. Okabe, Kose, and Nishimura (1999).
10. *Nikkei Business*, September 20, 1999.
11. Ministry of Education, Wagakuni No Bunkyo Shisaku (Educational Policy of our Nations), 1998, p. 304.
12. Note that the importance of direct corporate R&D subsidies has declined over the last 30 years.
13. US data are for 1994; German data are for 1995. Ministry of Education, 'Kyoiku shisuu no Kokusai Hikaku' (International Comparison of Education Indices), 1998.
14. *The Nikkei Weekly*, 'Venture Companies Begin to Take Root', June 14, 1999, p. 4.
15. Forbes (1997).
16. Hori (1993).
17. International patents are defined as patents filed not only in the home country but also with the US Patent Office. They represent the best available measure of new-to-the-world innovations that are commercially important. Porter *et al.* (1999) examined the causes of differences in international patenting across countries. Also see Stern, Porter and Furman (1999).
18. For example, Sakakibara and Branstetter (1999a) found little evidence that the introduction of the multi-claim system in 1988 increased innovative efforts or R&D output.
19. *Nikkei Newspaper*, March 23, 1999.
20. See Porter (1998b), Chapter 7.
21. Chiaki Moriguchi contributed to the section on Kyoto.

CHAPTER 6

Transforming the Japanese Company

Despite the persistent problems confronting Japan's companies throughout the 1990s, few corporate leaders have questioned their fundamental approach to competing. In response to slow growth, companies have diversified into unrelated businesses instead of fixing the problems in their core businesses. In response to poor profitability, Japanese companies have migrated offshore in search of cheap labor and lower costs for other inputs. Recently, some have begun pruning product lines, shrinking the number of employees, and streamlining organizational structure. By and large, however, these steps represent merely a continuation of operational thinking, not a different way of competing. None of these approaches will address corporate Japan's real problem. Japanese companies need a new model of competition.

The New Corporate Agenda

The challenge for Japan's business leaders will be as great as or greater than those facing its government policy makers. Japanese companies must build on the genuine strengths of the past but, at the same time, they must be prepared to compete differently. The new corporate agenda includes the following elements.

Create Distinctive, Long-term Strategies

Although operational effectiveness can continue to be a source of competitive strength, it will not achieve superior performance on its own. Perhaps the most fundamental challenge facing Japanese companies is to embrace strategy, and begin the process of distinguishing themselves from rivals.

Strategy requires hard choices about what *not* to do. In a nation where imitation has been the rule, companies need to either choose a set of activities that are *different* from competitors or perform activities *differently* than rivals do.

Good strategy requires trade-offs, but Japanese companies have trouble making them. They have gotten so used to competing by extending the productivity frontier – pursuing both cost and quality advantages equally – that they fail to see that the real issue now is where on the frontier they want to compete.

Many internal barriers stand in the way of strategy in Japanese companies. The cultural norm of consensus, for example, exacerbates the tendency to try to be all things to all people. One of the first sayings a child learns in Japan is 'A nail that sticks out will be hammered down.' Being different is not a virtue in Japanese society. The same mind-set pervades corporate Japan. Consider the recruiting process. Until the so-called 'employment agreement' was formally abolished in 1997, student job seekers could not visit companies until July 1 or receive a formal offer before October 1. All new recruits throughout Japan started officially on April 1 each year.

Decision making within Japanese companies is based on consensus. Japanese companies rely on systems such as *ringisho* or *nemawashi* to ensure that no one is excluded from the decision-making process. In the *ringisho*, or proposal, system, the originator of a proposal makes sure that managers at every level have signed off before it reaches the top for approval. *Nemawashi*, or root tying, refers to the informal process of laying the groundwork before a formal proposal is set in motion. Both systems require a lengthy process of consultation and consensus building. At Mitsubishi Electric, for example, more than 25 managers in the semi-conductor division had to sign off on the expansion of production of 64-megabit memory chips in the early 1990s before the decision reached the board. There, about 50 directors also had to give their approval of what turned out to be a huge blunder.

Such a process has important adverse consequences for strategic positioning. First, the need to obtain so many approvals almost guarantees that bold or distinctive strategies will not be pursued. The chances of making choices and trade-offs that favor one unit or division over another are minimal. Second, once so many have signed off on a decision, it is very difficult to exit unsuccessful product lines or businesses.

Another potent barrier to strategy is the deeply ingrained tradition of customer service as it is practiced in Japan. In the automobile industry, for example, it is customary for a dealer salesperson to visit the customer's home to have the purchase and sales agreement signed. In most cases, the salesperson not only delivers the new car to the customer's home but also picks it up and drops it off for dealer-recommended checkups.

Although customer attentiveness is a strength, Japanese executives have bought into the notion that every customer need is equally valid. The tendency, therefore, is to respond to any need expressed by any customer. The end result is what we saw in the semiconductor example in Chapter 3, where the product lines of all Japanese manufacturers proliferated to include everything from transistors to microprocessors. Companies rarely choose which customers to serve and which customers to leave to competitors. The pervasive mentality is to try to be all things to all people. Instead, managers must understand that the essence of strategy is choosing *which* customers to serve and *which* of their needs to address.

Strategic competition is actually good for customers. It might seem that symmetric strategies and price competition would produce the best outcome from a customer standpoint. However, customers' needs differ. Where companies have distinctive strategies, customers can select the product or service that best meets their needs. Moreover, when companies make trade-offs, they align their activities to serve the unique needs of their chosen customers more efficiently. Again, the customer benefits.

Another impediment to strategy is that Japanese executives often rely on the same sources of information about markets and industries. Reports and white papers published by government and other groups such as *Keidanren* and *Shingikai* are widely circulated. The result is that executives from different companies often share the same view of the future and will therefore pursue similar actions.

At the broadest level, the Ministry of International Trade and Industry (MITI) has been providing companies with a 'vision' every ten years of where various industry sectors are headed. Its latest publication, *Vision of Industrial Policy in the 1990s*, offers an in-depth analysis of the outlook for eighteen industry sectors and the key issues confronting each of them. In its previous 'vision' books, MITI stated in no uncertain terms which industries would be 'sunrise' industries and which would be 'sunset' industries. With such official encouragement, companies have tended to pile into the same favored sectors.

MITI and the other ministries also make heavy use of advisory boards. These groups discuss industrial policies and review proposed legislation. The advisory boards, which are referred to as *shingikai, shinsakai, kyogikai, chosakai, iinkai,* or *kondankai* (in descending formality), are composed of private sector experts hand-picked by the ministry. An advisory board organized by MITI in 1996 included more than a dozen CEOs in six different industries – automobiles, semiconductors, consumer electronics, computers, software, and robotics. The board met with MITI officials and university professors to discuss the competitive challenges facing Japanese companies and to develop likely scenarios for each industry for the year 2005. The board met eight times over a six-month period. A confidential memo prepared by MITI officials, which contained detailed analyses and recommendations, was circulated to all members.

This approach continues the unhealthy tradition of government intervention in the competitive processes that we discussed in Chapter 5. Yet there is also a danger for companies. With so much sharing of competitive information, it is not surprising that companies develop a homogeneous view of their industry. The process also risks reducing the vitality of local rivalry.

When Japanese companies could succeed solely on the basis of operational effectiveness, developing and circulating information from multiple sources was clearly an advantage. This helped to disseminate best practices quickly and efficiently within an industry. But now Japanese companies must search for distinctive ways of competing, which requires a more creative, individualized process.

Finally, the *keiretsu* structure may have unwittingly undermined the pursuit of distinctive strategies. The large *keiretsu* have tended to enter the same industries. Table 6-1 shows the number of companies by sector in the six largest *keiretsu* in 1993. Their parallel presence in the same industries is striking. Mitsui and Mitsubishi, for example, are present in all sectors of the Japanese economy, except for one and two respectively. The arch rivals have almost the same number of sister companies.

The requirement that *keiretsu* companies buy from and sell to sister companies also works against strategy. It deters focus on segments of the market and adds to already strong tendencies toward product proliferation. The pressure to be all things to all people is intensified.

As we discussed in Chapter 3, Japanese companies need not look far to discover companies with distinctive strategies that are winning in the global market. In video games, Nintendo, Sega, and Sony have all prospered for extended periods. In carbon fibers, Toray chose to serve the needs of one customer group, sports equipment manufacturers, over others in the aerospace and defense sectors. In sewing machines, Juki decided to concentrate on the industrial sewing machine segment instead of the home segment. Many of the companies with the most distinctive strategies are not the well-established, traditional Japanese companies but a new generation founded in the 1980s and 90s. These companies seem to be less shackled by the traditional Japanese corporate model. Denied the power and resources that come from affiliation with a large group, they have sought areas of differentiation and made trade-offs that the larger companies were unwilling to make. Today, the need for strategy has become pressing throughout the economy, and large, established Japanese companies must find ways to remake themselves.

Table 6-1 Number of *keiretsu* companies
by industry, 1993 (cross-holding equity ration > 10%)

Industry	Mitsui	Mitsubishi	Sumitomo	Fuji	Dai-ichi Kangyo	Sanwa
Manufacturing						
Agriculture, fishery	0	0	0	0	0	0
Mining	3	0	1	0	0	0
Construction	14	10	10	14	7	7
Food processing	5	12	6	10	8	0
Fabrics/apparel	7	7	3	7	3	5
Paper/pulp	4	2	4	4	1	0
Chemicals	10	19	8	10	9	7
Pharmaceuticals	3	6	8	0	2	4
Petroleum/coal products	2	1	0	1	1	0
Rubber	1	0	2	2	1	2
Glass	3	7	5	7	1	2
Steel	3	1	5	6	2	4
Nonferrous metals	2	3	4	1	2	0
Wire, cables	2	3	1	1	2	0
Metal working	5	2	2	3	5	0
Machinery	9	5	9	11	7	4
Electronics	16	12	22	10	14	5
Shipbuilding	1	1	0	0	2	1
Railroad trucks	0	1	0	0	0	1
Automobiles	7	3	2	10	3	2
Precision instruments	4	2	1	2	3	1
Other manufacturing industries	2	2	3	3	5	4
Subtotal	*103*	*99*	*96*	*102*	*78*	*49*
Services						
Bank	2	2	1	2	1	2
Insurance	1	1	2	1	0	0
Trading	11	15	12	12	9	6
Retail	4	5	1	5	6	3
Real estate	3	2	2	1	0	1
Land transportation	3	5	2	3	2	2
Marine transportation	3	5	2	1	1	0
Air transportation	1	0	0	0	0	0
Warehouses	3	2	1	0	1	0
Utilities	3	1	1	0	1	0
Communications	1	3	1	0	0	0
Leisure	2	1	1	3	2	2
Subtotal	*37*	*42*	*26*	*28*	*23*	*16*
TOTAL	**140**	**141**	**122**	**130**	**101**	**65**

Source: Study on *Keiretsu*, Economic Research Association, 1993

Expand the Focus of Operational Effectiveness

OE improvement must continue, but it will require more disruptive change than it has in the past. The new frontiers of OE are in such areas as office productivity, IT, e-commerce, and marketing, where Japan has traditionally been weak. Internet diffusion, for example, is low in Japan, with only about 17 million users as of March 1999, compared with at least 92 million in the United States. Twenty percent of large companies (those with 7,800 employees or more) are still not connected to the Internet, while 80% of smaller companies remain unconnected. Most corporate PCs are shared among several employees.

Japan must aggressively embrace the productivity potential of information technology. Industry has not yet fully adopted the last generation of information technology, much less unleashed the transformational power of the Internet. Although the Japanese language has posed a major barrier to the adoption of earlier generations of technology, those problems have largely been solved. Slowness in adopting IT advances means that Japanese companies are bearing huge, unnecessary costs and foregoing important new growth opportunities.

Rapid adoption of information technology should become a national priority. It will require efforts not only by companies and trade associations but also by government. Government, for its part, must incorporate computer literacy into school curricula and provide the infrastructure, incentives, and competitive pressure that will stimulate hardware, software, and service providers to spread the technology into homes and offices throughout the country.

Japanese white-collar productivity also leaves plenty of room for improvement. During the growth era of the 1980s, front-office costs could be ignored. Now that many Japanese companies are facing declining sales and profits, they have begun to realize that no amount of economizing in factories can compensate for overstaffed offices. According to the Japan Institute of Office Automation, the number of white-collar workers increased to 54.2% of all employees in 1995, up from 38.7% in 1971.[1] Today, improving the productivity of white-collar workers should be pursued with the same level of commitment and vigor that was earlier directed at manufacturing.

Some companies began to tackle these issues in the early 1990s. Matsushita Electric, for example, began what it calls the 'Simple, Small, Strategic, and Speedy' campaign. One of its primary goals was to improve white-collar productivity by 30%. To do so, Matsushita eliminated an entire layer of senior management, rationalized dozens of vaguely defined product units into ten autonomous lines of business, and consolidated the company's 27 research labs into two. While moving in the right direction, these steps appear timid in light of experience in the United States and elsewhere.

It is also illuminating to note that while Matsushita was taking these steps, it was also pouring resources into entering unrelated new businesses, hopeful that they could absorb the displaced white-collar workers. This case highlights the difficulty of change – even pioneering companies fall back on old habits.

At Toyota, each administrative department has been asked to give up 20% of its employees to task forces that will identify new business opportunities or explore ways to improve white-collar productivity. In part, the program aims to foster more entrepreneurial thinking and prove to employees that corporate administration can be handled by far fewer people. Again, however, note how timid these steps are compared with Western practice.

Omron, a maker of electric components and medical devices, provides another example. It has encouraged managers to become specialists in particular businesses. To this end, Omron introduced what it calls its 'Human Renaissance' plan, in which many of its managers were required to take extended vacations of up to three months to reflect on their careers, spend time with their families, and broaden their horizons. A secondary purpose was to encourage the managers' subordinates to take more initiative while their bosses were away.

Examples like these are multiplying in Japan. But their tentative character reveals the barriers to productivity improvement that remain. Japanese companies must embrace the modern equivalent of the quality circles and statistical process control to pursue OE improvement with the same aggressiveness as quality and factory productivity were improved in the 1960s, 70s, and 80s.

Japan will not catch up without embracing the Internet. The technology practices of companies such as GE, Cisco, and Dell must become the new models. Cisco, for example, received one-third of its customer orders for routers and other networking gear via the Internet in 1996. That number reached 80% in 1999. Cisco purchases almost 100% of its components online, and its staff works in a paperless environment. According to one estimate, Cisco's sales per employee is three times that of Fujitsu.[2]

Learn the Role of Industry Structure in Strategy

A pervasive weakness in the Japanese approach to competition is its disregard of the role of industry structure in deciding both where to compete and how. Profitability is influenced not only by a company's own position but also by the structure of its industry, as discussed in Chapter 3. Japanese companies regularly flock to 'high-tech', 'sunrise', or growing industries without fully understanding that none of these things guarantees industry attractiveness. As a result, they end up crowding into unattractive businesses or undermining the structure of what could be attractive industries by transferring power to customers, reducing barriers to entry, and driving the basis of rivalry toward price. Then they wonder why profits are poor or nonexistent.

Take the facsimile industry, which is representative of other office equipment businesses. In the early days, barriers to entry were high because of the need for proprietary technology, high fixed development costs, and the need to attain economies of scale. Corporate buyers who valued quality, features, and service were not very price sensitive. Component suppliers provided mostly commodities and had little clout. Rivalry was moderate and focused not on price cutting but on variables such as new features, resolution quality, and transmission time.

Over time, the attractiveness of the industry was undermined by the companies themselves. The proliferation of weakly branded me-too products undercut entry barriers. The practice of selling to all distribution channels weakened the manufacturers' power vis-à-vis buyers. The homogeneous strategies of Matsushita, Ricoh, Canon, Toshiba, NEC, Sharp, Hitachi, Mitsubishi, Fujitsu, Minolta, and Murata left little room for product specialization or differentiation, so competition gravitated inevitably to price cutting. The average unit price of facsimile machines in Japan declined from ¥78,717 in 1992 to ¥42,498 in 1998.[3] Japanese companies still dominate the facsimile industry, but profitability has dissipated.

Shift the Goal from Growth to Profitability

The Japanese corporate model derives, in large part, from the goals set by companies. Lifetime employment makes expansion an imperative. The stigma attached to laying people off, even during an economic downturn, has meant that Japanese companies have consistently opted for product proliferation and entry into new growth areas.

This was possible because shareholders are seen as secondary, and exert little or no influence on management. In most large Japanese companies, 60% to 70% of shares are held by stable and friendly shareholders such as banks, insurance companies, and affiliated companies for relationship purposes. Not sensitive to profits, these controlling shareholders have rarely sold their shares. Such an ownership structure encourages top managers to focus not on near-term profits but on growth, which creates more business for affiliated companies. Also, most top managers of large Japanese companies hold solely salaried positions, so they have little incentive to pursue profitability.

Not surprisingly, then, the metrics used by Japanese companies to measure performance are market share and growth. It is notable that market share data are more available in Japan than anywhere else in the world, yet profitability data are scarce and unreliable. There is no line of business reporting that allows comparisons of profitability in particular businesses.

Japanese companies have a near obsession with market share, pursuing it at the expense of profitability. For example, in 1996, when Toyota's domestic market share dropped below the 40% mark for the first time in fifteen years, the company shifted into crisis mode and pulled out all the stops to reverse the decline. If market share remained below 40%, President Hiroshi Okuda said, 'It will have a negative impact on morale.' [4]

In Japan, employees become emotionally charged about winning or losing market share points vis-à-vis an arch rival. At Sony's General Audio Division, for example, employees make constant reference to 'BMW', which stands for 'Beat Matsushita Whatever.' Such rivalry is a good thing when it is channeled by proper strategic focus and oriented to improving profit performance. However, there is a danger in pursuing market share for its own sake.

The preoccupation with market share drives imitation and competitive convergence. Instead of concentrating on certain products or groups of customers, Japanese companies succumb to the temptation of pursuing broadly based strategies. They resist making trade-offs because they fear any such limits will constrain growth. By doing everything, though, Japanese companies become unique at nothing.

An almost inevitable result of Japanese corporate goals is recurring excess capacity (Chapter 1 gave examples from a sample of industries), which only exacerbates profitability problems. Ultimately, pressure to grow also leads to unrelated diversification. Overall, the net result is poor capital productivity.

Profitability is the only reliable guide to developing strategy. Pursuing the goal of profitability will require fundamental shifts in the values that underlie Japanese business practice. Earning a good return on investment must be seen as the ultimate test of a company's success in creating economic, customer, and social value. Capital must be seen as a valuable resource to be used efficiently. Prestige and rewards must come not from size but from uniqueness.

There are some signs that companies are becoming more concerned with profitability, partly due to pressure from non-Japanese investors. The role of non-Japanese investors has been growing as markets have globalized over the past decade and restrictions on portfolio investment in Japan have eased. Companies with a high percentage of such investors are shown in Table 6-2. It is not surprising that many of these companies have moved furthest to modify their corporate goals. Notably, all the companies in Table 6-2 have higher ROEs than the average of Tokyo Stock Exchange-listed companies.

Though Japanese companies are beginning to get the message about profitability, it is not at all clear that they have yet made the connection between profitability, industry structure, and strategy. The vast majority of change today is focused on operational effectiveness. Paring of product lines is driven more by the desire to drop items that are a drag on profitability than by the pursuit of a distinctive competitive position.

Reverse Unrelated Diversification

Historically, the diversification track record of Japanese firms has been exemplary. Japan's leading companies have consistently pursued diversification anchored in their primary fields, unlike many in the West. Canon and Olympus are good examples. Canon was principally a camera

Table 6-2   Companies with high percentage of non-Japanese investors, 1999

Company	%
Sony	45
Rohm	42
Canon	39
Minebea	38
Fuji Photo Film	36
Orix	35
TDK	35

Source: Japan Company Handbook, 1999

company for its first 30 years. In 1962, the company built on its optics expertise to enter copiers. In 1977, Canon pioneered ink-jet printers, building on its base in office equipment. It has moved from printers into imaging, precision tools, and other applications for printing. Olympus began as a producer of microscopes in 1920. It moved into cameras in 1936, gastro-cameras and fiberscopes in 1950 and 1963, and medical testing equipment in 1983.

The pressure to grow, however, can tempt executives to pursue new businesses where the company brings little advantage. As operational advantages waned and the post-bubble downturn limited the opportunity to grow domestically, many Japanese companies turned to unrelated diversification. When Shin Nippon Steel's main business leveled off in the 1980s, for example, the company tried its hand at theme parks and athletic clubs. Similarly, Yamaha moved into sports equipment, apparel, and ski resort management when the piano market became saturated in the 1980s. Even a company as respected as Toyota diversified into businesses as disparate as housing, helicopters, banking, software, and telecommunications. Sony entered insurance and securities.

The tendency to try to be all things to all customers has also manifested itself in the diversification strategies of Japanese companies that modeled themselves on the *sogo shosha*, or general trading companies. *Sogo shoshas* such as Mitsubishi Corporation, Mitsui Trading Company, Sumitomo Trading, C. Itoh, and Marubeni trade every conceivable product – from missiles to noodles – and offer services ranging from engineering to financing. In the high-growth period of the 1970s and 80s, it was popular for Japanese companies to identify themselves as *sogo* companies of one sort or another: for example, *sogo denki* (consumer electronics), *sogo jutaku* (housing), *sogo seikatsu* (living), *sogo* leisure, *sogo* apparel, and so forth. The consequences have been disastrous. The three leading *sogo denki* – Hitachi, Toshiba, and Mitsubishi Electric – averaged 0.9% return on sales between 1989 and 1998, compared with 6.3% for four leading specialized electronics manufacturers (Nidec, Rohn, Murata, and Futaba Denshi).

Private railroad companies, such as Tokyu, Seibu, Keio, Odakyu, Tobu, Kintetsu, Hanshin, and Hankyu, epitomize the all-things-to-all-customers company, offering a broad array of services for people who live along the railway line. Typically, their businesses include a department store at the urban terminal as well as hotels, supermarkets, housing developments, driving schools, museums, restaurants, travel agents, athletic facilities, real estate agents, and amusement parks. It is inconceivable that any company could have a competitive advantage in even a fraction of such disparate activities.

Japanese companies should abandon the outmoded notion of becoming *sogo* manufacturers or diversified giants such as Toshiba, Hitachi, and Mitsubishi Electric, which make everything from microchips and batteries to power plants and automated assembly plants. This model has a role in developing countries where capital and management are scarce, but it is obsolete in an advanced economy. Contrast these companies, which are facing their worst crises in history, with the high-performing Japanese companies, many of which are still barely known. The high performers are invariably focused on a few, tightly connected businesses. The need for strategy and choice is equally important at the corporate level of diversified firms as it is in individual businesses.

Update the Japanese Organizational Model

Embracing strategy will inevitably challenge Japan's model of leadership and organization. Japanese leaders most often see their role as building consensus, ensuring continuity, and providing for orderly succession. What Japan needs today is a new generation of leaders like Nobuyuki Idei of Sony, Yoshihiko Miyauchi of Orix, and Masayoshi Son of Softbank. Seen as mavericks in Japan, they are not afraid to rock the boat. They exemplify a new type of Japanese leader: an innovative thinker and a risk taker.

The dominant organizational structure in Japan still fosters continuous and incremental improvement. Central control by the corporate level is overbearing. While the rigid hierarchical structure common to Japanese corporations can be effective in pursuing operational improvement – such as miniaturization of audio equipment or increasing the yield of memory chips – it dampens real change and innovative thinking. To develop a new airliner, for example, engineers need to challenge design decisions continually, no matter how high in the hierarchy they may have been made. Without such an approach, design improvement is impossible. Japanese engineers were neither allowed nor accustomed to operate in this way.

In most businesses, the rigid, hierarchical model is increasingly obsolete. A new organizational model, similar to the one Idei is implementing at Sony, is in order. Idei reorganized the company into four market-focused business units to enhance autonomy, foster innovation, accelerate decision making, and improve accountability. The role of corporate headquarters is being reduced drastically.

Japanese companies also need to take steps to improve governance. Boards of directors have been large and unwieldy, composed solely of insiders who are advocates for their units. This structure makes strategic choices – especially shrinking or eliminating lines of business – difficult. Sony cut its board to ten from 38, including three outside (nonexecutive) directors. Toshiba also reduced the number of its board members from 33 to twelve. Fuji Photo, Hitachi, Japan Energy, Komatsu, Sapporo Beer, Sanwa Bank, and Sega have also reduced the size of their boards, and other Japanese companies should follow suit.

Internal incentives must also be modified. Otherwise, Japanese companies will continue to suffer from imitation and lack of distinctive strategies. Existing incentives are egalitarian and seniority driven. The Japanese system penalizes mistakes, encouraging managers to be careful and diligently study competitors. But it does not reward successes or risk taking, creating strong pressures to maintain the status quo and follow competitors. Companies must start rewarding originality and profitability in compensation, advancement, and opportunities for entrepreneurial wealth creation. With growing labor mobility and probable worker shortages due to an aging population, Japanese companies will have to become much more creative in attracting and retaining employees.

Some companies are already moving in such directions. Sony is again a leader, having begun offering stock options to executives in 1997. Until then, stock options were legally banned in Japan, except at small venture companies. A growing number of other companies, including NEC, Sega, and Softbank, now offer stock options to executives. If offering stock options and other incentive pay systems were widely emulated in Japan, higher profits would become a real priority for Japanese managers.

Develop a New Role for the Private Sector in National and Regional Economic Progress

Getting Japan on track to address its public policy challenges will happen far more rapidly if executives take more responsibility. Japanese business leaders have tended to passively accept counterproductive government policies. It is time, however, for the business–government relationship to change. The business community needs to take a more forceful role in pressuring government to make changes in the business environment.

Japanese companies have also been largely absent in improving their local business environment outside the realm of their immediate suppliers. While companies participate in trade associations and federations, they permit these organizations to focus on government relations rather than on matters such as training and environmental technologies, which would enhance their ability to compete. In such areas, the pattern has been to rely almost solely on government.

In an advanced economy, this model is no longer sufficient. As the needs for human resources, infrastructure, and efficient regulation have become more advanced and specialized, an active role in working with government and other institutions is needed to get results. Companies must actively define the obstacles they face in competing instead of leaving the decision to bureaucrats who have no business experience and who are detached from the market.

Associations and other collective bodies can also play an active part in institutionalizing cluster linkages. In addition to providing a neutral forum for identifying common needs, constraints, and opportunities, associations can be the focal point for efforts to address them. Associations can take the lead in creating specialized training programs in conjunction with local institutions, establishing university-based research programs and testing facilities, investigating solutions to environmental issues, and pursuing other common interests.

Associations can fill an especially important role for clusters consisting of many small- and medium-sized firms (for example, the clusters in tourism, metal fabrication, and agriculture). Such clusters have a particularly great need for a collective body to take on scale-sensitive functions. In the Netherlands, for example, grower cooperatives built the specialized auction and handling facilities that constitute one of the Dutch flower cluster's greatest competitive advantages. The Dutch Flower Council and the Association of Dutch Flower Growers Research Groups, in which most growers participate, also take on functions such as applied research and marketing.

Japan's hundreds of trade associations can be an important vehicle for private-sector initiatives to improve the business environment. They can also be a powerful force for change if they are less deferential to government and they broaden their focus from government relations to collective industry initiatives.

The New Japanese Company

The agenda laid out here is daunting. It will require nothing less than a major reorientation in thinking and practice. However, the seeds of the new Japanese company are already evident. A growing number of relatively new, emerging companies, many founded in the 1970s and 80s, are competing very differently from the large companies that led Japanese industry in previous decades. Interestingly, most of the emerging companies are based outside Tokyo. Here we profile four of these companies: Nidec Corp. of Kyoto, Rohm Co. of Kyoto, Kyoden Company of Nagano, and Shimano of Osaka. Unlike the *sogo* companies, these high performers have a clear strategic focus.

Nidec Corp.

Nidec controls about 73% of the world market for spindle micromotors used in computer hard-disk drives. It also has a strong presence in miniature cooling fans, with a world-leading market share of 38%. Fiscal 1999 sales were ¥106.0 billion (about US$1 billion), four times what they were ten years previously. Return on sales (ROS) in fiscal 1999 was 10.7%, and return on equity (ROE) was 9.4% (both high for a Japanese company). Exports represented 77% of sales.

From the beginning, Nidec pursued a clear strategy, competing differently than its more famous Japanese electronics rivals. It concentrated on a very limited set of products and resisted the temptation to vertically integrate. Spindle motors account for 80% of Nidec's sales. Microfans, which cater to the same customers as spindle motors, account for another 11%. The company's focus on spindle micromotors has led to a significant cost advantage over its two main competitors, Minebea and Sankyo Seiki. Because most of its customers are manufacturers of hard-disk drives, Nidec has accumulated a knowledge base in the field unmatched by its rivals.

Established in 1973, Nidec's first product breakthrough came at the end of the 1970s when it developed an all-in-one spindle motor for hard-disk drives using a brushless DC design, which cut heat output and space requirements. Nidec's innovation did not gain immediate acceptance in Japan because large domestic companies were reluctant to deal with an unknown supplier. But its innovative products and fast delivery times caught on quickly in the United States. Then Nidec used its strong international reputation to penetrate the domestic market.

Nidec aggressively recruits staff from established companies, a break from the typical Japanese corporate model. Approximately 40% of its staff have come from other companies, lured by generous financial incentives. Profit sharing is seen as a natural extension of a corporate culture that values results, action, and enthusiasm over age, seniority, and academic background. Since 1996, Nidec has been offering stock options, which have been almost nonexistent in larger Japanese firms.

Nidec began building a global production network in the 1980s. It serves customers globally out of plants in Japan, the United States, Singapore, Thailand, Taiwan, China, and the Philippines. Ninety-five percent of Nidec's manufacturing is conducted overseas. By locating close to its customers, Nidec offers high-speed, customized service that rivals cannot match.

Rohm

With sales of ¥272.8 billion in fiscal 1998, Rohm holds 34% of the world market in print heads for facsimile machines as well as substantial market shares in microsignal transistors (42%), silicon diodes (36%), and other products. In fiscal 1998, ROS was 22.5% and ROE was 11.0%.

Rohm's rivals are large, diversified manufacturers that offer a wide array of semiconductor products. In contrast, Rohm has a very limited product offering, focused on customized ICs and LSIs. The company chose not to follow traditional Japanese semiconductor makers into memory chips.

Rohm was established in 1954 by current CEO Kenichiro Sato. It began producing resistors, and over time, it moved into transistors, diodes, and integrated circuits. Rohm differs from its rivals in being very clear about what not to do. It does not get involved in state-of-the-art technologies. Throughout its history, Rohm has adhered to the practice of 'doing what big companies no longer do.' When a large company decides to halt the production of a certain electronic component, Rohm enters the market by contracting to become the OEM supplier. Rohm is also willing to exit low-profit product categories. It dropped one-third of the items in its product line in 1990 and redirected its focus from growth to profits.

Rohm assigns development engineers to a particular end product category, such as mobile phones, CDs, or video games, over a sustained period of time. This enables Rohm engineers to differentiate themselves from engineers working for the established companies, who are normally assigned to a particular technology or component segment. Rohm engineers have a much better understanding of technological advances and market developments in their fields, and can offer extensive consultation and advice and work closely with customers from the planning stages on to developing customized solutions. Since Rohm does not manufacture end products, customers can share ideas without jeopardizing their proprietary designs. Rohm can sell its chips to both Matsushita and Sony, even though these companies are fierce rivals.

To support its strategy, Rohm carefully measures performance by product category and by organizational unit. Sales, cost of goods sold, number of customer complaints, profits, and other measures are posted internally every month, and rankings by unit are disseminated within the company. Compensation is based on merit, and incentives encourage Rohm employees to work closely with their customers. The average age of Rohm's 2,800 employees in 1999 was 32.

Kyoden

Kyoden leads Japan's market for prototype printed circuit boards (PCBs) with a 50% share. It specializes in manufacturing prototypes for PC makers, consumer electronics producers, industrial machinery manufacturers, and a host of others. The company has more than 3,400 customers throughout Japan, to whom it sells an average of 22 prototypes at ¥10,000 each. Kyoden's prototypes command a price premium of up to 100 times more than mass-produced products. In 1998, the company recorded an ROE of 18.5% on sales of ¥10.9 billion.

Kyoden founder and CEO Hiroshi Hashimoto developed electronic products as a hobby while running a National (Matsushita-franchised) store in Nagano. Frustrated with having to wait as long as two months for PCBs, he decided in 1983 to start a company that would specialize in producing prototypes in small lots. To differentiate Kyoden from rivals, he came up with a slogan, 'PCB prototype produced in two days.' Today, Kyoden's uniqueness still comes from speed: it delivers prototypes to customers located in the Kanto and Kansai areas in one day, for a premium price.

Since Kyoden only produces prototypes, its manufacturing system is geared to large-variety, small-lot production. To deal with as many as 200 different orders a day, capacity utilization is set intentionally at 70% to support responsiveness and rapid delivery. Kyoden reinforces its differentiation from competitors by investing heavily in its 'quick-turnaround' system.

Each salesperson at Kyoden carries a notebook PC and transmits customer specifications directly to the Nagano production-planning department. Software developed by Kyoden breaks down the production process into twenty steps, calculates the estimated delivery time, and feeds the information back to salespeople on the spot. By working closely with customers and sharing confidential technical knowledge, Kyoden forms strong relationships that rivals have a hard time supplanting.

Shimano

Shimano, founded in Osaka in 1946, controls more than 70% of the world market for derailleurs, speed hubs, brakes, and other components for racing bicycles. Close to 90% of bicycle components sales are exported. The company recorded an ROS of 9.9% and an ROE of 8.6% on revenues of ¥145.8 billion in 1998.

Like the other high performers, Shimano has a clear strategy that it has maintained consistently for decades. The company concentrates on the premium bicycle component segment, initially in racing bikes and later in mountain bikes. Despite numerous opportunities, Shimano has deliberately opted out of making components for mass-market bicycles and motorcycles. The company seeks to produce components with the most advanced technology. Over almost two decades beginning in 1972, Shimano pioneered radical new technology that came to be accepted by the world's leading cyclists. While it took over a decade for Shimano to be accepted by top racers, today 65% of the teams participating in the Tour de France utilize Shimano components. Shimano has left its Italian and Japanese competitors behind with a much more rapid rate of new model introduction. When continuous improvement is combined with a clear strategy, the combination is unbeatable.

Shimano perceived an opportunity to extend its strategy to mountain bikes based on rugged, high-tech, shock-absorbing gear changers. It now commands 80% of the world market. Shimano builds brand equity through association with the winning racers and winning teams, PR, and sponsoring bike events. In a poll conducted by *Nikkei Newspaper* in 1998, Shimano came in eighth in the ranking of the best corporate brands. Shimano was the only component manufacturer to make the top 10 list, and it is known in Japan as the 'Wintel of the bicycle industry.'

Shimano pursued globalization more aggressively than its Japanese rivals. Starting in 1995, Shimano made English the company's official language. International meetings are held twice a year to coordinate global operations.

Conclusion

There is a pressing need for a new conception of the Japanese company. Good features of the Japanese corporate model should be retained – a long time horizon, treating employees as assets, close relationships with suppliers, aggressive investment to improve technology, continuous improvement in manufacturing productivity. But many other aspects of the way Japanese companies compete and are managed must be transformed, as we have outlined.

The emerging companies we profiled illustrate the competitive advantage that can be created by combining an orientation to profit, a clear strategy, and strong employee incentives with operational excellence and a long time horizon. Many other Japanese companies could prosper if all these elements were combined in a new approach to competition.

A number of Japanese companies have begun aggressive efforts to remake themselves, an encouraging development. However, reforms so far have focused on cost cutting, trimming product lines, modifying incentives, and enhancing governance. Cost cutting alone will not be successful. It is still not clear that Japanese managers have changed their approach to competing and begun to embrace strategic thinking.

There is a wave of optimism in 2000 that the Internet offers the key to restoring Japan's success. However, the Internet alone will not rescue the Japanese company. What is necessary is no less than a redefinition of corporate goals in Japan and a whole new conception of how competitive advantage is created and maintained.

Notes

1. *JMA Management Review*, August 1996, pp. 12–13.
2. *Nikkei Business*, March 1, 1999, pp. 30–4.
3. Chunichi-sha, *Denshi Kiki Nempo*, 1999, p. 353.
4. Alex Taylor III, 'Toyota's Boss Stands out in a Crowd', *Fortune*, November 25, 1996, p. 76.

CHAPTER 7

Can Japan Compete?

Can Japan compete? There are those who question whether Japan can prosper in the turn-of-the-century economy as it did in the less open, less dynamic, and less technologically intensive environment of the 1960s, 70s, and 80s. Many of Japan's strengths have become weaknesses. Its deeply ingrained social and cultural norms seem inconsistent with the innovation, entrepreneurship, and risk taking that are the hallmarks of today's competition.

We disagree. Japan has a history of competing successfully at the highest level and rapidly advancing national productivity, when competition was allowed to proceed unfettered. Japanese companies are still competitive in many fields, as our case studies illustrate. Some elements of the Japanese corporate model continue to be strengths. Based on decades of cumulative investment, Japan has moved to the world's top tier in commercial innovation, with high international patenting rates and rates of scientific citations *per capita*. Even as it suffers from gaping holes in its scientific and technology system, then, Japan is far ahead of most nations. Entrepreneurship is also on the rise, especially outside the traditional order in Tokyo and Osaka. Finally, Japanese workers and managers are almost universally well educated and extraordinarily dedicated, an asset few other nations can claim.

Japan can compete. To do so, however, will require the systemic changes in both business and government we have described. Japanese companies must be allowed to compete at the same time as they are forced to compete. The goals companies are judged against must change, and the way they are judged must change. A role for government in the economy will remain, but the nature of that role must be fundamentally altered.

The old model was internally consistent. Many individual practices and policies fit together. The challenge facing Japan is that numerous things must change simultaneously, not an easy task even if the right direction was well understood. Unfortunately, Japanese are still divided and puzzled about what went wrong and what to do about it.

A new strategy will nowhere be more difficult to accept than in government, where prestige and power have been concentrated. The instinct of the Japanese government to protect, cushion, and shelter companies and citizens is almost irresistible. In recent years, government has provided massive loan guarantees, by some estimates covering more than 10% of all outstanding loans, to prop up weak financial industry players. Deposit insurance reform has been delayed for fear it will hurt small lenders. Corporate tax reform is put off because it would force too much restructuring. Old habits will die hard.

This book offers a template with which those concerned with the nation's future, both inside and outside Japan, can evaluate progress. We have seen that many of the current developments fall short of what is needed – a new model for competing. Commentators have been prone to announce a recovery because the financial crisis has abated, and bouts of hopefulness produce upturns in the market. We have outlined the types of changes that, when they occur and cumulate, should lead to real optimism.

Can Japan Change?

Japan can compete. The real question is, Will it *choose* to compete? There is enormous skepticism – both abroad and inside Japan – about the nation's ability to embrace such fundamental change. Many argue that the generation now ruling Japan's government bureaucracies and corporations is wedded to things as they are. Japan's harshest critics accuse this generation of a failure of will.

We are more hopeful. We believe Japan has the will but lacks the vision and the direction. Japan's leaders are proud of their hard-won success, which is nothing short of miraculous. They are wary of Anglo-Saxon capitalism with its instability and excesses. Many have drawn the wrong lessons from Japan's past success. The conventional wisdom has been strongly reinforced by international opinion, from which some of the conventional wisdom emerged.

Japan is a nation that reveres its traditions. It is a nation that prizes stability. But it is also a nation that has demonstrated an extraordinary capacity to transform itself when its well-being is at stake. The Japan we know today was invented by a collective act of will following the devastation of World War II. This effort was successful because Japan had the flexibility to apply its own unique strengths to the best ideas then available – regardless of where those ideas came from. Edicts of the Allied Occupation Command became accepted parts of the post-World War II economic order. Japanese leaders recognized the realities of a devastated economy with few natural resources, and they undertook the extraordinary steps that were needed to rebuild.

This capacity for change under adversity was repeated at least two more times in Japan's postwar history. The Oil Shock of the 1970s triggered extraordinary upgrading in Japanese industry. When the price of crude oil quadrupled in 1973, the economy slowed from the 10% real GDP growth rate of the 1960s to negative growth in 1974, and the subsequent recession lasted four years. Under intense pressure, Japanese companies invested heavily in energy-conserving technologies and moved toward higher value products. The Oil Shock was the catalyst for Japan's global leadership in energy conservation, which has benefited many industries. The Oil Shock was also the impetus for innovations that established Japan in advanced industries such as automobiles and consumer electronics. In TV sets, for example, the desire to reduce power consumption triggered Japanese producers' early move from vacuum tubes to transistors – a move that carried many other benefits in terms of the reliability, functionality, and manufacturability of products.

The Yen Shock, which saw the Japanese yen appreciate by 100% in the two years after the Plaza Accord in September 1985, led to an equally rapid transformation. Almost overnight, Japanese products became expensive in international markets. And Japanese wages reached some of the highest levels in the world, a sharp reversal in an economy where low wages relative to the West for skilled workers had been an important advantage. Faced again with severe pressures, Japanese firms improved their productivity enormously, shifting the production of less sophisticated, lower value products to overseas locations, and moving to more sophisticated products that were less susceptible to price competition.

Japan's response to these two shocks provides cause for optimism, but there are some important differences this time around. Although the past and the present crises have generated a sense of urgency, the urgency today is perhaps less strongly felt. Whereas the causes of the previous shocks were clear and highly visible, today's difficulties are more puzzling and less well understood. There is a strong tendency today to blame everything on the bubble and to focus only on the financial sector rather than look deeper.

In the wake of the previous shocks, the nation's goal and the needed direction were evident. Japan had to make major strides in cost reduction, energy usage, and product sophistication. Today, the goal and sense of direction are anything but evident.

Finally, the actions needed to deal with the previous shocks were congruent with Japanese strengths in relentless operational improvement. The steps needed today will require major changes in how companies think and act, not to mention wholesale shifts in the behavior of government. The policymaking process in Japan will make bold and systemic changes difficult.

Catalysts for Change

What will be the catalysts for real change? We see them emanating from several sources. First, foreign investors are becoming much more significant equity shareholders in Japanese companies, as the old, quasi-permanent interlocking holdings are gradually liquidated. At Sony, for example, 45% of the shares are held by foreigners (see Table 6-2). One can already see signs that the new shareholders will be playing a different role; their greatest influence, perhaps, will be in educating and encouraging other Japanese shareholders to exercise more influence. The likely result will be greater emphasis on profitability, a greater willingness to exit unprofitable products and businesses, more attention to performance measurement, more transparent financial reporting, and improvements in corporate governance.

Second, foreign companies are entering Japan in growing numbers, increasingly by acquiring Japanese companies. Low equity prices and pressures on Japanese companies to find new sources of capital have begun to unfreeze the market for corporate control. Foreign companies either acquired (in whole or in part) or merged with 85 Japanese firms in 1998, a record number. By August 1999, the number had already reached 86.[1] In June 1999, after a bitter two-month battle with Nippon Telegraph and Telecommunications, the British company Cable & Wireless acquired a 53% stake of International Digital Communications. This was the first successful hostile takeover in Japan, and the ultimate choice by IDC's board appears to have been made on the price received by shareholders.[2] In early 2000, an effort to acquire Shoei Company was the first case of a Japanese investor making a hostile takeover bid for a Japanese company.

As owners with different outlooks populate more industries or pose a credible threat of doing so, new corporate goals and new approaches to competition should proliferate. For example, when GE Capital formed a joint venture in 1998 with Toho Mutual Life, an ailing insurer, it selected Toho's best employees and most profitable operations and established a new company called GE Edison. An integration team was created to coach Toho Mutual executives in the 'GE way.' The team studied Toho Mutual operations to identify processes that were unwieldy and inefficient. What they found in claims processing was typical: a customer seeking a benefit payment at a branch office filled out a form; the office entered the claim in its computer and then mailed the form to the head office; the head office retyped the claim into its computer. A series of major process changes were initiated, speeding up claims payments, reducing overhead, and achieving a 30% increase in productivity.[3]

Renault, after acquiring 37% of Nissan to become its largest shareholder in May 1999, appointed Carlos Ghosn as Nissan's new Chief Operating Officer. Nissan, which had lost money for seven of the previous eight years, divested assets ranging from equity stakes in parts suppliers to unprofitable telecommunication subsidiaries and has begun to streamline its dealership networks.[4] Ghosn even had Nissan's executives test-drive competitors' cars to compare them with their own – a new experience.

Third, the *keiretsu* system is in the process of change. In October 1999, Sumitomo Bank announced it would merge with Sakura Bank, following a consolidation plan involving the International Bank of Japan, Fuji Bank, and Dai Ichi Kango Bank. The *keiretsu* system, where these banks each served as a main bank, is likely to decline. Cross-holdings among companies are also being sold off. This will trigger a chain reaction of new possibilities, including new financing approaches and more focused strategies.

A fourth catalyst for change is the process of government organizational reform that is under way. The Central Government Ministries Reform Law, passed in July 1999, will reorganize the current 22 central government ministries and agencies into thirteen and reduce the cabinet from twenty members to seventeen by January 2001. The legislation provides for a reduction of 10% in the number of central government employees over a ten-year period, and party leaders are talking in terms of a 25% cut.[5] In addition, the legislation creates a new economic policy council whose members will include the prime minister as well as experts from outside the government. The prime minister's power to create the budget, a task now undertaken primarily by the Ministry of Finance (MOF), will be enhanced. MOF will become a treasury ministry; most of its authority to supervise financial institutions will be transferred to a new agency.

This organizational reform does not guarantee a change in direction for Japan's economic strategy. However, the process of government restructuring should spur new approaches. The new economic policy council, for example, could embrace new directions and reallocate the budget accordingly. Having the current Ministry of Education and the Science and Technology Agency under one umbrella, as is contemplated, could lead to a unified approach to increasing basic scientific research and improving technical education at all levels.

Fifth, a new generation of CEOs is assuming leadership in many Japanese companies. This generation is far less inhibited than its predecessors about changing long-standing practices. Leaders at Honda (President Hiroyuki Yoshino), Toyota (Chairman Hiroshi Okuda), Sony (President Nobuyuki Idei), Orix (President Yoshihiko Miyauchi), and Softbank (President Masayoshi Son) all have significant overseas experience. In the past, overseas experience would have been a negative for corporate advancement. Because these new CEOs possess greater familiarity with international business practices and are taking leadership at a time of financial and competitive pressure, they are likely to do things differently. These leaders share several other traits that differentiate them from past leaders. They see change as inevitable. Sony's Idei, for example, has already implemented three rounds of organizational changes since he took office. Toyota's Okuda has replaced older executives with younger ones. In addition, they do not mind being the nail that sticks out – all of them are outspoken and direct.

Sixth, the newer generation of entrepreneurial companies are getting larger; some are joining the ranks of major corporations. We profiled some of these companies in Chapter 6. Softbank, Orix, and Pasona are additional examples along with emerging Japanese dot-coms such as Rakuten and NetAge. Many of these companies are highly profit oriented, compete with clear strategies, and have developed distinctly un-Japanese organizational models. They will certainly influence the way other Japanese companies compete.

The emerging companies also have a very different attitude toward government, which should reinforce the kinds of policy changes we advocate. In June 1999, for example, Softbank announced the creation of Nasdaq Japan, a computerized stock market with a tie-in to the US National Association of Securities Dealers, by the end of 2000. This would do away with the onerous IPO requirements of established Japanese markets. Although this plan aims to circumvent MOF's carefully crafted rules, industry observers expect that MOF will be forced to approve the plan given the strong pressure in Japan for financial deregulation.[6]

A final catalyst for change will be the Japanese people themselves. Younger workers have a different orientation than their elders. Many joined the workforce during the prolonged recession of the 1990s, and they do not expect to be protected by lifetime employment. They are more comfortable with merit-based compensation, more literate in information technology, and more flexible in accepting change. They will become a driving force for changing their companies and government policy.

Japanese are also becoming equity investors. With the returns on postal savings accounts and other traditional savings vehicles looking more and more anemic, money is flowing into mutual funds and equity shares. As

Japanese citizens move from being savers to becoming investors, their outlook toward companies will change.

Many argue that culture is the hardest thing to change, and that cultural factors will thwart Japan's adjustment. They maintain that a society so group oriented that it hammers down the nail that sticks out is incompatible with the new economy. Yet much of economic culture is learned. It arises from the incentives and rules built into the prevailing economic system. Lifetime employment in Japan, for example, is a creature of post-World War II labor strife, not a culturally ordained relationship between Japanese managers and employees. Economic culture can and will change as the context changes. Japanese are well informed about developments in the West, and globalization is dramatically accelerating the adjustment process.

Signs of change are everywhere. Major standard bearers such as NEC and Hitachi are restructuring. Foreign firms are making major acquisitions without any public outcry. Managers are leaving their traditional companies. Bureaucrats are leaving their ministries early. Entrepreneurs are thriving outside of Tokyo and Osaka, and there are more than 300 venture companies in Kyoto. Cyber start-ups are clustering in Tokyo's Shibuya district, which translates literally to Bitter Valley and is now fashionably called Bit Valley.

Teenagers are setting up on-line services. Individuals are investing a portion of their savings into the stock market. Internet and cell phone use is taking off. College graduates are starting to work for foreign firms. Women are gaining more freedom at work. These may be incremental steps, but they signal a whole new approach to competition.

The Need for a New Japanese Model

Today in Japan, change is occurring piecemeal, out of fear and necessity. Individual steps are being taken in an effort to emulate international practice or to deal with things that are clearly not working. There are fits and starts. New initiatives are announced – for example, consolidated corporate tax accounting and deposit insurance reform – and then postponed.

What is still lacking is an overall understanding of the causes of Japan's current difficulties and a uniquely Japanese solution. We hope this book helps to address those needs through its careful study of the nation's successes and failures, its new theory for understanding competition and productivity in a global economy, and its directions for the future.

Some have questioned whether Japan should move from a stability-based system to a competition-based system. Our research suggests that this is not the right question. Japan has *already moved to the competition system* in those parts of the economy that are productive and successful. The real question is whether Japan can understand this and overcome the obstacles to spreading the competition system throughout the economy.

To develop a comprehensive solution, Japan will need to embrace some elements of the Western approach, much as it has done in the past. The result, however, will not be a clone of American capitalism but a new and distinctly Japanese conception of competition.

Where will the uniqueness lie? Here is some of the potential we see: While Western individualism is a strength, it can also be a weakness. Japanese have an extraordinary ability to work across disciplines, functions, and companies. When equipped with more specialized training, Internet technology, and new competitive thinking, this ability to work together could trigger breakthroughs in productivity and strategy.

Moreover, advances in knowledge increasingly come from cross-disciplinary work. With the proper investments in its university research system, better incentives, greater competition, and fewer regulatory distortions, Japan could emerge as an even stronger center of innovation.

Japan has benefited from strong clusters in many fields. As we discussed in Chapter 4, clusters work well in Japan, given the ability to cooperate while fiercely competing. With a greater orientation to regional specialization and with more responsibility pushed down to lower levels of government, Japan could set off a new era of entrepreneurship and cluster development. We see evidence of this in the Internet area.

In the area of demand conditions, Japan's living circumstances, culture, and demographics continue to provide advantages that could become even more important in the future. Japan has long been a cutting-edge market for compact, multifunctional, quiet products. Japanese are highly sensitive to look, style, and packaging. The nation has been a leader in energy efficiency. All these areas remain strengths and represent areas of growing importance worldwide.

Demand advantages could be amplified if Japanese consumers and businesses embrace environmental protection, a real possibility given the nation's crowded conditions. Japan could become a leading-edge market for meeting the needs of its aging population. Regulatory reform could unleash the pressure of well-educated, picky consumers in previously controlled fields such as communications, services, and health care.

Western economies are faced with many poorly educated citizens, whereas Japan's almost universally highly educated men and women are a potent asset in knowledge-intensive competition. Japan's women, in particular, represent an extraordinary resource that could transform the corporate sector and provide the cadre of new employees to support economic growth even with an aging population. Most Western nations have already benefited from the movement of women in the workforce and therefore lack this potential.

While Western nations struggle to maintain employee involvement and loyalty, Japanese companies, with new incentive systems, could also gain advantages through their practiced teamwork.

While Western capital markets and Western companies have ever-shorter time horizons, Japan's longer time horizons represent a strength of growing significance. The influence of shareholders must increase in Japan, and companies must become more profit oriented, but those goals are not at all inconsistent with long-term ownership. Instead of simply imitating Western capital market practices, then, Japan could offer tax incentives for long-term equity holding and ensure that corporate law institutionalizes the primacy of the long-term interests of shareholders in mergers and other corporate choices.

Finally, the ability of Japan's institutions to work together can be a potent strength, in contrast to the adversarial US system. Many of Japan's institutions need to change their roles, but a new order could benefit from strong linkages.

It is time for Japan to embrace a new economic strategy, one based on a deeper understanding of the strengths and limitations of its past approaches to competition coupled with a new and more sophisticated mind-set about the roles of government and companies in the global economy. We have tried to sketch some of the most important elements of that new approach, and illustrate its power with examples drawn from Japan's actual experiences. Japan's leaders have the responsibility – and the opportunity – to devise a uniquely Japanese approach and make it a reality.

Japan has changed its overall economic strategy once before in the post-World War II period. In the late 1940s and 1950s, Japan competed largely on *low price and low wages*, selling cheap imitations of Western goods. Understanding the limits of that approach, the nation underwent a stunning transformation to a new mode of competition. Drawing on the ideas of Deming and Juran, Japan began to compete not just on price but on *quality*. The practices and approaches Japan pioneered in doing so changed competition forever throughout the world.

At the beginning of 2000, however, the limits of the current model have become increasingly evident, as we have discussed. Today, Japan must move beyond just quality competition to competing on *strategy and inno-*

vation. Japanese companies will need to develop distinctive strategies that result in true profitability. In order to do so, incremental improvements in best practice will not be enough. Genuine innovation not only in products but also in approaches to competing will be required. As it has shown in earlier periods of transition, if mind-sets change, Japan has the capacity to move rapidly. A new national movement of no less significance than the quality movement will be needed. We are hopeful that the beginnings of this next great transformation are at hand.

Notes

1. *The Nikkei Weekly*, September 20, 1999.
2. *Financial Times*, June 10, 1999.
3. *The New York Times*, September 14, 1999.
4. *Business Week*, October 11, 1999.
5. *Asia Pulse*, July 9, 1999.
6. *The Washington Post*, June 16, 1999.

REFERENCES

Abegglen, J.C. and Rapp, W. (1970) Japanese Managerial Behavior and 'Excessive Competition.' *The Developing Economies* **8**(4): 427–44.

Abegglen, J.C. and Stalk, G. (1985) *Kaisha: The Japanese Corporation: The New Competitors in World Business*. New York: Basic Books.

Ad Hoc Administration Reform Promotion Council Coordination Office (1988) Deregulation. Tokyo, Japan: Gyosei.

Alexander, C.P. (1981) Learning from the Japanese. *Personnel Journal* **60**(8): 616–19.

Aoki, M. (1987) The Japanese Firm in Transition, in Yamamura, K. and Yasuba, Y. (eds) *The Political Economy of Japan, Vol. 1, The Domestic Transformation*. Stanford, California: Stanford University Press.

Asher, D. and Smithers, A. (1998) *Japan's Key Challenges for the 21st Century*. Washington DC: The Paul H. Nitze School of Advanced International Studies of the Johns Hopkins University.

Ballon, R.J. (ed.) (1968) *Doing Business in Japan*. Tokyo: Sophia-Tuttle.

Ballon, R.J. (ed.) (1969) *The Japanese Employee*. Tokyo: Sophia-Tuttle.

Barret, M.E. and Gehrke, J.A. (1974) Significant Differences Between Japanese and American Business. *MSU Business Topics* **22**(1): 41–50.

Bartlett, C.A., Elderkin, K.W. and McQuade, K. (1991) *Body Shop International*. 9-392-032. Boston, MA: Harvard Business School.

Branstetter, L. and Sakakibara, M. (1998) Japanese Research Consortia: A Micro-econometric Analysis of Industrial Policy. *Journal of Industrial Economics* **46**(2): 207–33.

Buzzell, R.D. (1978) *Note on the Motorcycle Industry, 1975*. 9-578-210. Boston, MA: Harvard Business School.

Calder, K.E. (1988) *Crisis and Compensation: Public Policy and Political Stability in Japan, 1949–1986*. Princeton, NJ: Princeton University Press.

Callon, S. (1995) *Divided Sun: MITI and the Breakdown of Japanese High-Tech Industrial Policy, 1975–1993*, Stanford: Stanford University Press.

Clark, K.B. and Fujimoto, T. (1991) *Product Development Performance: Strategy, Organization and Management in the World Auto Industry*. Boston: Harvard Business School Press.

Cole, R.E. (1971) The Theory of Institutionalization: Permanent Employment and Tradition in Japan. *Economic Development and Cultural Change* **20**(1): 47–70.

Cole, R.E. (1979) *Work, Mobility and Participation: A Comparative Study of American and Japanese Industry*. Berkeley, CA: University of California Press.

Cole, R.E. and Yakushiji, T. (eds) (1984) *The American and Japanese Auto Industries in Transition: Report of the Joint US–Japan Automobile Study*. Ann Arbor, MI: Center for Japanese Studies, the University of Michigan.

Dertouzos, M.L., Lester, R.K. and Solow, R.M. (1989) *Made in America: Regaining the Productive Edge*. Cambridge, MA: MIT Press.

Dore, R.P. (1973) *British Factory–Japanese Factory: The Origins of National Diversity in Industrial Relations*. Berkeley, CA: University of California Press.

Dore, R.P. (1986) *Flexible Rigidities: Industrial Policy and Structural Adjustment in the Japanese Economy*. Stanford, CA: Stanford University Press.

Dore, R.P. (1987) *Taking Japan Seriously*. London: Athlone Press.

Drucker, P. (1971) Behind Japan's Success. *Harvard Business Review* **59**(1): 83–90.

Eads, G.C. and Yamamura, K. (1987) The Future of Industrial Policy, in Yamamura, K. and Yasuba, Y. (eds) *The Political Economy of Japan*. Stanford, CA: Stanford University Press: 423–68.

Enright, M.J. (1991) *The Japanese Facsimile Industry in 1990*. 9-391-209. Boston, MA: Harvard Business School.

Fair Trade Commission (various years) *Fair Trade Commission Annual Report*. Tokyo: Fair Trade Association.

Fallows, J.M. (1989) 'Containing Japan', *The Atlantic Monthly*, May.

Feldman, R. (1996) *Nihon no Suijaku* (The Weakening of Japan). Tokyo: Toyo Keizai Shinpousha.

Forbes, May 5 (1997) First the Pain, Then the Gain.

Fujimoto, T. (1997) *Seisan System no Shinka-ron* (The Evolutionary Production System). Tokyo: Yuuhikaku.

Fujimoto, T. (1999) *The Evolution of a Manufacturing System at Toyota*. New York: Oxford University Press.

Furstenberg, F. (1974) *Why the Japanese Have Been So Successful in Business*. London: Leviathan.

Gibney, F. (1979) *Japan: The Fragile Superpower* (rev. edn). New York: Norton.

Glazer, H. (1969) The Japanese Executive, in Ballon, R.J. (ed.) *The Japanese Employee*. Tokyo: Sophia University: 77–98.

Gyoukaku 700-nin Iinkai (1999) *Min to Kan* (Civil and Public: Public Offices and Officials of 2001). Tokyo: Kodansha.

High-Tech Strategy Research Committee (1990) *Technological Competitiveness of Japan vs. U.S.: Thorough Investigation*. Tokyo: Nikkei Science.

Higuchi, H. and Karatsu, H. (1999) *Nihon-keizai Hinode wa Chikai!* (Japanese Economy: 'Sunrise' is Near). Tokyo: PHP Kenkyuujo.

Hori, S. (1993) Fixing Japan's White-Collar Economy: A Personal View. *Harvard Business Review* **6**(71): 157–72.

Imai, K. and Komiya, R. (1989) The Characteristics of Japanese Firms, in Imai, K. and Komiya, R. (eds) *Nihon no Kigyo* (Japanese Firms). Tokyo, Japan: University of Tokyo Press.

Inose, N. (1997) *Nihonkoku no Kenkyuu* (Study of Japan). Tokyo: Bungei Shunjuu.

Irwin, D. and Klenow, P. (1996) High Tech R&D Subsidies: The Effects of Sematech. *Journal of International Economics* (40): 323–44.

Ishikawa, A. and Nejou, T. (1999) *Nihon no Nakano Sekai-kigyou* (World-class Companies Within Japan). Tokyo: Sannou Daigaku Syuppanbu.

Itami, H. (1987) *Jinpon Shugi Kigyo* (Human-Capital Based Company). Tokyo: Chikuma Shobo.

Itami, H. (1990) *Yen ga Yureru Kigyo ga Ugoku* (As the Yen Fluctuates, So do Corporations). Tokyo: NTT Shuppan.

Itami, H. (1995) Top Management and the Adaptability of Corporations, in Corporate Behavior Study Group (ed.) *Nohon Kigyo no Tekiouryoku* (The Adaptability of Japanese Firms). Tokyo: Nippon Keizai Shinbunsha.

Itami, H., Kagono, T. and Ito, M. (1993) *Nihon no Kigyou shisutemu: Soshiki to Senryaku* (Japanese Corporate Systems: Organization and Strategy). Tokyo: Yuuhikaku.

Ito, H. (1995) The Economics of 'Company People', in Corporate Behavior Study Group (ed.) *Nohon Kigyo no Tekiouryoku* (The Adaptability of Japanese Firms). Tokyo: Nippon Keizai Shinbunsha.

Ito, M. and Kiyono, K. (1984) Trade and Foreign Direct Investment, in Komiya, R., Okuno, M. and Suzumura, K. (eds) *Nihon no Sangyo Seisaku* (The Japanese Industrial Policy). Tokyo: University of Tokyo Press.

Ito, T. (1992) *The Japanese Economy*. Cambridge, MA: MIT Press.

Iwasaki, A. (1984) Mergers and Reorganizations, in Komiya, R., Okuno, M. and Suzumura, K. (eds) *Nihon no Sangyo Seisaku* (The Japanese Industrial Policy). Tokyo: University of Tokyo Press.

Iwata, R. (1977) *Nihon Teki Keiei no Hensei Genri* (The Logic behind the Changing Japanese-Style Management). Tokyo: Bunshindo.

Japan Fair Trade Commission (1993) *Survey on the Flat Glass Distribution System* (Ita Garasu no Ryutsu ni Kansuru Kigyokan Torihiki no Jittai Chosa). Tokyo: Japan Fair Trade Commission.

Johnson, C. (1982) *MITI and the Japanese Miracle: The Growth of Industrial Policy, 1925–1975*. Stanford, CA: Stanford University Press.

Kagono, T. (1988) *Kigoka Seishin to Kigyoka Teki Kakushin* (Entrepreneurship and Entrepreneurial Innovation), in Itami, H., Kagono, T., Kobayashi, T., Sakakibara, K. and Ito, M., *Kyoso to Kakushin – Jidosha Sangyo no Kigyo Seicho* (Competition and Innovation – Corporate Growth in the Automobile Industry). Tokyo: Toyo Keizai Shinposha.

Kanamori, H. (1984) *Sengo Keizai no Tenkan to Hatten* (The Transition and Development of the Post-War Economy), in Kanamori, H. and Nihon Keizai Kenkyu Center (eds) *Nihon Keizai – Dai Tenkan no Jidai* (The Japanese Economy in the Major Transition Period). Tokyo: Nihon Keizai Shinbunsha.

Kaplan, E.G. (1972) *Japan: The Government–Business Relationship*. Washington, DC: United States Department of Commerce.

Karatsu, H. (1997) *Nihon Keizai no Sokojiikara* (Hidden Power of the Japanese Economy). Tokyo: Nihonkeizai Shinbunsha.

Kato, H. (1992) *Konton no Nakani Nihon ga Mieru* (Japan in the New Age of Chaos). Tokyo: Koudansha.

Kato, H. (1997) *Kanryou Shudou Kokka no Shippai* (Failure of Bureaucracy-Led Nation). Tokyo: Toyo Keizai Shinpousha.

Katz, R. (1999) *Kusariyuku Nihon to iu Shisutemu* (Japan: The System That Soured). Tokyo: Toyo Keizai Shinpousha.

Kawakami, T., Nagao, R., Itami, H., Kagono, T. and Okazaki, T. (1994) *Nihon-gata Keiei no Eichi* (Wisdom of Japanese-styled Management). Tokyo: PHP Kenkyuujo.

Kisugi, A. (1999) The Historical Overview of the Japanese Competition Policy (1): the Pre-War Period to the 1977 Amendment, in Goto, A. and Suzumura, K. (eds) *Nihon no Kyoso Seisaku* (The Japanese Competition Policy). Tokyo: University of Tokyo Press.

Koike, K. (1981) *Hinon no Jukuren* (Skill Formation in Japan). Tokyo: Yuuhikaku.

Koike, K. (1989) Skill Formation and Long-Term Competition, in Imai, K. and Komiya, R. (eds) *Nihon no Kigyo* (Japanese Firms). Tokyo: University of Tokyo Press.

Komiya, R., Sase, M. and Eto, M. (1997) *21-seiki ni Mukau Nihon-keizai* (Japanese Economy for the 21st Century). Tokyo: Toyo Keizai Shinpousha.

Koo, R.C. (1999) *Nihon-keizai Kaifuku eno Aojashin* (Japan's Economy: Blueprint for Recovery). Tokyo: PHP Kenkyuujo.

Kosaka, M. (1992) *Nihon Sonbou no Toki* (The World Is Not One and Yet the World Is One). Tokyo: Kodansha.

Koshiro, M. (1999) The Historical Overview of the Japanese Competition Policy (2): the 1977 Amendment and the Tightened Antitrust Law Afterwards, in Goto, A. and Suzumura, K. (eds) *Nihon no Kyoso Seisaku* (The Japanese Competition Policy). Tokyo: University of Tokyo Press.

McCraw, T. (1986) From Partners to Competitors: An Overview of the Period Since World War II, in McCraw, T. (ed.) *America versus Japan*. Boston, MA: Harvard Business School Press.

Ministry of International Trade and Industry (1963) *Wagakuni Sangyo Kozo Kohdoka no Kihonteki Houkoh* (The Basic Direction and Challenges for the Upgrading of the Japanese Industrial Structure). Tokyo: MITI.

Miyazaki, Y. (1992) *Fukugou Fukyou* (Compounded Recession). Tokyo: Chuou Kouronsha.

Mizutani, K. (1996) *Migikata Sagari no Nihon-keizai* (Japan's Economy on the Downslope). Tokyo: PHP Kenkyuujo.

Nakane, C. (1970) *Japanese Society*. Berkeley, CA: University of California Press.

Nakatani, I. (1984) The Economic Role of Financial Corporate Grouping, in Aoki, M. (ed.) *The Economic Analysis of the Japanese Firm*. Amsterdam: North-Holland: 227–58.

Nakatani, I. (1996) *Nihon-keizai no Rekishiteki Tenkan* (Historical Transformation of the Japanese Economy). Tokyo: Toyo Keizai Shinpousha.

Nakatani, I. and Ota, H. (1994) *Keizai-kaikaku no Bijon* (Beyond the 'Hiraiwa Report' Vision of Economic Reform). Tokyo: Toyo Keizai Shinpousha.

Naono, N. (1996) *Semiconductor and Liquid Crystal Industries in Transition*. Nikkei: BP Books.

Nathan, J. (1999) *Sony: The Private Life*. Boston/New York: Houghton Mifflin.

Nihon Keizai Shinbunsha (ed.) (1997) *2020-nen Kara No Keishou* (Warning from the Year 2020: Japan Will Vanish). Tokyo: Nihon Keizai Shibunsha.

Nihon Keizai Shinbunsha (ed.) (1999) *Keihan Barei* (Kei-Han Valley). Tokyo: Nihon Keizai Shibunsha.

Noguchi, Y. (1993) *Nihon no Keizai Kaikaku no Kouzu* (Composition of Economic Reform in Japan). Tokyo: Toyo Keizai Shinpousha.

Noguchi, Y. (1995) *1940-nen Taisei* (The 1940 System). Tokyo: Toyo Keizai Shinpousha.

Nonaka, I. and Takeuchi, H. (1995) *The Knowledge-Creating Company*. New York: Oxford University Press.

OECD (1995) *Purchasing Power Parities and Real Expenditures 1993*. Paris: OECD Statistics Directorate.

Ohara, I. (1999) *Nihon Saisei no Jouken* (Conditions for Japan's Recovery). Tokyo: Toyo Keizai Shinpousha.

Ohmae, K. (1989) *Heisei Ishin* (Zero-Based Organization and Constitution). Tokyo: Koudansha.

Ohmae, K. (1995) *The End of the Nation State*. New York: Free Press.

Ohmae, K. (1998) *Kawaru Sekai Kaware Nihon!* (Change Japan to Survive the New Order). Tokyo: PHP Kenkyuujo.

Okabe, K., Kose, N. and Nishimura, K. (1999) *College Students Who Cannot Calculate Fractions* (Bunsu ga Dekinai Daigakusei). Tokyo: Toyo Keizai Shinpousha.

Okamoto, Y. (1995) *Saraba Hyouryuu Nihon* (Farewell to Drifting Japan). Tokyo: Toyo Keizai Shinpousha.

Okimoto, D.I. (1989) *Between MITI and the Market: Japanese Industrial Policy for High Technology*. Stanford, CA: Stanford University Press.

Ouchi, W.G. (1981) *Theory Z: How American Business Can Meet the Japanese Challenge*. Reading, MA: Addison-Wesley.

Patrick, H. and Rosovsky, H. (1976) Japan's Economic Performance: An Overview, in Patrick, H. and Rosovsky, H. (eds) *Asia's New Giant: How the Japanese Economy Works*. Washington, DC: Brookings Institution: 1–61.

Porter, M.E. (1980) *Competitive Strategy: Techniques for Analyzing Industries and Competitors*. New York: Free Press.

Porter, M.E. (1990) *The Competitive Advantage of Nations*. New York: Free Press.

Porter, M.E. (1992) *Capital Choices: Changing the Way America Invests in Industry*. Washington, DC: Council on Competitiveness and Harvard Business School.

Porter, M.E. (1996) What is Strategy? *Harvard Business Review* **74**(6).

Porter, M.E. (1998a) The Microeconomic Foundations of Economic Development. *The Global Competitiveness Report 1998*. Geneva, Switzerland: World Economic Forum.

Porter, M.E. (1998b) *On Competition*. Boston, MA: Harvard Business School Press. (Contains reprint of Porter, 1996.)

Porter, M.E. (1999) Microeconomic Competitiveness: Findings from the 1999 Executive Survey. *The Global Competitiveness Report 1999*. Geneva, Switzerland: World Economic Forum.

Porter, M.E. and McGahan, A. (1997) How Much Does Industry Matter, Really? *Strategic Management Journal* **18**: 15–30.

Porter, M.E. and Bond, G.C. (1999) Innovative Capacity and Prosperity: The Next Competitiveness Challenge. *The Global Competitiveness Report 1999*. Geneva, Switzerland: World Economic Forum.

Porter, M.E. and Takeuchi, H. (1999) Fixing what Really Ails Japan. *Foreign Affairs*, May/June.

Porter, M.E., Stern, S. and Council on Competitiveness (1999) *The New Challenge to America's Prosperity: Findings from the Innovation Index*. Washington, DC: Council on Competitiveness.

Prestowitz, C.V. (1988) *Trading Places: How We Allowed Japan to Take the Lead*. New York: Basic Books.

Rohlen, T.P. (1975) The Company Work Group, in Vogel, E.F. (ed.) *Modern Japanese Organization and Decision-Making*. Berkeley, CA: University of California Press: 185–209.

Sachs, J. and Warner, A. (1995) Economic Reform and the Process of Global Integration. *Brookings Papers on Economic Activity* **1**(1): 1–118.

Sakaiya, T. (1997) *Tsugi wa Kounaru* (This will be 'Next'). Tokyo: Koudansha.

Sakaiya, T. (1998) *Arubeki Ashita* (Dawn of a New Japan). Tokyo: PHP Kenkyuujo.

Sakakibara, E. (1990) *Shihonshugi o Koeta Nihon* (Japan beyond Capitalism). Tokyo: Toyo Keizai Shinpousha.

Sakakibara, E. (1993) *Bunmei toshiteno Nihon-gata Shihonshugi* (Japanese-style Capitalism as Civilization). Tokyo: Toyo Keizai Shinpousha.

Sakakibara, E. (1996) *Shinpo-shugi karano Ketsubetsu* (Farewell to Progressivism). Tokyo: Yomiuri Shinbunsha.

Sakakibara, M. (1994) *Cooperative Research and Development: Theory and Evidence on Japanese Practice*, PhD thesis, Harvard University.

Sakakibara, M. (1997a) Heterogeneity of Firm Capabilities and Cooperative Research and Development: An Empirical Examination of Motives. *Strategic Management Journal* **18** (special issue): 143–64.

Sakakibara, M. (1997b) Evaluating Government-Sponsored R&D Consortia in Japan: Who Benefits and How? *Research Policy* **26**(4–5): 447–73.

Sakakibara, M. (1999a) Knowledge Sharing in Cooperative Research and Development. Working paper, presented at the 1999 annual meeting of the American Economic Association, New York.

Sakakibara, M. (1999b) Does R&D Cooperation Stimulate Competition? Evidence from Japanese Research Consortia. Working paper.

Sakakibara, M. and Branstetter, L. (1999a) Do Stronger Patents Induce More Innovation? Evidence from the 1988 Japanese Patent Law Reforms. Working paper.

Sakakibara, M. and Branstetter, L. (1999b) Developing a Framework for the Impact Assessment of Research Consortia Using Japanese and U.S. Data. Working paper.

Sakakibara, M. and Porter, M.E. (in press) Competing at Home to Win Abroad: Evidence from Japanese Industry. *Review of Economics and Statistics*.

Sasaki, N. (1998) Nihon Keiei ni Kokusaika wo Semaru Soto Karano Chikara (The External Pressure to Force the Internationalization of Japanese Management) in Uchino T. and Abegglen, J.C. (eds) *Tenki ni Tatsu Nihongata Kigyo* (The Japanese-Model Corporation at Crossroads). Tokyo: Chuo Keizai Sha.

Saxonhouse, G.R. (1985) Japanese Cooperative R&D Ventures: A Market Evaluation. Research Seminar in International Economics, Seminar Discussion Paper No. 156. Dept. of Economics, University of Michigan.

Schonberger, R.J. (1982) *Japanese Manufacturing Techniques: Nine Hidden Lessons in Simplicity*. New York: Free Press.

Seki, M. (1997) *Kuudouka o Koete* (Beyond Hollowing Out: Technology and Area Restructuring). Tokyo: Nihon Keizai Shinbunsha.

Sheff, D. (1993) *Game Over: How Nintendo Conquered the World*. New York: Vintage Press.

Shimada, H. (1995) *Japan Kuraisisu* (Japan Crisis). Tokyo: Koudansha.

Shimada, H. (1995) *Nihon Kaikakuron* (Japanese Reform). Tokyo: PHP Kenkyuujo.

Shimada, H. (1997) *Nihon Saifujou no Kousou* (The Concept of Japan Resurfacing). Tokyo: Toyo Keizai Shinpousha.

Shinpo, S. (1994) *Daisan no Kaikoku o Mezasu Nihon-keizai* (The Third Opening of the Japanese Economy). Tokyo: Toyo Keizai Shinpousha.

Society of Japanese Aerospace Companies (1987) *The Result of YS-11*. Tokyo: Society of Japanese Aerospace Companies.

Stern, S., Porter, M.E. and Furman, J.L. (1999) The Determinants of National Innovative Capacity. *Harvard Business School Working Paper* 00–034, October 19.

Suzuki, Y. (1994) *Nihon-keizai no Shouraizou* (Future Image of the Japanese Economy). Tokyo: Toyo Keizai Shinpousha.

Takenaka, H. (1994) *Minfuron* (Common Wealth).Tokyo: Koudansha.

Takeuchi, H. (1991) Small and Better: The Consumer-driven Advantage in Japanese Product Design. *Design Management Journal*, winter.

Takeuchi, H. (1992) Nihon-gata Kouporeito Gabanansu (Japanese-styled Corporate Governance). *Business Review* **39**(3).

Takeuchi, H. (1999) Nihonkigyou no Shinseihin Kaihatsu niokeru Gojuunen no Hensen (The Transition of New Product Development in Japanese Companies in the Last 50 years), in *Seihin Kaihatsu Kakushin* (Product Development Innovation). Tokyo: Yuuhikaku.

Takeuchi, H. and Nonaka, I. (1986) The New New Product Development Game. *Harvard Business Review* **61**(1).

Takeuchi, H. and Nonaka, I. (1995) *The Knowledge-Creating Company*. New York: Oxford University Press.

Takeuchi, H. and Ishikura, Y. (1994) *Ishitsu no Manejimento* (Management of Heterogeneity). Tokyo: Diamond-sha.

Takeuchi, Y. (1998) *Nihon no Owari* (The End of Japan). Tokyo: Nihon Keizai Shinbunsha.

Tanaka, N. (1992) *Saigo no Jyuunen* (Towards the Twenty-first Century: A Vision for the Japanese Economy). Tokyo: Nihon Keizai Shinbunsha.

Tanaka, N. (1996) *Atarashii Sangyou-shakai no Kousou* (A Vision of New Industrial Society). Tokyo: Nihon Keizai Shinbunsha.

Tasker, P. (1994) *Nihon wa Yomigaeruka* (Will Japan Be Ready in Time for the Coming Second Golden Age of Capitalism?). Tokyo: Koudansha.

Tasker, P. (1997) *Fukigen Na Jidai* (Japan 2020). Tokyo: Koudansha.

Thurow, L. (1998) *Nihon wa Kanarazu Fukkatsu Suru* (Japan's Economic Recovery). Tokyo: TBS Britannica.

Tracy, P. and Azumi, K. (1976) Determinants of Administrative Control – A Test of a Theory with Japanese Factories. *American Sociological Review* **41**(1): 80–94.

Tsuruta, T. (1984) The Rapid Growth Era, in Komiya, R., Okuno, M. and Suzumura, K. (eds) *Nihon no Sangyo Seisaku* (The Japanese Industrial Policy). Tokyo: University of Tokyo Press.

Tyson, L.D. and Zysman, J. (1989) Developmental Strategy and Production Innovation in Japan, in Johnson, C., Tyson, L.D. and Zysman, J. (eds) *Politics and Productivity: The Real Story of Why Japan Works*. Cambridge, MA: Ballinger Publishing Company.

Uchino, T. (1988) Kawaru Nihongata Kigyo Keiei (The Changing Japanese-style Management), in Uchino, T. and Abegglen, J.C. (eds) *Tenki ni Tatsu Nihongara Kigyo* (The Japanese-Model Corporation at Crossroads). Tokyo: Chuo Keizai Sha.

Urabe, K. (1978) *Nihon Teki Keiei wo Kangaeru* (Thoughts on the Japanese-Style Management). Tokyo: Chuo Keizai Sha.

Van Wolferen, K. (1989) *The Enigma of Japanese Power: People and Politics in a Stateless Nation*. New York: A.A. Knopf.

Van Wolferen, K. (1994) *Ningen o Koufuku nishinai Nihon toiu Shisutemu* (The False Realities of A Politicized Society). Tokyo: Mainichi Shinbunsha.

Vogel, E.Z. (1975) *Modern Japanese Organization and Decision Making*. Berkeley, CA: University of California Press.

Wada, H. (1999) *Gakuryoku Houkai* (The Collapse in Scholarship). Tokyo: PHP Kenkyuujo.

Weinstein, D. and Yafeh, Y. (1995) Japan's Corporate Groups: Collusive or Competitive? An Empirical Investigation of *Keiretsu* Behavior. *Journal of Industrial Economics* **43**: 359–76.

Whitehill, A.M. and Takezawa, S. (1978) Workplace Harmony: Another Japanese 'Miracle'? *Columbia Journal of World Business* **13**(3): 25–39.

Womack, J., Jones, D.T. and Roos, D. (1990) *The Machine that Changed the World*. New York: Rawson Associates.

Yashiro, N. (1997) *Nihon-teki Koyou Kankou no Keizaigaku* (The Economics of Japanese Employment Customs). Tokyo: Nihon Keizai Shimbun-sha.

Yoffie, D. (1986) Protecting World Markets, in McCraw, T. (ed.) *America versus Japan*. Boston, MA: Harvard Business School Press.

Yoshino, M.Y. (1968) *Japan's Managerial System: Tradition and Innovation*. Cambridge, MA: Harvard University Press.